—— The ——
Gallup
—— Poll ——

Public Opinion 1989

Other Gallup Poll Publications Available from Scholarly Resources

The Gallup Poll: Public Opinion Annual Series

1988 (ISBN 0-8420-2330-5) *1981* (ISBN 0-8420-2200-7)
1987 (ISBN 0-8420-2292-9) *1980* (ISBN 0-8420-2181-7)
1986 (ISBN 0-8420-2274-0) *1979* (ISBN 0-8420-2170-1)
1985 (ISBN 0-8420-2249-X) *1978* (ISBN 0-8420-2159-0)
1984 (ISBN 0-8420-2234-1) *1972–77* (ISBN 0-8420-2129-9, 2 vols.)
1983 (ISBN 0-8420-2220-1) *1935–71* (ISBN 0-394-47270-5, 3 vols.)
1982 (ISBN 0-8420-2214-7)

International Polls

The International Gallup Polls: Public Opinion, 1979
ISBN 0-8420-2180-9 (1981)

The International Gallup Polls: Public Opinion, 1978
ISBN 0-8420-2162-0 (1980)

The Gallup International Public Opinion Polls:
France, 1939, 1944–1975
2 volumes ISBN 0-394-40998-1 (1976)

The Gallup International Public Opinion Polls:
Great Britain, 1937–1975
2 volumes ISBN 0-394-40992-2 (1976)

The Gallup Poll

Public Opinion 1989

George Gallup, Jr.

SR Scholarly Resources Inc.
Wilmington, Delaware

ACKNOWLEDGMENTS

The preparation of this volume has involved the entire staff of the
Gallup Poll, and their contributions are gratefully acknowledged. I
particularly wish to thank Graham Hueber, executive editor of *The
Gallup Report*, and Professor Fred L. Israel of the City College of
New York, who was the principal coordinator.

G.G., Jr.

The paper used in this publication meets the minimum require-
ments of the American National Standard for permanence of
paper for printed library materials, Z39.48, 1984.

Scholarly Resources Inc.
104 Greenhill Avenue
Wilmington, DE 19805-1897

Library of Congress Catalog Card Number: 79-56557
International Standard Serial Number: 0195-962X
International Standard Book Number: 0-8420-2344-5

CONTENTS

DESIGN OF THE SAMPLE

The Gallup Poll gathers information both in personal interviews and in interviews conducted by telephone. Although the method for selecting households in which to conduct interviews is different, the goal is the same: to provide representative samples of adults living in the United States. In either case the standard size for Gallup Polls is 1000 interviews. More interviews are conducted in specific instances where greater survey accuracy is desired.

Design of the Sample for Personal Surveys

The design of the sample for personal (face-to-face) surveys is that of a replicated area probability sample down to the block level in the case of urban areas and to segments of townships in the case of rural areas.

After stratifying the nation geographically and by size of community according to information derived from the most recent census, over 350 different sampling locations are selected on a mathematically random basis from within cities, towns, and counties that, in turn, have been selected on a mathematically random basis.

The interviewers are given no leeway in selecting the areas in which they are to conduct their interviews. Each interviewer is given a map on which a specific starting point is marked and is instructed to contact households according to a predetermined travel pattern. At each occupied .dwelling unit, the interviewer selects respondents by following a systematic procedure that is repeated until the assigned number of interviews has been completed.

Design of the Sample for Telephone Surveys

The samples of telephone numbers used in telephone interview surveys are based on a random digit stratified probability design. The sampling procedure involves selecting listed "seed" numbers, deleting the last two digits, and randomly generating two digits to replace them. This procedure provides telephone samples that are geographically representative. The random digit aspect, since it allows for the inclusion of unlisted and unpublished numbers, protects the samples from "listing bias"—the unrepresentativeness of telephone samples that can occur if the distinctive households whose telephone numbers are unlisted or unpublished are excluded from the sample.

Weighting Procedures

After the survey data have been collected and processed, each respondent is assigned a weight so that the demographic characteristics of the total weighted sample of respondents match the latest estimates of the demographic characteristics of the adult population available from the U.S. Census Bureau. Telephone surveys are weighted to match the characteristics of the adult population living in households with access to a telephone. The weighting of personal interview data includes a factor to improve the representation of the kind of people who are less likely to be found at home.

The procedures described above are designed to produce samples approximating the adult civilian population (18 and older) living in private households (that is, excluding those in prisons, hospitals, hotels, religious and educational institutions, and those living on reservations or military bases)—and in the case of telephone surveys, households with access to a telephone. Survey percentages may be applied to census estimates of the size of these populations to project percentages into numbers of people. The manner in which the sample is drawn also produces a sample that approximates the distribution of private households in the United States. Therefore, survey results also can be projected to numbers of households.

Sampling Tolerances

In interpreting survey results, it should be borne in mind that all sample surveys are subject to sampling error—that is, the extent to which the results may differ from what would be obtained if the whole population surveyed had been interviewed. The size of such sampling errors depends largely on the number of interviews.

The following tables may be used in estimating the sampling error of any percentage. The computed allowances have taken into account the effect of the sample design upon sampling error. They may be interpreted as indicating the range (plus or minus the figure shown) within which the results of repeated samplings in the same time period could be expected to vary, 95 percent of the time, assuming the same sampling procedure, the same interviewers, and the same questionnaire.

Table A shows how much allowance should be made for the sampling error of a percentage. Let us say a reported percentage is 33 for a group that includes 1000 respondents. First, we go to the row headed "percentages near 30" and then go across to the column headed "1000." The number here is 4, which means that the 33 percent obtained in the sample is subject to a sampling error of plus or minus 4 points. Another way of saying it is that very probably (95 chances out of 100) the average of repeated samplings would be somewhere between 29 and 37, with the most likely figure being the 33 obtained.

In comparing survey results in two samples, such as for men and women, the question arises as to how large must a difference between them be before one can be reasonably sure that it reflects a real difference. In Tables B and C, the number of points that must be allowed for in such comparisons is indicated. Table B is for percentages near 20 or 80, and Table C is for percentages near 50. For percentages in between, the error to be allowed for is between those shown in the two tables.

TABLE A

Recommended Allowance for Sampling Error of a Percentage

	In Percentage Points (at 95 in 100 confidence level)* Sample Size					
	1000	750	600	400	200	100
Percentages near 10	2	3	3	4	5	7
Percentages near 20	3	4	4	5	7	9
Percentages near 30	4	4	4	6	8	10
Percentages near 40	4	4	5	6	8	11
Percentages near 50	4	4	5	6	8	11
Percentages near 60	4	4	5	6	8	11
Percentages near 70	4	4	4	6	8	10
Percentages near 80	3	4	4	5	7	9
Percentages near 90	2	3	3	4	5	7

*The chances are 95 in 100 that the sampling error is not larger than the figures shown.

TABLE B

Recommended Allowance for Sampling Error of the Difference

	In Percentage Points (at 95 in 100 confidence level)* Percentages near 20 or percentages near 80			
	750	600	400	200
Size of sample				
750	5			
600	5	6		
400	6	6	7	
200	8	8	8	10

TABLE C

	Percentages near 50			
	750	600	400	200
Size of sample				
750	6			
600	7	7		
400	7	8	8	
200	10	10	10	12

*The chances are 95 in 100 that the sampling error is not larger than the figures shown.

Here is an example of how the tables would be used: Let us say that 50 percent of men respond a certain way and 40 percent of women also respond that way, for a difference of 10 percentage points between them. Can we say with any assurance that the 10-point difference reflects a real difference between men and women on the question? The sample contains approximately 600 men and 600 women.

Since the percentages are near 50, we consult Table B, and since the two samples are about 600 persons each, we look for the number in the column headed "600" that is also in the row designated "600." We find the number 7 here. This means that the allowance for error should be 7 points, and that in concluding that the percentage among men is somewhere between 3 and 17 points higher than the percentage among women, we should be wrong only about 5 percent of the time. In other words, we can conclude with considerable confidence that a difference exists in the direction observed and that it amounts to at least 3 percentage points.

If, in another case, men's responses amount to 22 percent and women's 24 percent, we consult Table B because these percentages are near 20. We look in the column headed "600" that is also in the row headed "600" and see that the number is 6. Obviously, then, the 2-point difference is inconclusive.

RECORD OF
GALLUP POLL ACCURACY

Year	Gallup Final Survey*		Election Result*	
1988	56.0%	Bush	53.9%	Bush
1984	59.0	Reagan	59.2	Reagan
1982	55.0	Democratic	55.8	Democratic
1980	47.0	Reagan	50.8	Reagan
1978	55.0	Democratic	54.0	Democratic
1976	48.0	Carter	50.0	Carter
1974	60.0	Democratic	58.9	Democratic
1972	62.0	Nixon	61.8	Nixon
1970	53.0	Democratic	54.3	Democratic
1968	43.0	Nixon	43.5	Nixon
1966	52.5	Democratic	51.9	Democratic
1964	64.0	Johnson	61.3	Johnson
1962	55.5	Democratic	52.7	Democratic
1960	51.0	Kennedy	50.1	Kennedy
1958	57.0	Democratic	56.5	Democratic
1956	59.5	Eisenhower	57.8	Eisenhower
1954	51.5	Democratic	52.7	Democratic
1952	51.0	Eisenhower	55.4	Eisenhower
1950	51.0	Democratic	50.3	Democratic

* The figure shown is the winner's percentage of the Democratic-Republican vote except in the elections of 1948, 1968, and 1976. Because the Thurmond and Wallace voters in 1948 were largely split-offs from the normally Democratic vote, they were made a part of the final Gallup Poll preelection estimate of the division of the vote. In 1968, Wallace's candidacy was supported by such a large minority that he was clearly a major candidate, and the 1968 percentages are based on the total Nixon-Humphrey-Wallace vote. In 1976, because of interest in McCarthy's candidacy and its potential effect on the Carter vote, the final Gallup Poll estimate included Carter, Ford, McCarthy, and all other candidates as a group.

1948	44.5	Truman	49.9	Truman
1946	58.0	Republican	54.3	Republican
1944	51.5	Roosevelt	53.5*	Roosevelt
1942	52.0	Democratic	48.0	Democratic
1940	52.0	Roosevelt	55.0	Roosevelt
1938	54.0	Democratic	50.8	Democratic
1936	55.7	Roosevelt	62.5	Roosevelt

*Civilian vote 53.3, Roosevelt soldier vote 0.5 = 53.8% Roosevelt. Gallup final survey based on civilian vote.

Average Deviation for 26
   National Elections ....2.2 percentage points

Average Deviation for 19
   National Elections
   Since 1950, inclusive ....1.5 percentage points

Trend in Deviation

Elections	Average Error
1936–1950	3.6
1952–1960	1.7
1962–1970	1.6
1972–1988	1.4

CHRONOLOGY

This chronology is provided to enable the reader to relate poll results to specific events, or series of events, that may have influenced public opinion.

1988

December 2   The Labor Department reports that 450,000 new jobs were generated in November.

December 7   Soviet General Secretary Mikhail Gorbachev announces at the United Nations that the USSR will sharply cut its military forces.

December 8   A devastating earthquake strikes Soviet Armenia.

December 13   Angola, Cuba, and South Africa conclude an agreement on independence for Namibia.

December 14   President Ronald Reagan authorizes the start of a "substantive dialogue" with the Palestine Liberation Organization.

December 21   More than 250 people are killed as a TWA plane blows up over Scotland en route from London to New York.

1989

January 4   The Congressional Budget Office estimates that the federal deficit for the 1990 fiscal year will be $141 billion, much higher than the White House's calculations.

January 6   The Labor Department reports that unemployment stood at 5.3%, a fourteen-year low, at the end of 1988.

January 7   Emperor Hirohito of Japan dies after a reign of sixty-two years.

January 9   President Reagan submits his final budget, for fiscal 1990, of $1.15 trillion. More funds are targeted for AIDS research, rescuing insolvent savings and loan institutions, and cleaning up contaminated nuclear waste facilities.

January 11   In his farewell address, President Reagan says that he perceives his eight-year administration as a time of "rediscovery of our values and our common sense." He now finds the country "more prosperous, more secure, and happier than it was eight years ago."

January 19   The Labor Department reports that consumer prices rose 4.4% in 1988, thus matching the 1987 increase.

January 20   George Bush and Dan Quayle are inaugurated as president and vice president of the United States.

January 25   President Bush appoints an eight-member commission to propose a code of ethics for government officials.

January 27	The Commerce Department reports that the gross national product grew at an annual rate of 2% in the fourth quarter of 1988. For the year as a whole the economy grew at 3.8%, its strongest showing in four years.
February 1	The Commerce Department reports that its Index of Leading Economic Indicators rose 0.6% in December.
February 2	The Senate rejects a pay increase for its members. The House of Representatives also will reject the pay increase on February 7.
February 5	The Soviet Union, ending its nine-year military intervention, completes its withdrawal of troops from Afghanistan.
February 6	President Bush proposes to close or sell 350 savings and loan institutions that are in financial trouble.
February 10	Leading banks raise their prime lending rate to 11%, the highest level since 1984.
February 14	Five Central American presidents sign an agreement that would disarm and repatriate *contra* rebels opposing the Nicaraguan regime.
February 15	Iran's Ayatollah Khomeini calls on Moslems around the world to assassinate author Salman Rushdie because a character in Rushdie's novel, *The Satanic Verses*, disparages the prophet Mohammed.
February 16	President Bush states his opposition to banning the import or sale of semiautomatic assault rifles.

February 17	The Commerce Department announces that, for the first time in eight years, the trade deficit had declined in 1988.
February 21	The first of the Iran-*contra* trials begins in a federal district court in Washington, DC.
March 9	Eastern Airlines files for bankruptcy.
	The Senate, in a rare rebuff to a president, rejects the nomination of John Tower as secretary of defense. On the following day President Bush nominates Richard Cheney, a U.S. representative from Wyoming, to that position.
March 10	The Labor Department reports that the unemployment rate in February fell to 5.1%, the lowest level since May 1974.
March 13	The space shuttle *Discovery*, with a five-person crew, is launched from Cape Canaveral, Florida. The crew intends to film Earth in an effort to document damage to the planet from various natural and human causes.
March 14	In a reversal of policy, President Bush bans imports of semiautomatic assault rifles.
March 24	The largest oil spill in U.S. history occurs after an Exxon tanker strikes a reef in Alaska's Prince William Sound.
March 26	A historic election in the Soviet Union sends a strong signal to the Kremlin that the citizenry wants a faster pace in economic, social, and political reforms.

April 7	The decline in the nation's unemployment rate continued in March. The rate of 4.9%, the lowest since 1973, is considered by some economists as virtually equivalent to full employment.
	Amid reports that the Alaskan oil-spill cleanup is proceeding too slowly, President Bush orders federal troops and equipment to assist in the effort.
April 9	A massive turnout of people in Washington, DC, officially estimated at 300,000, supports a woman's right to choose to have an abortion.
April 21	The Dow Jones Industrial Average closes above 2400 for the first time since the sharp decline in stock prices began in the summer of 1987.
April 26	The Commerce Department reports that the economy showed strength in the first quarter of 1989, with the gross national product expanding at an annual rate of 5.5%.
May 2	The citizens of Panama vote for a president, but the regime dominated by General Manuel Noriega voids the election.
	Hungary begins to dismantle a 150-mile-long fence marking its border with Austria.
May 4	Oliver North becomes the first person to be convicted in the Iran-*contra* scandal.
	The shuttle *Atlantis*, with five crew members, lifts off from Cape Canaveral. Later that day the crew deploys the *Magellan* spacecraft on a

fifteen-month, 800-million-mile journey to Venus.

May 5   The Labor Department reports that unemployment, after reaching a fifteen-year low, edged upward in April to 5.2%. Other data released also show that the economy is not growing as fast as previously indicated.

May 10–11   Secretary of State James Baker and Soviet Foreign Minister Eduard Shevardnadze agree to reopen the strategic arms reduction talks in Geneva.

May 18   Congress approves a compromise budget worked out between the president and House and Senate leaders.

May 25   Former Secretary of Housing and Urban Development Samuel Pierce admits that he had been lobbied by former government officials and that he had asked his staff to give "careful consideration" to certain projects.

         Mikhail Gorbachev is elected president of the Soviet Union by its new parliament.

May 31   House Speaker Jim Wright resigns after revelation of serious ethical charges against him.

June 3   Iran's Ayatollah Khomeini dies at the age of eighty-six.

June 4–9   More than 11,000 researchers and public health officials meet in Montreal at the Fifth International Conference on AIDS.

June 6	U.S. Representative Tom Foley of the state of Washington is elected speaker of the House of Representatives.
June 9	Testimony before Congress reveals further and greater mismanagement and corruption in the Department of Housing and Urban Development. Such revelations will continue throughout June and July.
June 12	President Bush proposes a series of legislation to clean up the nation's air.
June 13	President Bush vetos a bill that would have raised the minimum wage from $3.35 per hour to $4.55 per hour.
June 21	The Supreme Court rules that burning the American flag is a form of political protest protected by the Constitution.
July 3	The Supreme Court, in a sharply divided 5-to-4 decision, puts new restraints on a woman's right to have an abortion.
July 4	Poland's new legislature convenes with members of the trade union, Solidarity, holding almost one half of the seats.
July 7	Figures released by the government further ease concerns about inflation.
July 9–13	President Bush visits Poland and Hungary.
July 14	The heads of seven major non-Communist industrial nations meet in Paris at a summit scheduled concurrently with the observance of the bicentennial of the French Revolution.

July 27	The Commerce Department reports that the gross national product grew at an annual rate of 1.7% in the second quarter of 1989, the slowest rate of economic expansion in three years.
July 28	Terrorists in Lebanon claim that they have executed a U.S. Marine colonel whom they had abducted in 1988. They contend that they acted in retaliation for the Israeli abduction of Sheik Abdul Karim Obeid.
August 2	Forty-six futures traders at the Chicago Mercantile Exchange are indicted for racketeering.
August 4	Newly released government figures indicate that inflation remains well under control.

Five Central American presidents reach an agreement to dismantle *contra* bases in Honduras. |
August 7	West Germany refuses to expel more than 45,000 East Germans who have emigrated across the border.
August 8	Popular protests in Estonia, Latvia, and Lithuania denounce Soviet domination of these countries.
August 9	Legislation to rescue the savings and loan industry is signed into law by President Bush.
August 23	On the fiftieth anniversary of the Hitler-Stalin pact, more than one million persons join hands in the Baltic States to form a 400-mile-long line as a means of protesting their current status in the Soviet bloc.

August 24	Cincinnati Reds' manager Pete Rose is banned for life from baseball on charges that he had repeatedly placed bets on games.
September 1	Government figures released in September appear to bode well for the nation's economy.
September 5	President Bush announces a broad plan to combat drug use and trafficking.
September 6	The United States closes its embassy in Lebanon.
September 11–14	The number of refugees fleeing from East Germany increases. In mid-September more than 13,000 enter West Germany from Hungary.
September 21–22	Hurricane Hugo causes enormous devastation in the Carolinas.
September 25	President Gorbachev warns leaders of the Soviet republics of Armenia and Azerbaijan to reduce tensions between their peoples.
October 1	East Germany celebrates its fortieth anniversary, but street protests and a continuing outward flow of emigrants mar the event.
October 2	Soviet workers obtain the right to strike.
October 3	Rebel officers in Panama fail to oust General Noriega from power.
October 5	Television evangelist Jim Bakker is convicted of fraud and conspiracy.

October 6	Producer prices rose during September after declining for three months.
October 13	Stock prices decline sharply in the second-highest one-day drop in history.
October 17	A major earthquake strikes northern California.
October 18	The space shuttle *Atlantis* rockets into orbit to send the *Galileo* spacecraft on its planned six-year journey to Jupiter.
November 2	Senate Republicans drop efforts to cut the capital gains tax in this congressional session.
November 5	Thousands of East Germans continue to flee to West Germany.
November 7	David Dinkins is elected mayor of New York. He is the first black to preside over the nation's largest city. Congress raises the federal government's debt ceiling to $3.123 trillion.
November 9	East Berlin officials lift travel and emigration restrictions to the West. As the Wall no longer divides the city, tens of thousands rush to West Berlin.
November 14	President Gorbachev warns Western leaders against exploiting the political turmoil in Eastern Europe.
November 24–30	The prodemocracy movement in Czechoslovakia makes major gains as the nation's Communist party virtually collapses.

November 26   Hungary holds free elections, its first in forty years.

December 2–3   Presidents Bush and Gorbachev meet at sea off the coast of Malta.

December 8   The Labor Department reports a slight increase to 5.3% in the November unemployment rate.

December 20   President Bush dispatches U.S. troops to Panama to overthrow the government of General Noriega.

December 24   General Noriega takes refuge in the Vatican's diplomatic mission in Panama City.

December 25   In Romania, President Nicolae Ceausescu and Communist party leaders are overthrown.

Female

All of the time 40%
Most of the time.............................30
Not very often 10
Never 16
Not sure 4

By Education

Attended College

All of the time 33%
Most of the time.............................30
Not very often 18
Never 17
Not sure 2

No College

All of the time 35%
Most of the time.............................26
Not very often 13
Never 24
Not sure 2

By Age

18–29 Years

All of the time 40%
Most of the time.............................32
Not very often 14
Never 13
Not sure 1

30–49 Years

All of the time 31%
Most of the time.............................24
Not very often 19
Never 21
Not sure 5

50 Years and Over

All of the time 31%
Most of the time.............................22
Not very often 11
Never 31
Not sure 5

Asked of the entire sample: During the last three months, on about how many different occasions, if any, did you happen to see

JANUARY 1
DESIGNATED DRIVER

Interviewing Date: 9/25–10/1/88
Special Survey*

Asked of those who attend parties where alcoholic beverages are served: At social occasions, do you and your friends select a "designated driver" all of the time, most of the time, not very often, or never?

All of the time 34%
Most of the time.............................28
Not very often 15
Never 21
Not sure 2

By Sex

Male

All of the time 28%
Most of the time.............................26
Not very often 21
Never 25
Not sure ....**

*This survey was conducted by the Gallup Organization in conjunction with the Center for Health Communications of the Harvard University School of Public Health. It excludes persons who do not attend parties where alcoholic beverages are served (33% nationally).

** Less than 1%

television commercials promoting the "designated driver" concept?

Have seen commercials 54%
   1–5 times..................................31
   6 or more times........................23
Have not seen; no answer....................46

By Sex

Male

Have seen commercials 55%
   1–5 times..................................34
   6 or more times........................21
Have not seen; no answer....................45

Female

Have seen commercials 53%
   1–5 times..................................28
   6 or more times........................25
Have not seen; no answer....................47

By Education

Attended College

Have seen commercials 55%
   1–5 times..................................39
   6 or more times.........................16
Have not seen; no answer....................45

No College

Have seen commercials 53%
   1–5 times..................................25
   6 or more times........................28
Have not seen; no answer....................47

By Age

18–29 Years

Have seen commercials 63%
   1–5 times..................................33
   6 or more times........................30
Have not seen; no answer....................37

30–49 Years

Have seen commercials 57%
   1–5 times..................................35
   6 or more times........................22
Have not seen; no answer....................43

50 Years and Over

Have seen commercials 46%
   1–5 times..................................26
   6 or more times........................20
Have not seen; no answer....................54

Those Who Attend Parties Where Alcohol Is Served

Have seen commercials 56%
   1–5 times..................................33
   6 or more times........................23
Have not seen; no answer....................44

Note: Most U.S. adults have been exposed to the "designated driver" television ad campaign aimed at reducing drunken driving. A majority of those who attend parties where alcoholic beverages are served say that they try to put the designated driver concept into practice when traveling in a group. The latest Gallup Poll results are a hopeful sign that these public service commercials may be having an impact on people's behavior. If statistics show a decrease in the number of alcohol-related highway fatalities this New Year's Eve, then those promoting such antidrunken-driving programs can claim some of the credit.

Under the designated driver concept, a group of people attending a social affair asks one of its members to abstain voluntarily from drinking alcohol in order to drive the others home safely. Over one half of Americans (54%) say that they have seen television commercials promoting this concept on one or more occasions in the past three months. One in four (23%) has seen the ads six or more times. Among the age group with the highest incidence of alcohol-related highway fatalities—those under 30 years—close to two thirds (63%) have seen the ads.

A majority (62%) of those who have occasion to attend parties where alcohol is served say that they try to designate a driver all or most of the time when they are in such situations. Only one fifth (21%) reply that they have never thought to select one. Women are more likely than men to designate a driver regularly when going out to a social affair with a group of friends. And young people, an obvious target of the television ads, are more likely than older people to say that they have adopted the concept.

JANUARY 5
MOST ADMIRED MAN

Interviewing Date: 12/9–12/88
Survey #APIO 296-G

What man whom you have heard or read about, living today in any part of the world, do you admire the most? And who is your second choice?

The following are listed in order of frequency of mention, with first and second choices combined:

Ronald Reagan
Mikhail Gorbachev
George Bush
Pope John Paul II
Jesse Jackson
Billy Graham
Lee Iacocca
Edward Kennedy
Bill Cosby
Donald Trump

By way of comparison, the following are the results of the 1987 audit:

Ronald Reagan
Pope John Paul II
Jesse Jackson
Gary Hart
George Bush
Billy Graham
Oliver North
Mikhail Gorbachev
Lee Iacocca
Jimmy Carter

Note: Soviet leader Mikhail Gorbachev is the second most admired man in America. Only President Ronald Reagan is held in higher esteem by the American people, and more respondents in the survey chose the Soviet premier than chose President-elect George Bush as the man they admire most. Gorbachev's popularity is unique. He finished in eighth place last year, the first time any Soviet head of state made this list since this question was first asked in 1946.

Gorbachev's popularity in the United States and in other Western nations is in response to the political and economic reforms he has championed within the Soviet Union as well as to the signing of the historic INF Treaty. His ranking in this particular survey also may have been helped by the fact that the poll was conducted immediately after his trip to the United Nations in New York, where he was very well received and where he announced plans for a unilateral reduction in conventional armaments.

President Reagan is at the top of the list for the eighth consecutive year. Following Reagan and Gorbachev are Bush, Pope John Paul II, and the Reverend Jesse Jackson. Rounding out the roster of most admired men are the Reverend Billy Graham, Chrysler chairman Lee Iacocca, Senator Edward Kennedy, television star Bill Cosby, and businessman Donald Trump. Graham has ranked among the top ten since 1955, while Jackson first appeared on the list in 1981 and Bush and Iacocca in 1984. Although not chosen among the most admired in 1987, Kennedy had made the top ten for the previous sixteen years.

Named to the list for the first time are Cosby and Trump. Missing, however, for the first time in ten years is former President Jimmy Carter. Two others who also are absent this year are former Democratic presidential candidate Gary Hart and the Iran-*contra* affair's Colonel Oliver North; each had been named for the first time in 1987.

Others frequently named but who did not make the top ten include North, Carter, Michael Dukakis, Lech Walesa, and Henry Kissinger. Interestingly, since Gallup began asking the public for their choices more than four decades ago, Dukakis is the first major-party presidential candidate not to be included among the ten most admired men in an election year.

The list is compiled by asking respondents to volunteer their first and second choices of men whom they most admire. Accordingly, political figures and personalities who receive extensive media exposure dominate the selections.

JANUARY 8
MOST ADMIRED WOMAN

Interviewing Date: 12/9–12/88
Survey #APIO 296-G

What woman whom you have heard or read about, living today in any part of the world, do you admire the most? And who is your second choice?

The following are listed in order of frequency of mention, with first and second choices combined:

Margaret Thatcher
Mother Teresa of Calcutta
Nancy Reagan
Oprah Winfrey
Betty Ford
Barbara Walters
Corazon Aquino
Jacqueline Kennedy Onassis
Elizabeth Taylor
Barbara Bush

By way of comparison, the following are the results of the 1987 audit:

Nancy Reagan
Margaret Thatcher
Mother Teresa of Calcutta
Corazon Aquino
Jeane Kirkpatrick
Pat Schroeder
Betty Ford
Coretta Scott King ⎫
Raisa Gorbachev ⎬ tied
Elizabeth Dole ⎪
Geraldine Ferraro ⎭

Note: Once again, British Prime Minister Margaret Thatcher ranks first, ahead of Mother Teresa of Calcutta and First Lady Nancy Reagan, as the woman most admired by the American public. Since 1981 each of these women has held one of the top four positions, with only slight shifts each year in their relative rankings.

Fourth on the list of most admired women is television talk-show hostess Oprah Winfrey, followed by former First Lady Betty Ford and television personality Barbara Walters. The seventh position is held by Corazon Aquino, president of the Philippines; eighth, former First Lady Jacqueline Kennedy Onassis; and ninth, actress Elizabeth Taylor. Rounding out the list is the president-elect's wife, Barbara Bush.

There is significant turnover in the top ten women chosen as the most admired. Six who were named last year did not make the list in 1988: Jeane Kirkpatrick, the former U.S. ambassador to the United Nations; Pat Schroeder, U.S. representative from Colorado; Coretta Scott King, widow of the Reverend Dr. Martin Luther King, Jr.; Raisa Gorbachev, wife of Soviet Premier Mikhail Gorbachev; Elizabeth Dole, the former transportation secretary; and Geraldine Ferraro, the 1984 Democratic vice-presidential nominee. With the exception of Gorbachev and Schroeder, however, each of these women frequently was mentioned by respondents in 1988, as were Princess Diana of Great Britain and Sandra Day O'Connor, associate justice of the Supreme Court.

Among the top ten women, Jacqueline Kennedy Onassis has been on the list the most often, with twenty-three mentions over the last three decades. She is followed by Betty Ford, who has appeared annually since 1974. Barbara Walters was first named as one of the most admired women in 1977, and she has periodically made the list since then. On the other hand, Oprah Winfrey, Elizabeth Taylor, and Barbara Bush are named to the top ten for the first time this year.

JANUARY 12
PRESIDENT REAGAN

Interviewing Date: 12/27–29/88
Survey #GO 89024

Do you approve or disapprove of the way Ronald Reagan is handling his job as president?

Approve...63%
Disapprove.......................................29
No opinion.. 8

By Sex

Male

Approve...66%
Disapprove...26
No opinion... 8

Female

Approve...59%
Disapprove...32
No opinion... 9

By Ethnic Background

White

Approve...67%
Disapprove...26
No opinion... 7

Nonwhite

Approve...34%
Disapprove...50
No opinion...16

Black

Approve...30%
Disapprove...56
No opinion...14

By Education

College Graduate

Approve...69%
Disapprove...30
No opinion... 1

College Incomplete

Approve...65%
Disapprove...32
No opinion... 3

High-School Graduate

Approve...62%
Disapprove...28
No opinion...10

Less Than High-School Graduate

Approve...56%
Disapprove...27
No opinion...17

By Region

East

Approve...64%
Disapprove...27
No opinion... 9

Midwest

Approve...60%
Disapprove...32
No opinion... 8

South

Approve...67%
Disapprove...27
No opinion... 6

West

Approve...58%
Disapprove...31
No opinion...11

By Age

18-29 Years

Approve...71%
Disapprove...22
No opinion... 7

30-49 Years

Approve...63%
Disapprove...30
No opinion... 7

50-64 Years

Approve...56%
Disapprove...33
No opinion...11

65 Years and Over

Approve..52%
Disapprove...38
No opinion...10

By Household Income
$40,000 and Over

Approve..74%
Disapprove...23
No opinion...3

$25,000–$39,999

Approve..69%
Disapprove...25
No opinion...6

$15,000–$24,999

Approve..62%
Disapprove...31
No opinion...7

Under $15,000

Approve..48%
Disapprove...38
No opinion...14

By Politics
Republicans

Approve..93%
Disapprove...5
No opinion...2

Democrats

Approve..38%
Disapprove...51
No opinion...11

Independents

Approve..58%
Disapprove...31
No opinion...11

By Religion
Protestants

Approve..64%
Disapprove...29
No opinion...7

Catholics

Approve..64%
Disapprove...26
No opinion...10

By Importance of Religion
Very Important

Approve..62%
Disapprove...29
No opinion...9

Fairly Important

Approve..66%
Disapprove...26
No opinion...8

Not Important

Approve..59%
Disapprove...36
No opinion...5

By Work Status
Full Time

Approve..70%
Disapprove...23
No opinion...7

Part Time

Approve..65%
Disapprove...29
No opinion...6

Not Employed

Approve..51%
Disapprove...38
No opinion...11

All Working Women

Approve..68%
Disapprove...25
No opinion...7

Full-Time Working Women

Approve..69%
Disapprove...24
No opinion...7

Selected National Trend

1988	Approve	Dis-approve	No opinion
November 11–14....	57%	35%	8%
September 25– October 1.........	54	37	9
August 19–22........	53	37	10
July 15–18	54	36	10
June 10–13...........	51	39	10
May 13–22...........	48	43	9
April 8–11............	50	39	11
March 4–7............	50	42	8
January 22–25.......	49	40	11

The following table compares the approval ratings of President Reagan and his predecessors:

Presidential Performance Ratings
(Percent Approval)

	High	Low	Last	Average
Reagan	68%*	35%**	63%	52%
Carter	75	21	34	47
Ford	71	37	53	46
Nixon	68	24	24	48
Johnson	80	35	49	55
Kennedy	83	57	58	70
Eisenhower	79	49	59	66
Truman	87	23	31	46
Roosevelt	84	54	66	68

* May 1981; May 1986
** January 1983

How do you think Ronald Reagan will go down in history—as an outstanding president, above average, below average, or poor?

Outstanding	17%
Above average......................	42
Average (volunteered).............	25
Below average	9
Poor................................	5
No opinion	2

By Sex

Male

Outstanding	20%
Above average......................	44
Average (volunteered).............	22
Below average	8
Poor................................	5
No opinion.........................	1

Female

Outstanding	15%
Above average......................	39
Average (volunteered).............	28
Below average	10
Poor................................	5
No opinion.........................	3

By Ethnic Background

White

Outstanding	18%
Above average......................	44
Average (volunteered).............	23
Below average	9
Poor................................	4
No opinion.........................	2

Nonwhite

Outstanding	15%
Above average......................	26
Average (volunteered).............	36
Below average	11
Poor................................	10
No opinion.........................	2

Black

Outstanding	12%
Above average......................	20
Average (volunteered).............	40
Below average	13
Poor................................	12
No opinion.........................	3

By Education

College Graduate

Outstanding	19%
Above average......................	47
Average (volunteered).............	15
Below average	13
Poor................................	5
No opinion.........................	1

College Incomplete

Outstanding 15%
Above average....................................46
Average (volunteered)..........................24
Below average 8
Poor...6
No opinion...1

High-School Graduate

Outstanding 17%
Above average....................................43
Average (volunteered)..........................26
Below average 8
Poor...5
No opinion...1

Less Than High-School Graduate

Outstanding 19%
Above average....................................28
Average (volunteered)..........................34
Below average 8
Poor...5
No opinion...6

By Region

East

Outstanding 15%
Above average....................................42
Average (volunteered)..........................25
Below average 12
Poor...5
No opinion...1

Midwest

Outstanding 12%
Above average....................................42
Average (volunteered)..........................30
Below average 10
Poor...5
No opinion...1

South

Outstanding 24%
Above average....................................38
Average (volunteered)..........................24
Below average 7
Poor...4
No opinion...3

West

Outstanding 17%
Above average....................................45
Average (volunteered)..........................21
Below average 8
Poor...8
No opinion...1

By Age

18–29 Years

Outstanding 15%
Above average....................................55
Average (volunteered)..........................19
Below average 6
Poor...4
No opinion...1

30–49 Years

Outstanding 19%
Above average....................................43
Average (volunteered)..........................24
Below average 10
Poor...3
No opinion...1

50–64 Years

Outstanding 18%
Above average....................................30
Average (volunteered)..........................29
Below average 10
Poor...9
No opinion...4

65 Years and Over

Outstanding 17%
Above average....................................24
Average (volunteered)..........................35
Below average 7
Poor...10
No opinion...7

By Household Income

$40,000 and Over

Outstanding 19%
Above average....................................47
Average (volunteered)..........................19
Below average 11

Poor..3
No opinion..1

$25,000–$39,999

Outstanding 16%
Above average..................................48
Average (volunteered)........................23
Below average 8
Poor..5
No opinion...*

$15,000–$24,999

Outstanding 15%
Above average..................................45
Average (volunteered)........................23
Below average 10
Poor..6
No opinion..1

Under $15,000

Outstanding 21%
Above average..................................26
Average (volunteered)........................33
Below average 10
Poor..6
No opinion..4

By Politics

Republicans

Outstanding 28%
Above average..................................53
Average (volunteered)........................17
Below average 1
Poor...*
No opinion..1

Democrats

Outstanding 11%
Above average..................................31
Average (volunteered)........................29
Below average 17
Poor..9
No opinion..3

Independents

Outstanding 14%
Above average..................................41
Average (volunteered)........................28
Below average 10

Poor..5
No opinion..2

By Religion

Protestants

Outstanding 20%
Above average..................................39
Average (volunteered)........................26
Below average 8
Poor..5
No opinion..2

Catholics

Outstanding 12%
Above average..................................49
Average (volunteered)........................26
Below average 9
Poor..3
No opinion..1

By Importance of Religion

Very Important

Outstanding 19%
Above average..................................36
Average (volunteered)........................28
Below average 9
Poor..5
No opinion..3

Fairly Important

Outstanding 18%
Above average..................................49
Average (volunteered)........................22
Below average 7
Poor..3
No opinion..1

Not Important

Outstanding 10%
Above average..................................47
Average (volunteered)........................19
Below average 14
Poor...10
No opinion...*

By Work Status

Full Time

Outstanding 17%
Above average..................................48

Average (volunteered)............................23
Below average 9
Poor... 3
No opinion... *

Part Time

Outstanding 16%
Above average......................................48
Average (volunteered)............................22
Below average 9
Poor... 4
No opinion... 1

Not Employed

Outstanding 19%
Above average......................................30
Average (volunteered)............................29
Below average 10
Poor... 8
No opinion... 4

All Working Women

Outstanding 15%
Above average......................................46
Average (volunteered)............................27
Below average 9
Poor... 3
No opinion... *

Full-Time Working Women

Outstanding 13%
Above average......................................46
Average (volunteered)............................28
Below average 10
Poor... 3
No opinion... *

*Less than 1%

Selected National Trend

	July 1987	March 1986
Outstanding	9%	16%
Above average	30	46
Average (volunteered)	34	23
Below average	16	8
Poor	9	5
No opinion	2	2

The following are the national comparisons for Presidents Jimmy Carter and Gerald Ford in December of their final years in office (1980 and 1976, respectively):

Evaluations of Carter and Ford

	Carter	Ford
Outstanding	3%	5%
Above average	11	20
Average (volunteered)	37	50
Below average	31	15
Poor	15	6
No opinion	3	4

Apart from whether you approve or disapprove of the way Ronald Reagan is handling his job as president, what do you think of Reagan as a person? Would you say you approve or disapprove of him?

Approve...79%
Disapprove...13
No opinion... 8

By Sex

Male

Approve...81%
Disapprove...13
No opinion... 6

Female

Approve...81%
Disapprove...13
No opinion... 6

By Ethnic Background

White

Approve...81%
Disapprove...12
No opinion... 7

Nonwhite

Approve...69%
Disapprove...22
No opinion... 9

Black

Approve...66%
Disapprove......................................25
No opinion.......................................9

By Education

College Graduate

Approve...84%
Disapprove......................................12
    No opinion....................................4

College Incomplete

Approve...79%
Disapprove......................................11
No opinion.......................................10

High-School Graduate

Approve...82%
Disapprove......................................12
No opinion.......................................6

Less Than High-School Graduate

Approve...70%
Disapprove......................................19
No opinion.......................................11

By Region

East

Approve...79%
Disapprove......................................16
No opinion.......................................5

Midwest

Approve...78%
Disapprove......................................14
No opinion.......................................8

South

Approve...83%
Disapprove......................................9
No opinion.......................................8

West

Approve...77%
Disapprove......................................14
No opinion.......................................9

By Age

18–29 Years

Approve...87%
Disapprove......................................8
No opinion.......................................5

30–49 Years

Approve...78%
Disapprove......................................14
No opinion.......................................8

50–64 Years

Approve...76%
Disapprove......................................16
No opinion.......................................8

65 Years and Over

Approve...73%
Disapprove......................................19
No opinion.......................................8

By Household Income

$40,000 and Over

Approve...82%
Disapprove......................................12
No opinion.......................................6

$25,000–$39,999

Approve...81%
Disapprove......................................13
No opinion.......................................6

$15,000–$24,999

Approve...84%
Disapprove......................................10
No opinion.......................................6

Under $15,000

Approve...72%
Disapprove......................................19
No opinion.......................................9

By Politics

Republicans

Approve...94%
Disapprove......................................2
No opinion.......................................4

Democrats

Approve..66%
Disapprove..26
No opinion...8

Independents

Approve..79%
Disapprove..12
No opinion...9

By Religion

Protestants

Approve..80%
Disapprove..13
No opinion...7

Catholics

Approve..82%
Disapprove..11
No opinion...7

By Importance of Religion

Very Important

Approve..80%
Disapprove..14
No opinion...6

Fairly Important

Approve..80%
Disapprove..12
No opinion...8

Not Important

Approve..77%
Disapprove..15
No opinion...8

By Work Status

Full Time

Approve..83%
Disapprove..10
No opinion...7

Part Time

Approve..84%
Disapprove..11
No opinion...5

Not Employed

Approve..73%
Disapprove..19
No opinion...8

All Working Women

Approve..84%
Disapprove..9
No opinion...7

Full-Time Working Women

Approve..83%
Disapprove..8
No opinion...9

Selected National Trend

	Approve	Dis-approve	No opinion
1987			
July 73%		20%	7%
1986			
December 75		18	7
September 80		12	8
1985			
November............. 81		10	9
1983			
August................. 67		21	12
1982			
February.............. 70		20	10
1981			
July 78		13	9

Note: Ronald Reagan ends his term in office with the highest approval rating of any president since Franklin Roosevelt. Sixty-three percent approve of the job Reagan has done. This compares with final approval ratings of 58% for John Kennedy and 59% for Dwight Eisenhower, the presidents who previously had the highest ratings since Roosevelt's 66%. In addition, as Reagan's final term draws to a close, public confidence in his leadership has returned to the level he enjoyed before the Iran-*contra* scandal broke. And unlike his modern predecessors, his final standing with the public is near the high points of his tenure.

Currently, 63% approve and 29% disapprove of the way Reagan is handling his presidential duties, identical to the job performance ratings he received in October 1986 before the revelation of his administration's sale of arms to Iran. Until recently the president's popularity languished near the 50% mark. He enjoys the unique distinction among modern presidents of ending his tenure very near his high points. In contrast, his eight predecessors, as monitored by one half-century of Gallup Polls, finished well below their peaks.

In addition, a 59% majority now says that Reagan will go down in history as an outstanding (17%) or above-average (42%) president, a percentage substantially higher than the 39% who held these views in mid-1987 and statistically equivalent to the 62% recorded in early 1986. Reagan fares much better in public expectations today than did his two immediate predecessors toward the end of their presidencies: in December 1980 only 14% thought that history would regard Jimmy Carter as an outstanding or above-average president, and only 25% thought this way about Gerald Ford in December 1976.

Reagan failed to achieve peak performance ratings as high as seven of his eight predecessors (Nixon was the exception). His average of 52% approval throughout his tenure, however, is surpassed only by Kennedy (70%), Roosevelt (68%), Eisenhower (66%), and Johnson (55%). Next to Reagan, the least attrition from high point to final assessment was suffered by Roosevelt and Ford, down 18 percentage points each; the greatest befell Harry Truman (off 56 points), followed by Nixon (down 44) and Carter (down 41). For all eight men the average loss was almost 32 points.

Reagan's political resilience, exemplified by his ability to surmount crises such as the Iran-*contra* affair, doubtless owes much to his enduring personal appeal. Throughout his tenure the percentage of Americans approving of Reagan as a person moved in a narrow range, from a low of 67% in mid-1983 to a high of 81% in late 1985. Currently, 79% approve of him as a person while 13% disapprove. Majorities from all walks of life and political persuasions, including those who disapprove

of his performance in office, hold positive opinions of Reagan, the man.

JANUARY 15
MIDDLE EAST SITUATION

Interviewing Date: 12/27–29/88
Survey #GO 89024

How closely would you say you have followed the recent situation in the Middle East?

Very closely......................................17%
Fairly closely....................................54
Not closely.......................................29
No opinion.. *

*Less than 1%

Asked of those who responded "very closely" (17%) or "fairly closely" (54%): In the Middle East situation, are your sympathies more with the Israelis or more with the Palestinian Arabs?

Israelis...46%
Palestinian Arabs 24
Both; neither (volunteered)....................16
No opinion..14

By Sex
Male

Israelis...52%
Palestinian Arabs 23
Both; neither (volunteered)....................15
No opinion..10

Female

Israelis...40%
Palestinian Arabs 24
Both; neither (volunteered)....................18
No opinion..18

By Ethnic Background
White

Israelis...48%
Palestinian Arabs 24

Both; neither (volunteered) 15
No opinion...13

Nonwhite

Israelis 39%
Palestinian Arabs 20
Both; neither (volunteered) 24
No opinion...17

Black

Israelis 42%
Palestinian Arabs 16
Both; neither (volunteered) 28
No opinion...14

By Education

College Graduate

Israelis 53%
Palestinian Arabs 24
Both; neither (volunteered) 20
No opinion... 3

College Incomplete

Israelis 47%
Palestinian Arabs 23
Both; neither (volunteered) 20
No opinion...10

High-School Graduate

Israelis 47%
Palestinian Arabs 24
Both; neither (volunteered) 15
No opinion...14

Less Than High-School Graduate

Israelis 35%
Palestinian Arabs 23
Both; neither (volunteered) 9
No opinion...33

By Region

East

Israelis 49%
Palestinian Arabs 25
Both; neither (volunteered) 15
No opinion...11

Midwest

Israelis 43%
Palestinian Arabs 25
Both; neither (volunteered) 17
No opinion...15

South

Israelis 50%
Palestinian Arabs 19
Both; neither (volunteered) 16
No opinion...15

West

Israelis 41%
Palestinian Arabs 28
Both; neither (volunteered) 18
No opinion...13

By Age

18–29 Years

Israelis 48%
Palestinian Arabs 29
Both; neither (volunteered) 15
No opinion... 8

30–49 Years

Israelis 53%
Palestinian Arabs 23
Both; neither (volunteered) 13
No opinion...11

50–64 Years

Israelis 38%
Palestinian Arabs 22
Both; neither (volunteered) 21
No opinion...19

65 Years and Over

Israelis 36%
Palestinian Arabs 21
Both; neither (volunteered) 21
No opinion...22

By Household Income

$40,000 and Over

Israelis 55%
Palestinian Arabs 22
Both; neither (volunteered) 16
No opinion... 7

$25,000-$39,999

Israelis 51%
Palestinian Arabs 26
Both; neither (volunteered) 13
No opinion.......................................10

$15,000-$24,999

Israelis 46%
Palestinian Arabs 24
Both; neither (volunteered) 15
No opinion.......................................15

Under $15,000

Israelis 38%
Palestinian Arabs 26
Both; neither (volunteered) 20
No opinion.......................................16

By Politics

Republicans

Israelis 52%
Palestinian Arabs 21
Both; neither (volunteered) 17
No opinion.......................................10

Democrats

Israelis 41%
Palestinian Arabs 28
Both; neither (volunteered) 15
No opinion.......................................16

Independents

Israelis 45%
Palestinian Arabs 22
Both; neither (volunteered) 18
No opinion.......................................15

By Religion

Protestants

Israelis 48%
Palestinian Arabs 22
Both; neither (volunteered) 16
No opinion.......................................14

Catholics

Israelis 42%
Palestinian Arabs 27

Both; neither (volunteered) 17
No opinion.......................................14

Also asked of the informed group (71% of the sample): Do you think there will or will not come a time when Israel and the Arab nations will be able to settle their differences and live in peace? [Those who responded affirmatively were asked: Do you think this will happen during the next five years, or not?]

Will settle differences............................55%
   During next 5 years............ 23
   Not during next 5 years....... 28
   Not sure............................4
Will not settle differences.....................42
No opinion... 3

Asked of the entire sample: The United States agreed to talks to open discussions with the Palestine Liberation Organization. Do you approve or disapprove of this decision?

Approve...72%
Disapprove.......................................20
No opinion... 8

By Sex

Male

Approve...74%
Disapprove.......................................22
No opinion... 4

Female

Approve...70%
Disapprove.......................................19
No opinion.......................................11

By Ethnic Background

White

Approve...73%
Disapprove.......................................19
No opinion... 8

Nonwhite

Approve...68%
Disapprove.......................................28
No opinion... 4

Black

Approve...70%
Disapprove...26
No opinion.. 4

By Education

College Graduate

Approve...86%
Disapprove...11
No opinion.. 3

College Incomplete

Approve...75%
Disapprove...20
No opinion.. 5

High-School Graduate

Approve...73%
Disapprove...19
No opinion.. 8

Less Than High-School Graduate

Approve...54%
Disapprove...30
No opinion...16

By Region

East

Approve...75%
Disapprove...17
No opinion.. 8

Midwest

Approve...72%
Disapprove...19
No opinion.. 9

South

Approve...70%
Disapprove...22
No opinion.. 8

West

Approve...70%
Disapprove...24
No opinion.. 6

By Age

18–29 Years

Approve...75%
Disapprove...20
No opinion.. 5

30–49 Years

Approve...75%
Disapprove...21
No opinion.. 4

50–64 Years

Approve...67%
Disapprove...20
No opinion...13

65 Years and Over

Approve...66%
Disapprove...20
No opinion...14

By Politics

Republicans

Approve...74%
Disapprove...17
No opinion.. 9

Democrats

Approve...70%
Disapprove...24
No opinion.. 6

Independents

Approve...73%
Disapprove...20
No opinion.. 7

By Religion

Protestants

Approve...71%
Disapprove...21
No opinion.. 8

Catholics

Approve...75%
Disapprove...17
No opinion.. 8

By Importance of Religion

Very Important

Approve...70%
Disapprove......................................21
No opinion....................................... 9

Fairly Important

Approve...77%
Disapprove......................................16
No opinion....................................... 7

Not Important

Approve...72%
Disapprove......................................23
No opinion....................................... 5

Middle East Sympathies

With Israelis

Approve...67%
Disapprove......................................28
No opinion....................................... 5

With Palestinian Arabs

Approve...86%
Disapprove......................................12
No opinion....................................... 2

With Both; Neither

Approve...73%
Disapprove......................................17
No opinion......................................10

Also asked of the entire sample: Do you think this improves or worsens the chances for peace in the Middle East?

Improves...67%
Worsens...15
No change (volunteered)......................... 8
No opinion......................................10

By Sex

Male

Improves...71%
Worsens...15
No change (volunteered)......................... 8
No opinion....................................... 6

Female

Improves...64%
Worsens...14
No change (volunteered)......................... 8
No opinion......................................14

By Ethnic Background

White

Improves...68%
Worsens...14
No change (volunteered)......................... 8
No opinion......................................10

Nonwhite

Improves...64%
Worsens...20
No change (volunteered)......................... 7
No opinion....................................... 9

Black

Improves...62%
Worsens...20
No change (volunteered)......................... 8
No opinion......................................10

By Education

College Graduate

Improves...81%
Worsens... 9
No change (volunteered)......................... 6
No opinion....................................... 4

College Incomplete

Improves...71%
Worsens...14
No change (volunteered)......................10
No opinion....................................... 5

High-School Graduate

Improves...68%
Worsens...14
No change (volunteered)......................... 8
No opinion......................................10

Less Than High-School Graduate

Improves...51%
Worsens...20
No change (volunteered)......................... 8
No opinion......................................21

By Region

East

Improves...69%
Worsens...14
No change (volunteered).........................7
No opinion..10

Midwest

Improves...61%
Worsens...15
No change (volunteered)........................13
No opinion..11

South

Improves...68%
Worsens...15
No change (volunteered).........................8
No opinion...9

West

Improves...72%
Worsens...14
No change (volunteered).........................4
No opinion..10

By Age

18–29 Years

Improves...74%
Worsens...16
No change (volunteered).........................4
No opinion...6

30–49 Years

Improves...70%
Worsens...15
No change (volunteered).........................9
No opinion...6

50–64 Years

Improves...61%
Worsens...13
No change (volunteered).........................10
No opinion..16

65 Years and Over

Improves...57%
Worsens...13
No change (volunteered).........................10
No opinion..20

By Politics

Republicans

Improves...68%
Worsens...12
No change (volunteered).........................8
No opinion..12

Democrats

Improves...68%
Worsens...15
No change (volunteered).........................8
No opinion...9

Independents

Improves...68%
Worsens...16
No change (volunteered).........................8
No opinion...8

By Religion

Protestants

Improves...66%
Worsens...16
No change (volunteered).........................8
No opinion..10

Catholics

Improves...70%
Worsens...13
No change (volunteered).........................8
No opinion...9

By Importance of Religion

Very Important

Improves...64%
Worsens...16
No change (volunteered).........................8
No opinion..12

Fairly Important

Improves...73%
Worsens...13
No change (volunteered).........................8
No opinion...6

Not Important

Improves...71%
Worsens..14
No change (volunteered)........................ 9
No opinion.. 6

Middle East Sympathies

With Israelis

Improves...66%
Worsens..19
No change (volunteered)........................ 9
No opinion.. 6

With Palestinian Arabs

Improves...78%
Worsens..13
No change (volunteered)........................ 6
No opinion.. 3

With Both; Neither

Improves...70%
Worsens.. 6
No change (volunteered)........................15
No opinion.. 9

Note: A large majority of Americans endorses the Reagan administration's recent decision to initiate talks with the Palestine Liberation Organization (PLO), with most respondents believing that negotiations with the PLO will improve the chances for peace in the Middle East. Almost three fourths (72%) approve of the U.S. move, while 20% disapprove and 8% are undecided. Little difference is found on the basis of sex, race, age, or political affiliation, but support for the decision increases with education. College graduates, for example, back the decision by an 86%-to-11% margin, while support drops to 54% to 30% among those who did not finish high school. Palestinian sympathizers also tend to uphold the U.S. decision (86%) more than those who side with the Israelis (67%).

Moreover, two thirds (67%) believe that the opening of talks between the United States and the PLO will enhance the chances for peace in the Middle East, while 15% disagree, 8% foresee little change, and 10% are undecided. Again, the well educated and those whose sympathies lie with the Palestinian Arabs are slightly more optimistic about the administration's initiative.

A slight majority of those who have followed the Middle East situation is optimistic about the long-term prospects for peace. Relatively few, however, think that an accommodation between Israel and its Arab neighbors is likely at any time in the near future. In fact, the same proportion now as in a Gallup survey last May (55%) says that the two adversaries eventually will be able to resolve their differences and live in peace. And the 23% who currently believe that this will occur within the next five years is not significantly greater than the 18% who felt this way last spring, before the Reagan administration's decision to begin a dialogue with the PLO.

In earlier surveys, informed Americans were sharply critical of Israel's handling of the Palestinian riots. Nevertheless, they remain more sympathetic toward the Israelis (46%) than toward the Palestinian Arabs (24%). Many respondents are ambivalent, however, with 16% siding equally with both factions (or neither) and 14% undecided.

JANUARY 19
SATISFACTION INDEX

Interviewing Date: 9/25–10/1/88
Survey #AI 875

Please tell me whether you are satisfied or dissatisfied with the following aspects of your life: Your present housing? Your standard of living? Your household income? Your family life? Your health today? Your job—the work you do? Your free time—the time when you are not working at your job?

Satisfaction Index
(Percent Satisfied)

	1988	1984
Family life	94%	88%
Health	88	85
Free time	87	78
Housing	87	81
Standard of living	85	78
Job	76	70
Household income	69	63

1988 Satisfaction Index by Ethnic Background
(Percent Satisfied)

	White	Black
Family life	94%	91%
Housing	89	74
Health	88	84
Free time	88	81
Standard of living	87	68
Job	76	71
Household income	71	52

1988 Satisfaction Index by Country
(Percent Satisfied)

	United States	Great Britain*
Free time	87%	76%
Housing	87	77
Standard of living	85	71
Job	76	61
Household income	69	56

*Based on a survey conducted during June 1988 by the Gallup affiliate in Great Britain

Note: George Bush's first 100 days will be buoyed by a public that currently are more upbeat and satisfied with the basic aspects of their lives than they have been for many years. Solid and growing majorities of citizens express satisfaction with each of seven components of their day-to-day existence— their family life, health, free time, housing, standard of living, job, and household income.

Satisfaction with family life has grown from 88% to 94% over the last four years, while over the same period of time satisfaction with health has increased from 85% to 88%; free time, from 78% to 87%; housing, from 81% to 87%; standard of living, from 78% to 85%; and job, from 70% to 76%. An increase also is noted in those who are satisfied with their household income, from 63% to 69%.

While the overall levels of reported satisfaction are encouragingly high for both white and black respondents on most items, some sharp differences exist. For example, only 52% of blacks, compared to 71% of whites, are satisfied with their household income. Marked differences also are recorded

for standard of living and housing. However, racial differences are slight on health, job, family life, and free time.

The remarkably high level of satisfaction with the amenities of life among Americans is underscored by comparisons with the British. Americans score higher on each of the five items included in both polls, with the differences most marked on job.

JANUARY 22
ABORTION

Interviewing Date: 12/27–29/88
Survey #GO 89024

In 1973 the Supreme Court ruled that states cannot place restrictions on a woman's right to an abortion during the first three months of pregnancy. Would you like to see this ruling overturned, or not?

Yes	37%
No	57
No opinion	6

By Sex
Male

Yes	36%
No	57
No opinion	7

Female

Yes	37%
No	59
No opinion	4

By Ethnic Background
White

Yes	36%
No	58
No opinion	6

Nonwhite

Yes	39%
No	56
No opinion	5

Black

Yes...37%
No...59
No opinion...4

By Education

College Graduate

Yes...29%
No...66
No opinion...5

College Incomplete

Yes...33%
No...62
No opinion...5

High-School Graduate

Yes...34%
No...59
No opinion...7

Less Than High-School Graduate

Yes...53%
No...41
No opinion...6

By Region

East

Yes...36%
No...60
No opinion...4

Midwest

Yes...34%
No...59
No opinion...7

South

Yes...44%
No...51
No opinion...5

West

Yes...31%
No...64
No opinion...5

By Age

18-29 Years

Yes...30%
No...69
No opinion...1

30-49 Years

Yes...37%
No...57
No opinion...6

50-64 Years

Yes...41%
No...51
No opinion...8

65 Years and Over

Yes...42%
No...48
No opinion...10

By Household Income

$40,000 and Over

Yes...31%
No...65
No opinion...4

$25,000-$39,999

Yes...33%
No...63
No opinion...4

$15,000-$24,999

Yes...38%
No...57
No opinion...5

Under $15,000

Yes...44%
No...51
No opinion...5

By Politics

Republicans

Yes...41%
No...54
No opinion...5

Democrats

Yes..36%
No...59
No opinion......................................5

Independents

Yes..33%
No...61
No opinion......................................6

By Religion

Protestants

Yes..39%
No...56
No opinion......................................5

Catholics

Yes..39%
No...54
No opinion......................................7

By Importance of Religion

Very Important

Yes..48%
No...45
No opinion......................................7

Fairly Important

Yes..24%
No...72
No opinion......................................4

Not Important

Yes..19%
No...77
No opinion......................................4

By Work Status

Full Time

Yes..34%
No...60
No opinion......................................6

Part Time

Yes..36%
No...59
No opinion......................................5

Not Employed

Yes..40%
No...54
No opinion......................................6

All Working Women

Yes..34%
No...62
No opinion......................................4

Full-Time Working Women

Yes..33%
No...63
No opinion......................................4

Do you ever wonder whether your own position on abortion is the right one, or not?

Yes..33%
No...60
Not sure 7

By Sex

Male

Yes..32%
No...61
Not sure 7

Female

Yes..34%
No...60
Not sure 6

By Ethnic Background

White

Yes..33%
No...61
Not sure 6

Nonwhite

Yes..34%
No...56
Not sure 10

Black

Yes..35%
No..58
Not sure 7

By Education

College Graduate

Yes..30%
No..66
Not sure 4

College Incomplete

Yes..36%
No..62
Not sure 2

High-School Graduate

Yes..37%
No..58
Not sure 5

Less Than High-School Graduate

Yes..27%
No..57
Not sure 16

By Region

East

Yes..31%
No..63
Not sure 6

Midwest

Yes..35%
No..57
Not sure 8

South

Yes..38%
No..55
Not sure 7

West

Yes..27%
No..68
Not sure 5

By Age

18–29 Years

Yes..40%
No..57
Not sure 3

30–49 Years

Yes..33%
No..64
Not sure 3

50–64 Years

Yes..30%
No..58
Not sure 12

65 Years and Over

Yes..26%
No..56
Not sure 18

By Household Income

$40,000 and Over

Yes..32%
No..66
Not sure 2

$25,000–$39,999

Yes..37%
No..59
Not sure 4

$15,000–$24,999

Yes..39%
No..56
Not sure 5

Under $15,000

Yes..30%
No..57
Not sure 13

By Politics

Republicans

Yes..32%
No..62
Not sure 6

Democrats

Yes	37%
No	56
Not sure	7

Independents

Yes	32%
No	62
Not sure	6

By Religion

Protestants

Yes	35%
No	59
Not sure	6

Catholics

Yes	32%
No	60
Not sure	8

By Importance of Religion

Very Important

Yes	34%
No	58
Not sure	8

Fairly Important

Yes	35%
No	60
Not sure	5

Not Important

Yes	28%
No	70
Not sure	2

By Work Status

Full Time

Yes	35%
No	61
Not sure	4

Part Time

Yes	31%
No	65
Not sure	4

Not Employed

Yes	32%
No	57
Not sure	11

All Working Women

Yes	34%
No	63
Not sure	3

Full-Time Working Women

Yes	35%
No	62
Not sure	3

Compared to a decade ago, medical scientists have learned significantly more about the first stages of life. Has this made you more in favor or less in favor of abortion—or hasn't this changed your opinion on the issue?

More in favor	5%
Less in favor	20
Have not changed opinion	71
Not sure	4

By Sex

Male

More in favor	4%
Less in favor	18
Have not changed opinion	75
Not sure	3

Female

More in favor	6%
Less in favor	22
Have not changed opinion	68
Not sure	4

By Ethnic Background

White

More in favor 4%
Less in favor 20
Have not changed opinion 72
Not sure 4

Nonwhite

More in favor 11%
Less in favor 24
Have not changed opinion 61
Not sure 4

Black

More in favor 12%
Less in favor 29
Have not changed opinion 56
Not sure 3

By Education

College Graduate

More in favor 4%
Less in favor 17
Have not changed opinion 79
Not sure .... *

College Incomplete

More in favor 7%
Less in favor 20
Have not changed opinion 72
Not sure 1

High-School Graduate

More in favor 5%
Less in favor 22
Have not changed opinion 70
Not sure 3

Less Than High-School Graduate

More in favor 7%
Less in favor 20
Have not changed opinion 64
Not sure 9

By Region

East

More in favor 6%
Less in favor 14

Have not changed opinion 75
Not sure 5

Midwest

More in favor 5%
Less in favor 25
Have not changed opinion 68
Not sure 2

South

More in favor 5%
Less in favor 23
Have not changed opinion 68
Not sure 4

West

More in favor 5%
Less in favor 18
Have not changed opinion 74
Not sure 3

By Age

18–29 Years

More in favor 7%
Less in favor 23
Have not changed opinion 69
Not sure 1

30–49 Years

More in favor 6%
Less in favor 17
Have not changed opinion 70
Not sure 7

50–64 Years

More in favor 6%
Less in favor 16
Have not changed opinion 70
Not sure 8

65 Years and Over

More in favor 6%
Less in favor 16
Have not changed opinion 70
Not sure 8

By Household Income

$40,000 and Over

More in favor 3%
Less in favor 17
Have not changed opinion 79
Not sure 1

$25,000–$39,999

More in favor 4%
Less in favor 23
Have not changed opinion 72
Not sure 1

$15,000–$24,999

More in favor 8%
Less in favor 24
Have not changed opinion 64
Not sure 4

Under $15,000

More in favor 6%
Less in favor 21
Have not changed opinion 67
Not sure 6

By Politics

Republicans

More in favor 5%
Less in favor 19
Have not changed opinion 71
Not sure 5

Democrats

More in favor 5%
Less in favor 18
Have not changed opinion 74
Not sure 3

Independents

More in favor 5%
Less in favor 23
Have not changed opinion 69
Not sure 3

By Religion

Protestants

More in favor 5%
Less in favor 23

Have not changed opinion 69
Not sure 3

Catholics

More in favor 6%
Less in favor 17
Have not changed opinion 72
Not sure 5

By Importance of Religion

Very Important

More in favor 5%
Less in favor 25
Have not changed opinion 66
Not sure 4

Fairly Important

More in favor 7%
Less in favor 17
Have not changed opinion 73
Not sure 3

Not Important

More in favor 2%
Less in favor 11
Have not changed opinion 87
Not sure .... *

By Work Status

Full Time

More in favor 4%
Less in favor 20
Have not changed opinion 73
Not sure 3

Part Time

More in favor 7%
Less in favor 27
Have not changed opinion 64
Not sure 2

Not Employed

More in favor 5%
Less in favor 20
Have not changed opinion 70
Not sure 5

All Working Women

More in favor 7%
Less in favor 23
Have not changed opinion 67
Not sure 3

Full-Time Working Women

More in favor 7%
Less in favor 21
Have not changed opinion 69
Not sure 3

Impact of Medical Advances on Attitude toward *Roe v. Wade*

Should Be Overturned

More in favor 5%
Less in favor 20
Have not changed opinion 71
Not sure 4

Should Not Be Overturned

More in favor 6%
Less in favor 17
Have not changed opinion 74
Not sure 3

*Less than 1%

Note: A substantial majority of Americans is opposed to the Supreme Court's overturning its 1973 affirmation of women's right to obtain abortions, one possible outcome of the Court's recent decision to rule on the constitutionality of a Missouri law that places severe restrictions on abortion rights. In a new Gallup Poll, 37% say that they would like to see *Roe v. Wade* overturned, while 57% are opposed and 6% undecided.

The Court has struck down previous challenges to its landmark 1973 ruling that the states cannot restrict women's right to abortions during the first three months of pregnancy, but President Ronald Reagan's appointment of Justices Antonin Scalia and Anthony Kennedy now has given the Court a conservative ideological balance. Legal experts think it is possible the Court, in its review of the Missouri case, will either overturn the 1973 ruling or weaken some of its provisions, with complete reaffirmation considered unlikely.

Opposition to the Court's overturning *Roe v. Wade* outweighs support in all major demographic groups. Little difference is found on the basis of sex, religious preference, or political affiliation, but opposition is higher among adults under age 30 (69%) than among 30 to 49-year-olds (57%) or those 50 and older (51%). Opposition also is more prevalent among well-educated, affluent Americans. Opponents barely outnumber proponents in the South, 51% to 44%, compared to an average of 61% to 34% in other regions of the nation.

Statistically equivalent percentages of people who consider religion very important in their lives favor (48%) and oppose (45%) having the Court overturn *Roe v. Wade*. In sharp contrast, among those for whom religion is less important, 24% favor this and 72% are opposed. .

One third (33%) say that they sometimes wonder whether their position on abortion is the right one, while 60% have not had doubts. When this question was asked four years ago, 38% expressed some uncertainty but 55% did not. Indeed, few issues in recent years have so sharply divided the American people as a woman's right to have an abortion. In a September 1988 poll, 57% favored legal abortions under certain circumstances, while 24% backed unlimited access and 17% an outright ban on all abortions. Public opinion on this question has remained virtually unchanged since the 1973 ruling.

Queried about the impact that advances in scientific knowledge on the early stages of life may have had on their attitudes about abortion, most respondents (71%) say that such evidence has not changed their opinions. However, among people whose opinions have changed, those who say that they are less inclined to favor abortions outnumber those who are more supportive, 20% to 5%. People who sometimes have had doubts about their stand on abortion are more apt to say that increased scientific knowledge has caused them to lean against rather than in favor of legal abortions.

JANUARY 26
SPORTS

Interviewing Date: 11/11–14; 12/9–12/88
Survey #APIO 295G; 296-G

Which of these sports and activities, if any, have you, yourself, participated in within the last twelve months? [Respondents were handed a card listing more than fifty recreational activities.]

Swimming..36%
Fishing...29
Bicycling..24
Bowling..21
Camping...19
Weight training*.............................19
Running, jogging............................17
Pool, billiards................................17
Softball..16
Hiking..16
Aerobics, dancercize.....................14
Basketball......................................14
Weight lifting................................14
Volleyball.......................................13
Hunting..12
Motorboating.................................12
Golf..12
Bicycle touring, racing..................11
Calisthenics...................................11
Bodybuilding.................................10
Baseball...10
Darts..10

Men's Top Activities

Fishing...41%
Swimming..38
Pool, billiards................................26
Weight training*.............................26
Bicycling..24
Bowling..23
Hunting..23
Camping...22
Softball..22
Weight lifting................................21
Basketball......................................21

Women's Top Activities

Swimming..34%
Bicycling..25
Aerobics, dancercize.....................23
Bowling..20
Fishing...17
Running, jogging............................16
Camping...16
Hiking..13

Weight training*.................................12
Calisthenics..11

*Any form of weight training, including weight lifting, bodybuilding, and Nautilus

Selected National Trend

	1987	1972	1959
Swimming	41%	42%	33%
Fishing	30	24	22
Bicycling	31	28	*
Bowling	23	28	18
Softball	19	13	*
Volleyball	16	12	4
Motorboating	14	20	*
Golf	13	14	8
Tennis	11	12	4

*Not asked

Note: Swimming continues to be Americans' favorite recreational activity, as it has been for more than one quarter of a century. More than one third of adults (36%) went swimming at least once during the last twelve months. Next most popular are fishing and bicycling, in which 29% and 24%, respectively, participated. These three sports have been among the leading activities since Gallup began auditing the public's preferences almost thirty years ago.

Bowling (21%), camping (19%), and weight training (19%) also rank high, as was determined by a national survey of over 2,000 adults who were asked to indicate in which of more than fifty pastimes they had taken part during a recent twelve-month period. Rounding out the top ten are jogging or running (17%), pool or billiards (17%), softball (16%), and hiking (16%).

Not surprisingly, participation in many of the activities listed was greater among men than women. Hunting, for example, was engaged in by 23% of men but only 3% of women. And while the percentage of women who went fishing last year (17%) was large enough to make it their fifth-ranking pastime, it led among men, with 41% participating. By the same token, weight training appears in the top ten of both sexes, but the proportion of men who worked out with weights was about twice that of women, 26% to 12%.

Four of the leading leisure activities, however, were equally popular with both sexes: swimming, bicycling, bowling, and running or jogging. Only aerobics was markedly more popular among women (23%) than men (5%).

Participation in most of the activities studied was about the same in both the 1988 and 1987 audits. The newer study, however, found that no sport had an increased participation rate, although significant declines were noted in swimming, bicycling, and hiking, among others.

JANUARY 29
ADULT RELATIONSHIPS

Interviewing Date: 9/24–10/9/88
Survey #GO 88273*

How would you rate the quality of the communication between you and your husband/wife/romantic partner? Is the communication in your relationship excellent, good, only fair, or poor?

Excellent...40%
Good...47
Fair..10
Poor.. 2
No opinion.. 1

By Sex

Male

Excellent...42%
Good...48
Fair... 8
Poor.. 2
No opinion.. *

*This survey was conducted for Cosgrove-Meurer Productions Inc. by the Gallup Organization. The findings are based on interviews with adults, age 18 and older, who are married, widowed, or unmarried and involved in a romantic relationship.

Female

Excellent...39%
Good...46
Fair..11
Poor.. 3
No opinion.. 1

By Ethnic Background

White

Excellent...42%
Good...46
Fair... 9
Poor.. 2
No opinion.. 1

Nonwhite

Excellent...28%
Good...48
Fair..19
Poor.. 4
No opinion.. 1

By Education
College Graduate

Excellent...42%
Good...49
Fair... 8
Poor.. 1
No opinion.. *

College Incomplete

Excellent...45%
Good...44
Fair... 6
Poor.. 3
No opinion.. 2

High-School Graduate

Excellent...39%
Good...48
Fair..10
Poor.. 3
No opinion.. *

Less Than High-School Graduate

Excellent...36%
Good...45

Fair...17
Poor...1
No opinion.................................1

By Age

18–29 Years

Excellent.................................43%
Good..48
Fair...5
Poor..3
No opinion..................................1

30–49 Years

Excellent.................................37%
Good..50
Fair..10
Poor..2
No opinion..................................1

50 Years and Over

Excellent.................................42%
Good..42
Fair..13
Poor..2
No opinion..................................1

By Household Income

$50,000 and Over

Excellent.................................45%
Good..45
Fair...8
Poor..2
No opinion...................................*

$30,000–$49,999

Excellent.................................40%
Good..50
Fair...7
Poor..2
No opinion..................................1

$15,000–$29,999

Excellent.................................37%
Good..49
Fair..10
Poor..3
No opinion..................................1

Under $15,000

Excellent.................................40%
Good..41
Fair..13
Poor..4
No opinion..................................2

By Relationship Status

Married/Widowed

Excellent.................................40%
Good..47
Fair..10
Poor..2
No opinion..................................1

Divorced/Separated

Excellent.................................46%
Good..33
Fair..20
Poor...*
No opinion..................................1

Never Married

Excellent.................................39%
Good..50
Fair...7
Poor..4
No opinion...................................*

Total Not Married

Excellent.................................41%
Good..45
Fair..11
Poor..3
No opinion...................................*

By Satisfaction with Relationship

Completely Satisfied

Excellent.................................55%
Good..41
Fair...3
Poor...*
No opinion..................................1

Mostly Satisfied

Excellent.................................18%
Good..58

Fair...19
Poor...5
No opinion...................................*

Mostly Dissatisfied

Excellent.....................................6%
Good..29
Fair...45
Poor...20
No opinion...................................*

Completely Dissatisfied

Excellent.....................................*%
Good..23
Fair...13
Poor...64
No opinion...................................*

By Satisfaction with Sexual Relationship

Total Satisfied

Excellent.....................................42%
Good..47
Fair...9
Poor...2
No opinion...................................*

Total Dissatisfied

Excellent.....................................3%
Good..44
Fair...21
Poor...32
No opinion...................................*

*Less than 1%

Looking back over your entire marriage/romantic relationship, if you could do it all over again, would you marry/get romantically involved with the same person again, or not?

Would..88%
Would not......................................8
Not sure 4

By Sex

Male

Would..90%
Would not......................................7
Not sure 3

Female

Would..86%
Would not......................................9
Not sure 5

By Ethnic Background

White

Would..90%
Would not......................................6
Not sure 4

Nonwhite

Would..73%
Would not......................................22
Not sure 5

By Education

College Graduate

Would..92%
Would not......................................3
Not sure 5

College Incomplete

Would..87%
Would not......................................9
Not sure 4

High-School Graduate

Would..88%
Would not......................................8
Not sure 4

Less Than High-School Graduate

Would..86%
Would not......................................11
Not sure 3

By Age

18–29 Years

Would..87%
Would not.....................................11
Not sure 2

30–49 Years

Would..89%
Would not.......................................7
Not sure 4

50 Years and Over

Would..87%
Would not.......................................8
Not sure 5

By Household Income

$50,000 and Over

Would..90%
Would not.......................................7
Not sure 3

$30,000–$49,999

Would..93%
Would not.......................................4
Not sure 3

$15,000–$29,999

Would..87%
Would not.......................................8
Not sure 5

Under $15,000

Would..83%
Would not......................................12
Not sure 5

By Relationship Status

Married/Widowed

Would..90%
Would not.......................................6
Not sure 4

Divorced/Separated

Would..72%
Would not......................................22
Not sure 6

Never Married

Would..83%
Would not......................................13
Not sure 4

Total Not Married

Would..79%
Would not......................................16
Not sure 5

By Satisfaction with Relationship

Completely Satisfied

Would..97%
Would not.......................................2
Not sure 1

Mostly Satisfied

Would..77%
Would not......................................15
Not sure 8

Mostly Dissatisfied

Would..26%
Would not......................................61
Not sure 13

Completely Dissatisfied

Would..23%
Would not......................................77
Not sure ....*

By Quality of Communication

Excellent

Would..97%
Would not.......................................2
Not sure 1

Good

Would..89%
Would not.......................................7
Not sure 4

Fair

Would..63%
Would not......................................24
Not sure 13

Poor

Would...28%
Would not.......................................61
Not sure 11

By Satisfaction with Sexual Relationship

Total Satisfied

Would...89%
Would not...7
Not sure 4

Total Dissatisfied

Would...59%
Would not..35
Not sure 6

*Less than 1%

Does your husband/wife/romantic partner fulfill your emotional needs all of the time, most of the time, only some of the time, or never?

All of the time 31%
Most of the time................................56
Some of the time 11
Never 1
Not sure 1

By Sex

Male

All of the time 36%
Most of the time................................51
Some of the time 11
Never 1
Not sure 1

Female

All of the time 26%
Most of the time................................60
Some of the time 11
Never 2
Not sure 1

By Ethnic Background

White

All of the time 32%
Most of the time................................56
Some of the time 10
Never 1
Not sure 1

Nonwhite

All of the time 22%
Most of the time................................56
Some of the time 17
Never 3
Not sure 2

By Education

College Graduate

All of the time 33%
Most of the time................................61
Some of the time 5
Never 1
Not sure ....*

College Incomplete

All of the time 26%
Most of the time................................62
Some of the time 10
Never 1
Not sure 1

High-School Graduate

All of the time 31%
Most of the time................................56
Some of the time 12
Never 1
Not sure ....*

Less Than High-School Graduate

All of the time 31%
Most of the time................................56
Some of the time 12
Never 1
Not sure ....*

By Age

18-29 Years

All of the time	26%
Most of the time	66
Some of the time	8
Never	*
Not sure	*

30-49 Years

All of the time	26%
Most of the time	62
Some of the time	11
Never	1
Not sure	*

50 Years and Over

All of the time	37%
Most of the time	46
Some of the time	13
Never	2
Not sure	2

By Household Income

$50,000 and Over

All of the time	28%
Most of the time	64
Some of the time	8
Never	*
Not sure	*

$30,000-$49,999

All of the time	30%
Most of the time	62
Some of the time	8
Never	*
Not sure	*

$15,000-$29,999

All of the time	31%
Most of the time	55
Some of the time	13
Never	1
Not sure	*

Under $15,000

All of the time	33%
Most of the time	47
Some of the time	13

Never	4
Not sure	3

By Relationship Status

Married/Widowed

All of the time	33%
Most of the time	55
Some of the time	10
Never	1
Not sure	1

Divorced/Separated

All of the time	24%
Most of the time	48
Some of the time	27
Never	*
Not sure	1

Never Married

All of the time	21%
Most of the time	70
Some of the time	9
Never	*
Not sure	*

Total Not Married

All of the time	22%
Most of the time	63
Some of the time	15
Never	*
Not sure	*

By Satisfaction with Relationship

Completely Satisfied

All of the time	42%
Most of the time	51
Some of the time	5
Never	1
Not sure	1

Mostly Satisfied

All of the time	13%
Most of the time	66
Some of the time	19
Never	1
Not sure	1

Mostly Dissatisfied

All of the time ....*%
Most of the time................................42
Some of the time 45
Never 13
Not sure ....*

Completely Dissatisfied

All of the time 23%
Most of the time................................*
Some of the time 64
Never 13
Not sure ....*

By Quality of Communication

Excellent

All of the time 49%
Most of the time................................49
Some of the time 2
Never ....*
Not sure ....*

Good

All of the time 21%
Most of the time................................68
Some of the time 9
Never 1
Not sure 1

Fair

All of the time 8%
Most of the time................................42
Some of the time 47
Never 3
Not sure ....*

Poor

All of the time 8%
Most of the time................................13
Some of the time 64
Never 11
Not sure 4

By Satisfaction with Sexual Relationship

Total Satisfied

All of the time 31%
Most of the time................................58

Some of the time 10
Never 1
Not sure ....*

Total Dissatisfied

All of the time 6%
Most of the time................................32
Some of the time 44
Never 18
Not sure ....*

*Less than 1%

Do you feel that you can trust your husband/wife/romantic partner all of the time, most of the time, only some of the time, or never?

All of the time 78%
Most of the time................................16
Some of the time 4
Never 1
Not sure 1

By Sex

Male

All of the time 85%
Most of the time................................11
Some of the time 3
Never ....*
Not sure 1

Female

All of the time 72%
Most of the time................................20
Some of the time 5
Never 2
Not sure 1

By Ethnic Background

White

All of the time 81%
Most of the time................................15
Some of the time 3
Never ....*
Not sure 1

Nonwhite

All of the time 56%
Most of the time................................28
Some of the time 12
Never 3
Not sure 1

By Education

College Graduate

All of the time 85%
Most of the time................................14
Some of the time 1
Never ....*
Not sure ....*

College Incomplete

All of the time 76%
Most of the time................................18
Some of the time 5
Never ....*
Not sure 1

High-School Graduate

All of the time 80%
Most of the time................................14
Some of the time 4
Never 2
Not sure ....*

Less Than High-School Graduate

All of the time 72%
Most of the time................................20
Some of the time 6
Never 1
Not sure 1

By Age

18–29 Years

All of the time 75%
Most of the time................................16
Some of the time 8
Never 1
Not sure ....*

30–49 Years

All of the time 78%
Most of the time................................19

Some of the time 2
Never 1
Not sure ....*

50 Years and Over

All of the time 80%
Most of the time................................14
Some of the time 4
Never 1
Not sure 1

By Household Income

$50,000 and Over

All of the time 87%
Most of the time................................12
Some of the time ....*
Never 1
Not sure ....*

$30,000–$49,999

All of the time 81%
Most of the time................................17
Some of the time 2
Never ....*
Not sure ....*

$15,000–$29,999

All of the time 78%
Most of the time................................17
Some of the time 4
Never 1
Not sure ....*

Under $15,000

All of the time 67%
Most of the time................................21
Some of the time 8
Never 2
Not sure 2

By Relationship Status

Married/Widowed

All of the time 81%
Most of the time................................14
Some of the time 3
Never 1
Not sure 1

Divorced/Separated

All of the time 66%
Most of the time.................................24
Some of the time 6
Never 2
Not sure 2

Never Married

All of the time 65%
Most of the time.................................26
Some of the time 8
Never 1
Not sure ....*

Total Not Married

All of the time 65%
Most of the time.................................25
Some of the time 8
Never 1
Not sure 1

By Satisfaction with Relationship

Completely Satisfied

All of the time 90%
Most of the time.................................8
Some of the time 1
Never ....*
Not sure 1

Mostly Satisfied

All of the time 60%
Most of the time.................................30
Some of the time 8
Never 2
Not sure ....*

Mostly Dissatisfied

All of the time 24%
Most of the time.................................36
Some of the time 21
Never 19
Not sure ....*

Completely Dissatisfied

All of the time 37%
Most of the time.................................13
Some of the time 50
Never ....*
Not sure ....*

By Quality of Communication

Excellent

All of the time 92%
Most of the time.................................7
Some of the time 1
Never ....*
Not sure ....*

Good

All of the time 77%
Most of the time.................................20
Some of the time 3
Never ....*
Not sure ....*

Fair

All of the time 44%
Most of the time.................................34
Some of the time 16
Never 5
Not sure 1

Poor

All of the time 18%
Most of the time.................................40
Some of the time 31
Never 11
Not sure ....*

By Satisfaction with Sexual Relationship

Total Satisfied

All of the time 80%
Most of the time.................................16
Some of the time 4
Never ....*
Not sure ....*

Total Dissatisfied

All of the time 42%
Most of the time.................................29
Some of the time 17
Never 10
Not sure 2

*Less than 1%

How satisfied are you with the sexual relationship you share with your husband/wife/romantic partner?

Completely satisfied 56%
Mostly satisfied..................................38
Mostly dissatisfied 2
Completely dissatisfied.........................1
Not sure 3

By Sex

Male

Completely satisfied 56%
Mostly satisfied..................................40
Mostly dissatisfied 2
Completely dissatisfied.........................1
Not sure 1

Female

Completely satisfied 56%
Mostly satisfied..................................37
Mostly dissatisfied 1
Completely dissatisfied.........................1
Not sure 5

By Ethnic Background

White

Completely satisfied 56%
Mostly satisfied..................................38
Mostly dissatisfied 2
Completely dissatisfied.........................1
Not sure 3

Nonwhite

Completely satisfied 57%
Mostly satisfied..................................38
Mostly dissatisfied 1
Completely dissatisfied.........................1
Not sure 3

By Education

College Graduate

Completely satisfied 52%
Mostly satisfied..................................40
Mostly dissatisfied 4
Completely dissatisfied.........................2
Not sure 2

College Incomplete

Completely satisfied 52%
Mostly satisfied..................................43
Mostly dissatisfied 1
Completely dissatisfied.........................*
Not sure 4

High-School Graduate

Completely satisfied 57%
Mostly satisfied..................................38
Mostly dissatisfied 2
Completely dissatisfied.........................1
Not sure 2

Less Than High-School Graduate

Completely satisfied 61%
Mostly satisfied..................................30
Mostly dissatisfied 1
Completely dissatisfied.........................*
Not sure 8

By Age

18–29 Years

Completely satisfied 57%
Mostly satisfied..................................40
Mostly dissatisfied 1
Completely dissatisfied.........................*
Not sure 2

30–49 Years

Completely satisfied 52%
Mostly satisfied..................................43
Mostly dissatisfied 3
Completely dissatisfied.........................*
Not sure 2

50 Years and Over

Completely satisfied 60%
Mostly satisfied..................................32
Mostly dissatisfied 1
Completely dissatisfied.........................1
Not sure 6

By Household Income

$50,000 and Over

Completely satisfied 55%
Mostly satisfied..................................38

Mostly dissatisfied 3
Completely dissatisfied...........................1
Not sure 3

$30,000–$49,999

Completely satisfied 56%
Mostly satisfied...................................42
Mostly dissatisfied 1
Completely dissatisfied...........................*
Not sure 1

$15,000–$29,999

Completely satisfied 55%
Mostly satisfied...................................40
Mostly dissatisfied 2
Completely dissatisfied...........................1
Not sure 2

Under $15,000

Completely satisfied 59%
Mostly satisfied...................................31
Mostly dissatisfied 2
Completely dissatisfied...........................1
Not sure 7

By Relationship Status

Married/Widowed

Completely satisfied 57%
Mostly satisfied...................................36
Mostly dissatisfied 2
Completely dissatisfied...........................1
Not sure 4

Divorced/Separated

Completely satisfied 41%
Mostly satisfied...................................53
Mostly dissatisfied 1
Completely dissatisfied...........................*
Not sure 5

Never Married

Completely satisfied 53%
Mostly satisfied...................................42
Mostly dissatisfied 1
Completely dissatisfied...........................1
Not sure 3

Total Not Married

Completely satisfied 49%
Mostly satisfied...................................46

Mostly dissatisfied 1
Completely dissatisfied...........................*
Not sure 4

By Satisfaction with Relationship

Completely Satisfied

Completely satisfied 71%
Mostly satisfied...................................25
Mostly dissatisfied 1
Completely dissatisfied...........................*
Not sure 3

Mostly Satisfied

Completely satisfied 31%
Mostly satisfied...................................61
Mostly dissatisfied 3
Completely dissatisfied...........................1
Not sure 4

Mostly Dissatisfied

Completely satisfied 35%
Mostly satisfied...................................46
Mostly dissatisfied 6
Completely dissatisfied...........................*
Not sure 13

Completely Dissatisfied

Completely satisfied ....*%
Mostly satisfied...................................65
Mostly dissatisfied ....*
Completely dissatisfied...........................35
Not sure ....*

By Quality of Communication

Excellent

Completely satisfied 76%
Mostly satisfied...................................22
Mostly dissatisfied ....*
Completely dissatisfied...........................*
Not sure 2

Good

Completely satisfied 47%
Mostly satisfied...................................48
Mostly dissatisfied 2
Completely dissatisfied...........................*
Not sure 3

Fair

Completely satisfied 26%
Mostly satisfied................................61
Mostly dissatisfied 4
Completely dissatisfied.........................1
Not sure 8

Poor

Completely satisfied 13%
Mostly satisfied................................46
Mostly dissatisfied 16
Completely dissatisfied.........................19
Not sure 6

*Less than 1%

Note: In an era of increasingly fragile marriages, a couple's ability to communicate is the single most important factor contributing to a stable and satisfying relationship. In a new Gallup study of married and romantically involved adults, 40% rate their ability to communicate with their partner as excellent, 47% as good, and 12% as only fair or poor. The quality of the relationships among couples with excellent communication, however, is strikingly better than among those who rank lower. Comparing the two groups, the former are far more likely than the latter to feel completely satisfied with their overall relationship and to say that they would choose the same partner again.

The critical importance of communication also is evident in the more concrete aspects of these relationships. Couples whose ability to communicate is excellent are more apt than those who share their feelings less well to be completely satisfied with their sexual relationship, to say their emotional needs are always fulfilled, and to believe that they can trust their partner all of the time.

Of the participants in this survey of romantic relationships, 61% express complete satisfaction with their union, and 36% are mostly satisfied. This level of contentment is high enough to lead 88% of these people to claim that they would become romantically involved with their partner again if they had the chance to do it all over.

However, 84% of those whose communication is excellent say that they are completely satisfied with their overall relationship, compared to 53% of those with good communication and only 19% of those with fair or poor. Similarly, almost all (97%) of the respondents who rate their communication with their partner as excellent say that they would choose that person to be their partner again, compared to 89% of those with good communication and only 46% of those who rank fair or poor.

A majority (56%) of married or romantically involved adults report being wholly satisfied with the sexual relationship they share with their partner. However, three fourths (76%) of all persons in relationships with excellent communication express complete satisfaction with their sexual relationship, compared to 47% of those in relationships with good communication, and only 20% of those with fair or poor communication.

Communication also plays a key role in helping partners meet each other's emotional needs. About one third (31%) of all married and involved adults report that their emotional needs are always met by their partner. This proportion is significantly larger among persons in relationships characterized by excellent communication, with approximately one half (49%) of these respondents claiming that their emotional needs are met all of the time. Among persons in relationships with only good communication, on the other hand, only 21% say that their partner always satisfies their emotional needs. And only a very small percentage (8%) of persons in relationships hampered by fair or poor communication say that these needs are met by their partner all the time.

The level of trust also appears closely tied to a couple's ability to communicate. Although more than three fourths (78%) of all married and involved adults think that they can trust their partners all of the time, thorough confidence is much more prevalent in relationships with excellent communication. More than nine out of ten persons (92%) whose ability to share information with their partner is excellent say that they trust him or her all of the time. Somewhat fewer (77%) persons who rate their ability to communicate as good say that they can always trust their partner, while less than a majority (31%) of those who rate fair or poor have complete trust in their partner.

Marriage's Changing Role

Recent information from the U.S. Census Bureau and other sources reveals some startling facts about the changing role of marriage in the lives of Americans today. The decline in marriage rates, the tendency to postpone marriage, the high divorce rate, and the decline in the rate of remarriage all contribute to a significant revision of life-styles.

The marriage rate for single adults as a whole has dropped precipitously from its post-1950s high to a new low, in part from a trend toward postponing marriage until older ages and in part from a growing tendency to forgo it altogether. In the early 1960s the median age for first marriages was 20 years for women and 23 for men; by 1987 these median ages had climbed to 24 for women and 26 for men.

This trend toward postponement has been accompanied by a growth in the proportion of adults of all ages who remain single, thus suggesting that many may be choosing to forgo matrimony altogether. In 1970, for example, only 9% of male and 6% of female 30 to 34-year-olds had never been married. By 1987 these proportions had risen dramatically, with 23% of men and 15% of women in this age group counting themselves among the never-married.

The assault on marriage is not limited to increasing numbers of men and women who choose either to postpone or to forgo marriage. The divorce rate among married couples also remains high. The average number of years that women remain with their husbands has decreased substantially from the period between 1955 and 1960. In the twenty years since then, the average length of time that white women remained married fell from 37 to 26 years; among black women, it dropped from 26 to 16 years.

A final blow to the institution of marriage can be seen in the rapidly declining remarriage rate among divorced people. In fact, remarriage has been dropping even faster than the rate of first marriages among single adults.

These trends do not mean that Americans are forgoing intimacy and choosing to live their lives without a partner of the opposite sex. While the institution of marriage has suffered blows, rates of cohabitation have mushroomed. Approximately 2.5 million U.S. households are couples living together without being married, and the number of people cohabiting before marriage quadrupled between 1964 and 1984. Moreover, divorced persons now are more likely to cohabit than to remarry.

The story told by these trends is that marriage today is an optional life-style, not a necessity for successful and productive living. It has become an option because men and women have become less dependent on each other, both through the increasing similarity of their educational levels and earning power and through the greater availability of devices and services that make running the household a simpler task.

FEBRUARY 2
PRESIDENT BUSH

Interviewing Date: 1/24–26/89
Survey #AI 877

Do you approve or disapprove of the way George Bush is handling his job as president?

Approve...51%
Disapprove..6
No opinion..43

Bush, Reagan Comparisons
(Percent Approval)

	Bush January 1989	Reagan January 1981
Nationwide	51%	51%

By Sex

Male	53%	54%
Female	49	48

By Ethnic Background

White	52%	54%
Black	51	24

By Education

College.............................. 54%   56%
No college........................... 49   48

By Region

South 57%   52%
Non-South............................ 49   50

By Age

18–29 years......................... 54%   50%
30–49 years......................... 50   54
50 years and over.................. 50   49

By Household Income

Top 50 percent..................... 56%   57%
Bottom 50 percent................. 46   42

By Politics

Republicans.......................... 69%   74%
Democrats 38   38
Independents........................ 47   53

The following table shows how George Bush and the last eight presidents fared with the public during their first weeks in office:

Presidential Performance Ratings
(Percent Approval)

Bush ....January 1989   51%
Reagan ....January 1981   51
Carter..................February 1977   66
Ford.......................August 1974   71
Nixon...................January 1969   59
Johnson..............December 1963   78
Kennedy ....February 1961   72
Eisenhower...........February 1953   68
Truman ....May 1945   87

What kind of president do you think George Bush will be—an outstanding president, above average, below average, or poor?

Outstanding 6%
Above average.................................... 32
Average (volunteered) 31
Below average 16

Poor... 6
No opinion.. 9

Note: George Bush, like his predecessor, has begun his presidency with the approval of a thin majority of the American people. Less than one week after taking office, 51% approve of Bush's job performance while only 6% disapprove. High levels of uncertainty are characteristic of early surveys of incoming presidents, but an exceptionally large number (43%) have not yet formed their opinions about Bush. President Ronald Reagan also received a 51%-approval rating early in his tenure. He left office in January, however, riding an unprecedented wave of popularity, and Bush's high percentage of undecided replies may reflect some public uncertainty that he can measure up to Reagan.

In striking contrast to the initial views of Reagan, equal proportions of blacks (51%) and whites (52%) approve of Bush's handling of his presidential duties at this early stage in his administration. This suggests that his efforts to reach out to blacks and to other minorities may be paying off and that blacks bear little of the animus toward Bush that they did toward Reagan and his policies. Far fewer blacks (24%) than whites (54%) approved of Reagan in January 1981.

In a preinauguration assessment, almost four Americans in ten (38%) said that Bush would turn out to be an outstanding (6%) or above-average (31%) president. In the same late December poll, 59% thought that history would regard President Reagan in these terms.

Early measurements of presidential performance tend to be overwhelmingly positive, since the public typically has only a limited impression of incoming presidents and is inclined to give them the benefit of the doubt. Bush's initial job ratings are no exception, but because so many respondents are currently undecided about him, his approval score is well below the benchmark ratings received by other elected first-term presidents: Jimmy Carter (66%), Richard Nixon (59%), John Kennedy (72%), and Dwight Eisenhower (68%). Those presidents who took office after the resignation or death of their predecessors— Gerald Ford (71%), Lyndon Johnson (78%), and Harry Truman (87%)—had higher first ratings, largely because they were better known to the public. Johnson and Truman also benefited from an outpouring of sympathy after the deaths of Presidents Kennedy and Franklin Roosevelt.

If the polls run true to form, Bush can expect both his approval and disapproval ratings to rise during the next few months, as the public becomes more familiar with him. As a rule, at least one year is required for the public to have a good sense of the new man in the Oval Office.

The following table shows how the last eight presidents fared with the public during their first year in office:

Presidential Performance Ratings
(Percent Approval)

	Year	High	Low	Point difference
Reagan	1981	68%	49%	-19
Carter	1977	75	51	-24
Ford	1974–75	71	37	-34
Nixon	1969	68	56	-12
Johnson	1963–64	80	73	-7
Kennedy	1961	83	71	-12
Eisenhower	1953	75	58	-17
Truman	1945–46	87	50	-37

Reagan's ratings fell steadily throughout his first year with the onset of the 1981–82 recession. Carter's decline was not associated with any specific issue but rather with a growing belief that he was not up to the job. Ford's popularity plummeted within one month of taking office as a result of the Nixon pardon. Presidents Nixon, Johnson, Kennedy, and Eisenhower all maintained high levels of public support during their early years in office.

As noted, Bush and Reagan each won the approval of 51% in their first Gallup Poll assessment. A demographic comparison shows many points of similarity.

The 4-point difference between Bush's approval rating among men (53%) and women (49%) is too small to be statistically conclusive. However, it generally reflects last November's election results, in which Bush received proportionately fewer votes from women than men. It thus may presage a continuation of the gender gap found in Reagan's initial approval ratings among men

(54%) and women (48%), and in every Gallup Poll conducted during his two terms in office.

Bush's ratings by education and family income also closely resemble Reagan's. The age patterns for both are essentially flat, but Bush receives a slightly higher rating in the South (57% approve) than in other regions (49%). Reagan's later popularity in the South was not apparent in his earlier ratings.

FEBRUARY 5
CONGRESSIONAL SALARY INCREASE

Interviewing Date: 1/24–26/89
Survey #AI 877

Do you happen to know how much salary U.S. senators and representatives now are paid per year?

$91,000 or more	12%
$76,000–$90,000	20
$51,000–$75,000	10
$50,000 or less	2
Don't know	56

Recently, there has been a proposal to increase the salaries of members of Congress from $89,500 to $135,000 per year. In exchange, members would not be able to accept speaking fees from special-interest groups. Do you favor or oppose raising congressional salaries from $89,500 to $135,000 per year?

Favor	15%
Oppose	82
No opinion	3

By Politics

Republicans

Favor	16%
Oppose	80
No opinion	4

Democrats

Favor	10%
Oppose	87
No opinion	3

Favor	19%
Oppose	79
No opinion	2

Note: While a blue-ribbon panel recommends it and President George Bush and former President Ronald Reagan give it their blessing, the vast majority of Americans believes that members of Congress do not deserve a $45,500 pay raise. Boosting congressional salaries from the present $89,500 to $135,000 per year, as proposed by a nonpartisan commission, is favored by only 15% of the public and opposed by 82%, even when tied to a ban on speaking fees from special-interest groups.

The 50 percent raise for U.S. senators and representatives, as well as large salary increases for 2,000 other top federal officials, judges, and cabinet members, will automatically go into effect February 8 unless both the Senate and House vote against it. The survey found slightly less opposition to the pay raise among affluent, well-educated Americans, but in all population groups opposition outweighs support by at least a 2-to-1 ratio.

Public awareness of the salary that congressmen now are paid is scant. Only one person in five (20%) was able to cite a figure that is near the correct amount, while 12% think that legislators earn more and another 12%, less. More than one half (56%) were unable to specify any figure at all.

Knowledge of congressional salaries, however, has little bearing on respondents' attitudes toward the pay raise proposal. Whether they named a figure that is too high, about right, too low, or none, more than three fourths oppose increasing congressional pay. This opposition to the pay raise may reflect, in part, the generally low public esteem in which Congress is held. Asked to rate the honesty and ethical standards of people employed in twenty-five different professions in a survey last fall, only 16% gave congressmen a very high or high rating.

According to the commission that set the proposed new pay scales, "most members of Congress find it difficult to live on their current salaries." Proponents of the raise also argue that: 1) The cost of living has gone up twice as much as has congressional pay during the last twenty years; 2) legislators deserve salaries comparable to white-collar executives in the private sector; 3) most members maintain two residences, one in their home state or district and the other in Washington, where living costs are high; 4) unless congressmen and other civil servants receive substantial pay raises, top-quality people will be unwilling to run for Congress, serve as judges, or take high-level public jobs (only the rich will be able to hold public office); and 5) linking the pay hikes to new legislation banning most kinds of outside income would reduce the possibility that members are beholden to special-interest groups.

Opponents question the propriety of Congress legislating its own compensation. They contend, moreover, that the proposed increases are unnecessary and excessive, especially at a time of fiscal austerity. Critics also argue that: 1) members' current salaries already put them in the top 1 percent of all U.S. wage earners; 2) a majority in both houses of Congress have other sources of income, not including honoraria, that bring their total annual earnings to $135,000 or more; 3) the raises would be inflationary and would lead to salary hikes for other government employees; and 4) legislators should be willing to make financial sacrifices in order to serve the public interest.

FEBRUARY 9
EXPECTATIONS FOR THE
BUSH PRESIDENCY

Interviewing Date: 1/24–26/89
Survey #AI 877

Here are some questions about the tasks facing President Bush. Do you think the Bush administration will or will not be able to:

Reduce the federal budget deficit?

Will	39%
Will not	46
No opinion	15

By Politics

Republicans

Will	56%
Will not	30
No opinion	14

Democrats

Will	22%
Will not	62
No opinion	6

Independents

Will	40%
Will not	46
No opinion	14

Get the drug crisis under control?

Will	36%
Will not	51
No opinion	13

By Politics

Republicans

Will	73%
Will not	17
No opinion	10

Democrats

Will	49%
Will not	36
No opinion	15

Independents

Will	63%
Will not	26
No opinion	11

Keep America prosperous?

Will	74%
Will not	16
No opinion	10

By Politics

Republicans

Will	48%
Will not	41
No opinion	11

Democrats

Will	28%
Will not	59
No opinion	13

Independents

Will	31%
Will not	55
No opinion	14

Improve the quality of the environment?

Will	62%
Will not	26
No opinion	12

By Politics

Republicans

Will	88%
Will not	6
No opinion	6

Democrats

Will	63%
Will not	23
No opinion	14

Independents

Will	74%
Will not	16
No opinion	10

Keep the nation out of war?

Will	77%
Will not	11
No opinion	2

By Politics

Republicans

Will...85%
Will not...5
No opinion.......................................10

Democrats

Will...68%
Will not...17
No opinion.......................................15

Independents

Will...77%
Will not...12
No opinion.......................................11

Reduce the crime rate in the United States?

Will...39%
Will not...49
No opinion.......................................12

By Politics

Republicans

Will...48%
Will not...41
No opinion.......................................11

Democrats

Will...33%
Will not...55
No opinion.......................................12

Independents

Will...37%
Will not...50
No opinion.......................................13

Improve educational standards?

Will...74%
Will not...18
No opinion.......................................8

By Politics

Republicans

Will...82%
Will not...10
No opinion.......................................8

Democrats

Will...65%
Will not...25
No opinion.......................................10

Independents

Will...73%
Will not...20
No opinion.......................................7

Increase respect for the United States abroad?

Will 74%
Will not...15
No opinion.......................................11

By Politics

Republicans

Will...81%
Will not...11
No opinion.......................................8

Democrats

Will...67%
Will not...20
No opinion.......................................13

Independents

Will...75%
Will not...15
No opinion.......................................10

Improve the lot of minorities and the poor?

Will...53%
Will not...36
No opinion.......................................11

By Politics

Republicans

Will	65%
Will not	26
No opinion	9

Democrats

Will	42%
Will not	48
No opinion	10

Independents

Will	53%
Will not	35
No opinion	12

Avoid raising taxes?

Will	29%
Will not	64
No opinion	7

By Politics

Republicans

Will	38%
Will not	54
No opinion	8

Democrats

Will	19%
Will not	73
No opinion	8

Independents

Will	31%
Will not	64
No opinion	5

Note: The American people have mixed expectations for President George Bush's administration, but their confidence has grown since last November that Bush will be able to make good on many of his campaign promises. They are most optimistic that he will be able to keep the nation out of war (77%) and prosperous (74%), increase respect for the United States abroad (74%), and raise educational standards (74%). They are less confident that the new president can improve the quality of the environment (62%) and enhance the lot of minorities and the poor (53%).

The public is least sanguine about Bush's ability to lower the crime rate (39%), reduce the federal budget deficit (39%), bring the drug epidemic under control (36%), and avoid raising taxes (29%). In fact, more Americans believe that Bush cannot meet these four challenges than think he can.

As anticipated, voters' expectations are highly colored by their political loyalty. Republican majorities believe that Bush can accomplish all of the goals studied, except for crime, drugs, and taxes. They are closely divided over Bush's ability to reduce the crime rate and stem the drug crisis, each with 48% thinking he can resolve these problems and 41% doubtful, but a majority of the party faithful says that Bush cannot keep his campaign promise not to raise taxes, 54% to 38%.

Democrats remain more skeptical than Republicans that Bush can meet all these challenges, but the harsh views that Democrats expressed in the postelection poll in November have softened, in some cases dramatically. In November, for example, Bush's promise to keep the nation out of war was the only campaign vow that a majority of Democrats thought he could keep. Today, roughly two Democrats in three believe that the new president will keep us at peace (68%) and prosperous (63%), gain us respect abroad (67%), and raise educational standards (65%).

Since November, Bush has gained credibility among Democrats on most of the issues tested. Nevertheless, negative assessments continue to outweigh positive ones that he can reduce the budget, get the drug epidemic under control, bring down the crime rate, avoid raising taxes, or improve the lot of minorities and the poor.

FEBRUARY 12
PERSONAL FINANCES

Interviewing Date: 1/24–26/89
Survey #AI 877

We are interested in how people's financial situation may have changed. Would you say that you are financially better off now than you were a year ago, or are you financially worse off now?

Better..44%
Worse...26
Same (volunteered).............................28
No opinion...2

By Sex

Male

Better..51%
Worse...23
Same (volunteered).............................25
No opinion...1

Female

Better..39%
Worse...29
Same (volunteered).............................30
No opinion...2

By Ethnic Background

White

Better..44%
Worse...25
Same (volunteered).............................29
No opinion...2

Nonwhite

Better..47%
Worse...32
Same (volunteered).............................18
No opinion...3

Black

Better..45%
Worse...35
Same (volunteered).............................18
No opinion...2

By Education

College Graduate

Better..49%
Worse...25
Same (volunteered).............................26
No opinion...*

College Incomplete

Better..52%
Worse...18
Same (volunteered).............................28
No opinion...2

High-School Graduate

Better..45%
Worse...26
Same (volunteered).............................28
No opinion...1

Less Than High-School Graduate

Better..31%
Worse...36
Same (volunteered).............................28
No opinion...5

By Region

East

Better..38%
Worse...29
Same (volunteered).............................32
No opinion...1

Midwest

Better..47%
Worse...26
Same (volunteered).............................24
No opinion...3

South

Better..46%
Worse...25
Same (volunteered).............................27
No opinion...2

West

Better..46%
Worse...25
Same (volunteered).............................28
No opinion...1

By Age

18–29 Years

Better..62%
Worse...20

Same (volunteered)..............................8
No opinion......................................*

30–49 Years

Better...50%
Worse..28
Same (volunteered)............................22
No opinion......................................*

50 Years and Over

Better...28%
Worse..28
Same (volunteered)............................40
No opinion......................................4

By Household Income

$40,000 and Over

Better...55%
Worse..18
Same (volunteered)............................26
No opinion......................................1

$25,000–$39,999

Better...48%
Worse..25
Same (volunteered)............................27
No opinion......................................*

$15,000–$24,999

Better...41%
Worse..30
Same (volunteered)............................28
No opinion......................................1

Under $15,000

Better...34%
Worse..35
Same (volunteered)............................28
No opinion......................................3

By Politics

Republicans

Better...54%
Worse..18
Same (volunteered)............................26
No opinion......................................2

Democrats

Better...34%
Worse..35
Same (volunteered)............................29
No opinion......................................2

Independents

Better...48%
Worse..24
Same (volunteered)............................27
No opinion......................................1

*Less than 1%

Selected National Trend

	Better	Worse	Same	No opinion
1988				
September–October	53%	23%	23%	1%
May	47	24	28	1
January	41	28	29	2
1987				
August–September	43	29	27	1
March	46	30	23	1
January	39	28	33	*

*Less than 1%

Now, looking ahead, do you expect that at this time next year you will be financially better off than now, or worse off than now?

Better...61%
Worse..13
Same (volunteered)............................19
No opinion......................................7

The following are "super optimists," those who claim to be better off now than they were one year ago and expect to be still better off next year:

	Super optimists
National	37%

By Sex

Male	41%
Female	32

By Ethnic Background

White..36%
Black...39

By Education

College graduate.................................42%
College incomplete.............................45
High-school graduate..........................35
Less than high-school graduate...............22

By Region

East...31%
Midwest...39
South..38
West...39

By Age

18–29 years.......................................55%
30–49 years.......................................41
50 years and over.............................19

By Household Income

$40,000 and over...............................50%
$25,000–$39,999..............................37
$15,000–$24,999..............................33
Under $15,000..................................26

By Politics

Republicans.......................................47%
Democrats...27
Independents.....................................37

The following is the trend in "super optimists," those who claim to be better off now than they were one year ago and expect to be still better off next year:

Selected National Trend

	Super optimists
1988	
September–October	44%
May	38
January	32
1987	
August–September	34
March	36
January	29

1986	
September	32
January	31
1985	
October	28
March	37
1984	
November–December	32
March	28
1983	
June	20
March	18

Note: After rising steadily throughout 1988, Americans' financial optimism now shows signs of cooling off. Nevertheless, optimism continues to outweigh pessimism by a wide margin. In a new Gallup audit of consumers' financial outlooks, 61% expect to be better off one year from now, while 19% say that their situation will not change much and 13% predict a downturn. The latest figures represent a 6 percentage-point decrease in optimism since last fall, when 67% thought that their finances would improve, 17% remain the same, and 9% grow worse. Those findings marked the high point in consumer buoyancy since 1976, when Gallup began monitoring the public's financial mood.

Voters' perceptions of financial well-being and a strong national economy contributed importantly to George Bush's election last November. President Bush, however, is committed to addressing fiscal problems inherited from the Reagan administration, such as the huge budget deficit and the savings and loan crisis, with no increase in taxes. The decline in financial optimism may reflect public recognition that resolving these problems will require some personal sacrifices and belt-tightening.

Responses to a companion question also show a decline in consumers' perceptions of their current financial status vis-à-vis one year ago. At present 44% say that they are better off, 28% the same, and 26% worse off than at this time last year. Last fall optimists reached a peak in this trend, with 53% perceiving an improvement, 23% no change, and 23% a decline in their finances from the same period one year earlier.

The latest results also show a decline in "super optimists," from 44% last fall to 37% at present. Studies have shown that these people—who say that they now are better off than in the past and expect to be still more prosperous in the future—are likely to be buyers of big-ticket discretionary items, such as houses, cars, and major appliances, and to be heavy users of credit.

Super optimism is strongly influenced by demographic factors such as gender, age, education, and family income. Men are more likely than women to fit this description. Super optimists also tend to be younger, better educated, and more affluent than people who do not share this high degree of optimism. Republicans are far more likely than Democrats to qualify. Unlike earlier surveys, in which proportionately fewer blacks than whites have been super optimists, the current poll found no significant difference by race.

FEBRUARY 19
BALANCED BUDGET AMENDMENT/ LINE-ITEM VETO

Interviewing Date: 1/24–26/89
Survey #AI 877

Have you heard or read about the proposal for a constitutional amendment that would require the federal government to balance the national budget each year?

	Yes
National	48%

Asked of the entire sample: Under this proposed amendment, any federal budget passed by Congress would have projected tax revenues that are equal to projected government spending, unless a three-fifths majority of Congress voted not to do so. Would you favor or oppose this amendment to the Constitution?

Favor 59%
Oppose... 24
No opinion..................................... 17

By Politics

Republicans

Favor 58%
Oppose... 25
No opinion..................................... 17

Democrats

Favor 57%
Oppose... 24
No opinion..................................... 19

Independents

Favor 63%
Oppose... 24
No opinion..................................... 13

Selected National Trend*

	Favor	Oppose	No opinion
1987	53%	23%	24%
1985	49	27	24

*Earlier Gallup Polls, employing slightly different wording in the questions, also found heavy public backing for a balanced budget amendment.

At the present time, when Congress passes a bill, the president cannot veto parts of that bill but must accept or veto it in full. Do you think this should or should not be changed so that the president can veto some items in a bill without vetoing the entire bill?

Favor 70%
Oppose... 24
No opinion..................................... 6

By Politics

Republicans

Favor 82%
Oppose... 13
No opinion..................................... 5

Democrats

Favor 61%
Oppose... 31
No opinion..................................... 8

Independents

Favor 70%
Oppose... 27
No opinion..................................... 3

Selected National Trend

	Favor	Oppose	No opinion
1987	66%	23%	11%
1985	71	22	7
1983	67	25	8
1978	70	19	11
1975	69	20	11
1945	57	14	29

In your opinion, is the current federal budget deficit a very serious problem for the country, a fairly serious problem, not a serious problem, or is this something you haven't thought much about?

Very serious 63%
Fairly serious 20
Not serious 3
No opinion 14

By Politics

Republicans

Very serious 56%
Fairly serious 26
Not serious 5
No opinion 13

Democrats

Very serious 65%
Fairly serious 18
Not serious 2
No opinion 15

Independents

Very serious 70%
Fairly serious 16
Not serious 2
No opinion 12

Selected National Trend

	1985	1984
Very serious	61%	54%
Fairly serious	23	29
Not serious	3	5
No opinion	13	12

Note: In his 1990 budget proposal, President George Bush urged Congress to approve several measures to "make budgeting more sensible." Among the president's requests were two proposals for reform that have had bipartisan public support for many years: the balanced budget amendment and the line-item veto.

A new Gallup Poll found better than 2-to-1 public backing for a constitutional amendment requiring the federal government to balance its budget each year, with 59% in favor, 24% opposed, and 17% undecided. A balanced budget amendment is favored by voters of all political persuasions, including 58% of Republicans, 57% of Democrats, and 63% of independents. The amendment was one of President Ronald Reagan's top policy priorities; at one point he referred to it as the centerpiece of his "economic bill of rights."

The public has long favored the line-item veto, the other budget reform that President Bush called for in his message to Congress. Given this power, a president could veto some items in a bill without having to veto the entire measure, as at present. In the current survey, support outweighs opposition by almost a 3-to-1 ratio, 70% to 24%. Republicans overwhelmingly favor the item veto, 82% to 13%, while Democrats also express support by a narrower 61%-to-31% margin. Self-described independents mirror the national consensus, 70% to 27%.

Large majorities in Gallup surveys spanning more than four decades have favored changing the present system. In 1945, when this issue was first presented to the public, 57% voted for and 14% against the item veto. As President Bush said in his budget message to Congress, "Forty-three governors have the line item veto. Presidents should have it too."

Proponents argue that giving presidents the right to veto individual items in appropriations bills would put an end to "pork-barrel" legislation—the inclusion in the budget of items that primarily serve the narrow political interests of some members of Congress. Others contend that eliminating the expensive riders frequently tacked onto bills would save millions of dollars. The main argument, however, in favor of the present system is that it gives the legislative branch more power by forcing a president to accept items, especially in appropriations bills, that he might not otherwise accept.

Although economists are at odds about the importance of the $150-billion federal deficit in the $5-trillion U.S. economy, the public believes that it is a grave national problem. In the latest survey, 63% characterize the deficit as a very serious problem for the country and an additional 20% consider it fairly serious. Merely 3% say that it is not serious, while 14% are undecided. Democrats (65%) and independents (70%) are slightly more inclined than Republicans (56%) to think that the deficit is a very serious problem.

FEBRUARY 23
AIRLINE SAFETY

Interviewing Date: 1/24–26/89
Survey #AI 877

Compared to five years ago, do you think flying on commercial airliners in the United States has become safer, less safe, or stayed about the same?

Safer 9%
Less safe 52
Stayed the same 36
No opinion 3

By Sex

Male

Safer 13%
Less safe 42
Stayed the same 43
No opinion 2

Female

Safer 5%
Less safe 60
Stayed the same 30
No opinion 5

By Politics

Republicans

Safer 10%
Less safe 47
Stayed the same 39
No opinion 4

Democrats

Safer 5%
Less safe 58
Stayed the same 32
No opinion 5

Independents

Safer 11%
Less safe 50
Stayed the same 38
No opinion 1

Those Who Always Have
a Fear of Flying

Safer 10%
Less safe 66
Stayed the same 20
No opinion 4

Those Who Have a Fear of Flying
Most of the Time

Safer 14%
Less safe 60
Stayed the same 26
No opinion .... *

Those Who Sometimes Have
a Fear of Flying

Safer 6%
Less safe 54
Stayed the same 40
No opinion .... *

Those Who Never Have
a Fear of Flying

Safer 11%
Less safe 40
Stayed the same 46
No opinion 3

Those Who Think the Government
Is Doing All It Can with Safety

Safer 14%
Less safe 34
Stayed the same 48
No opinion 4

Those Who Think the Government
Is Not Doing Enough with Safety

Safer 7%
Less safe 60

Stayed the same...................................31
No opinion...2

*Less than 1%

In your opinion, is the federal government doing all it can to make commercial aviation safe, or not?

Doing all it can...................................29%
Not doing enough...............................62
No opinion...9

By Sex

Male

Doing all it can...................................32%
Not doing enough...............................62
No opinion...6

Female

Doing all it can...................................27%
Not doing enough...............................61
No opinion...12

By Politics

Republicans

Doing all it can...................................34%
Not doing enough...............................54
No opinion...12

Democrats

Doing all it can...................................22%
Not doing enough...............................68
No opinion...10

Independents

Doing all it can...................................29%
Not doing enough...............................64
No opinion...7

Those Who Always Have a Fear of Flying

Doing all it can...................................15%
Not doing enough...............................82
No opinion...3

Those Who Have a Fear of Flying Most of the Time

Doing all it can...................................21%
Not doing enough...............................75
No opinion...4

Those Who Sometimes Have a Fear of Flying

Doing all it can...................................25%
Not doing enough...............................72
No opinion...3

Those Who Never Have a Fear of Flying

Doing all it can...................................32%
Not doing enough...............................58
No opinion...10

Those Who Think Flying on Commercial Airliners Is Safer Compared to Five Years Ago

Doing all it can...................................45%
Not doing enough...............................48
No opinion...7

Those Who Think Flying on Commercial Airliners Is Less Safe Compared to Five Years Ago

Doing all it can...................................19%
Not doing enough...............................72
No opinion...9

Those Who Think Safety on Commercial Airliners Has Stayed the Same Compared to Five Years Ago

Doing all it can...................................39%
Not doing enough...............................53
No opinion...8

Asked of those who have flown on a commercial airliner in the past twelve months (39% of the sample): When you fly, how often, if ever, are you frightened— would you say always, most of the time, sometimes, or never?

Always 10%
Most of the time..................................8
Sometimes...26
Never 55
No opinion...1

By Sex

Male

Always 8%
Most of the time....................................5
Sometimes...20
Never 67
No opinion...*

Female

Always 12%
Most of the time..................................11
Sometimes...32
Never 44
No opinion..1

*Less than 1%

Selected National Trend*

	1987	1983
Always	12%	9%
Most of the time	6	3
Sometimes	30	21
Never	52	67
No opinion	**	**

*Based on those who had flown in the past year
**Less than 1%

Note: A majority of Americans believes that flying on commercial airliners is more dangerous today than it was five years ago. However, fewer now than in 1987 think that the trend in air travel safety has grown worse.

In a new Gallup Poll, 52% say that commercial flying has become riskier, 36% find it unchanged, and 9% think it is safer. In 1987, by comparison, 64% thought that commercial flying safety had declined, 28% perceived little change, and 5% said it was safer.

The latest findings show a shift in public opinion toward the view that air travel safety has neither improved nor deteriorated over the last five years and a drop in those who think that it has gotten worse. The belief that flying has become safer increased only slightly between the two surveys, from 5% in 1987 to 9% today. (It should be noted that the mid-1987 survey was conducted after a spate of airliner accidents and near collisions, and the 1989 poll was taken one month after the December 21 explosion of a Pan American 747 over Scotland.)

Although Americans appear to be slightly more sanguine about commercial air travel, the perception has grown since 1987 that the federal government's efforts to improve flight safety are inadequate. In the earlier survey, 31% thought that the government was "doing all it can to make commercial aviation safe," while 55% disagreed. Today, 29% say that Washington is doing a satisfactory job, while 62% think it has been remiss.

Fear of flying increased dramatically between 1983 and 1987, with the proportion of passengers reporting that they were at least occasionally afraid climbing from 33% to 48% during this four-year period. In the new survey, 44% say that they are always (10%), most of the time (8%), or sometimes (26%) afraid of flying. As in past surveys, women (55%) are far more likely than men (33%) to admit to this fear. Women also are more inclined than men to perceive the trend in aviation safety to have worsened in the last five years, 60% and 42%, respectively.

According to the National Transportation Safety Board, accident totals and accident rates for U.S. scheduled air carriers and commuter airlines declined in 1988 from the year before. The 1988 rate calculations do not include the explosion of Pan American Flight 103 over Lockerbie, Scotland, which resulted in the death of 270 people, because the crash was caused by a terrorist bomb.

FEBRUARY 26
SOCIAL VALUES

Interviewing Date: 1/24–26/89
Survey #AI 877

Using a scale from 10 to 0, please tell me how important each of the following is to you. If you think something is extremely important, you would call off the highest number, 10. If you think something is extremely unimportant, you would mention the lowest number, 0. If you think something is neither extremely important nor extremely unimportant, you would mention some number between 10 and 0— the higher the number, the more important you think it is, and the lower the number, the less important:

Having a good family life?

	Those saying very important (+10, +9)
National	89%

By Sex

Male	86%
Female	92

By Ethnic Background

White	89%
Nonwhite	88
Black	87

By Education

College graduate	87%
College incomplete	89
No college	90

By Age

18–29 years	90%
30–49 years	87
50 years and over	91

By Household Income

$40,000 and over	85%
$25,000–$39,999	89
Under $25,000	93

Having a good self-image or self-respect?

	Those saying very important (+10, +9)
National	85%

By Sex

Male	81%
Female	88

By Ethnic Background

White	85%
Nonwhite	86
Black	90

By Education

College graduate	85%
College incomplete	83
No college	85

By Age

18–29 years	84%
30–49 years	85
50 years and over	85

By Household Income

$40,000 and over	83%
$25,000–$39,999	84
Under $25,000	87

Being in good physical health?

	Those saying very important (+10, +9)
National	84%

By Sex

Male	81%
Female	86

By Ethnic Background

White	83%
Nonwhite	88
Black	91

By Education

College graduate	73%
College incomplete	82
No college	89

By Age

18–29 years	80%
30–49 years	83
50 years and over	87

By Household Income

$40,000 and over	76%
$25,000–$39,999	87
Under $25,000	87

Having a sense of accomplishment and lasting contribution?

	Those saying very important (+10, +9)
National	69%

By Sex

Male	65%
Female	73

By Ethnic Background

White	68%
Nonwhite	76
Black	76

By Education

College graduate	67%
College incomplete	71
No college	69

By Age

18–29 years	77%
30–49 years	67
50 years and over	65

By Household Income

$40,000 and over	68%
$25,000–$39,999	71
Under $25,000	68

Working for the betterment of American society?

	Those saying very important (+10, +9)
National	67%

By Sex

Male	59%
Female	74

By Ethnic Background

White	67%
Nonwhite	65
Black	68

By Education

College graduate	56%
College incomplete	62
No college	73

By Age

18–29 years	58%
30–49 years	63
50 years and over	77

By Household Income

$40,000 and over	62%
$25,000–$39,999	68
Under $25,000	71

Following a strict moral code?

	Those saying very important (+10, +9)
National	60%

By Sex

Male	54%
Female	66

By Ethnic Background

White	61%
Nonwhite	50
Black	51

By Education

College graduate	58%
College incomplete	63
No college	60

By Age

18–29 years	53%
30–49 years	58
50 years and over	66

By Household Income

$40,000 and over	60%
$25,000–$39,999	63
Under $25,000	61

Having an exciting, stimulating life?

	Those saying very important (+10, +9)
National	50%

By Sex

Male	51%
Female	50

By Ethnic Background

White...48%
Nonwhite 65
Black 68

By Education

College graduate...............................43%
College incomplete............................47
No college...55

By Age

18–29 years.......................................63%
30–49 years.......................................49
50 years and over..............................43

By Household Income

$40,000 and over 49%
$25,000–$39,999..............................50
Under $25,000...................................53

Having a nice home, car, and other belongings?

	Those saying very important (+10, +9)
National..41%

By Sex

Male..42%
Female...41

By Ethnic Background

White...37%
Nonwhite 71
Black 81

By Education

College graduate...............................30%
College incomplete............................31
No college...49

By Age

18–29 years.......................................44%
30–49 years.......................................38
50 years and over..............................42

By Household Income

$40,000 and over 36%
$25,000–$39,999..............................37
Under $25,000...................................46

Selected National Trend
(Percentage Rating Each "Very Important")

	1989	1981
Good family life....................	89%	82%
Good self-image....................	85	79
Good physical health.............	84	81
Sense of accomplishment........	69	63
Betterment of society............	67	51
Strict moral code	60	47
Exciting life.........................	50	51
Nice home, car.....................	41	39

Note: The American people consider the intangible aspects of their lives—their families, health, and self-respect—to be far more important than possessing material goods or leading exciting lives. Between these extremes lie other social values, such as having a sense of accomplishment, working to improve society, and following a strict moral code.

Nine in ten participants in a recent Gallup Poll (89%) assign one of the top two positions on an 11-point scale to the importance of having a good family life. Almost as many consider having a good self-image or self-respect (85%) and being in good physical health (84%) as very important.

Ranking somewhat lower are having a sense of accomplishment and lasting contribution (69%), working for the betterment of American society (67%), and following a strict moral code (60%). The lowest are leading an exciting and stimulating life (50%) and owning a nice home, car, and other belongings (41%).

For the most part, Americans' present values are similar to those recorded in a late 1981 poll. However, significantly more respondents now attach great importance to working for the betterment of society (67%) than did so in the earlier survey (51%). Following a strict moral code has also grown in acceptance, with 60% at present, compared to 47% in 1981, saying that this is very important to their lives. Interestingly, in his inaugural address, President George Bush stressed the need for high ethical standards in government and for volunteer efforts to help the disadvantaged.

The social values polled may be considered in terms of demographics. Large majorities in all major population groups attach a great deal of importance to their family lives and self-respect. Being in good physical health is considered very important by slightly more older than younger adults and by a larger proportion of noncollege attendees than college graduates. As in the 1981 study, women, older adults, the less well-to-do, and the less educated place a higher value on working for social betterment than do people from different socioeconomic backgrounds.

More women than men and more older than younger adults also consider following a strict moral code to be extremely important, but education and income levels have little bearing on the public's attitudes on this value. However, the wide gulf that separated the views of people of different ages in 1981 has narrowed sharply since then. In the earlier survey, for example, twice as many Americans age 50 and older (62%) as those under 30 (29%) thought that adherence to a strict moral code was extremely important. Age now plays a less dominant role in shaping opinion on this value, with 66% of older Americans and 53% in the youngest group placing a high degree of importance on following a strict moral code.

On the other hand, age continues to be the primary determinant of the importance that people attach to leading exciting and stimulating lives. Almost two thirds of adults under 30 (63%), compared to 49% of 30 to 49-year-olds and 43% of those 50 and older,l; consider this highly important. The appeal of an exciting life-style also drops as educational attainment rises: a larger proportion of Americans who did not attend college (55%) assign this a higher value than do those with some college training (47%) or a college degree (43%).

Not surprisingly, less affluent and less well-educated Americans prize material possessions, such as a nice home, car, or other belongings, more than do wealthier, college-trained people.

MARCH 2
CRIME

Interviewing Date: 1/24–26/89
Survey #AI 877

Is there any area near where you live—that is, within a mile—where you would be afraid to walk alone at night?

	Yes
National	43%

By Sex

Male	25%
Female	59

By Ethnic Background

White	41%
Nonwhite	55
Black	53

By Region

East	41%
Midwest	40
South	49
West	39

By Age

18–29 years	45%
30–49 years	32
50 years and over	52

By Household Income

$40,000 and over	28%
$25,000–$39,999	43
$15,000–$24,999	45
Under $15,000	55

Selected National Trend

1983	45%
1981	45
1977	45
1975	45
1972	42
1967	31
1965	34

How about at home at night—do you feel safe and secure, or not?

	Feel unsafe and insecure
National	10%

By Sex

Male	6%
Female	14

By Ethnic Background

White	9%
Nonwhite	18
Black	19

By Region

East 8%
Midwest 5
South ....,,14
West 12

By Age

18–29 years 11%
30–49 years 9
50 years and over...............................11

By Household Income

$40,000 and over 8%
$25,000–$39,999 8
$15,000–$24,999 11
Under $15,000 15

Selected National Trend

1983 ....16%
1981 16
1977 15
1975 20
1972 17

Note: Fear of crime pervades the nation. At least four Americans in ten are afraid to walk alone in their neighborhoods at night, while one tenth feel insecure in the refuge of their own homes and one half believe that there is more crime in their communities than there was one year ago.

Despite these alarming statistics, fear of neighborhood crime, after rising sharply in the early 1970s, has remained at about the same level. For example, the proportion afraid of walking alone near their homes at night, 43% today, is virtually identical to the 42% recorded in 1972. The trend since then has varied by only a few percentage points. By contrast, only 31% were afraid to venture out alone at night in 1967.

Fear of crime is strongly influenced by demographic factors such as sex, race, age, and income. More than twice the proportion of women (59%) than men (25%) and more blacks (53%) than whites (41%) are afraid to walk alone at night. Apprehension is higher among adults under age 30 (45%) and those 50 and older (52%) than it is among 30 to 49-year-olds (32%). Fear increases as family income declines: 28% of persons with yearly incomes of $40,000 or more, compared to 55% of those earning less than $15,000, are afraid to walk alone at night. Fear is slightly higher in the South (49%) than in other regions of the nation (40%).

This fear of crime is so pervasive that 10% of Americans feel unsafe in their own homes at night. The current findings mark a slight improvement in household security from earlier surveys, which found about one sixth of respondents fearful at home at night.

MARCH 3
JOHN TOWER

Interviewing Date: 2/28–3/2/89
Survey #AI 878

Have you heard or read about the nomination of John Tower to be secretary of defense?

| | Yes |
National 88%

Asked of the aware group (88% of the sample): From what you know about John Tower, do you favor or oppose his confirmation as secretary of defense?

Favor 35%
Oppose 53
No opinion 12

By Sex
Male

Favor 44%
Oppose 47
No opinion..9

Female

Favor 26%
Oppose 59
No opinion 15

By Ethnic Background
White

Favor 36%
Oppose 52
No opinion...12

Black

Favor 23%
Oppose...62
No opinion...15

By Education

College Graduate

Favor 34%
Oppose...59
No opinion... 7

College Incomplete

Favor 32%
Oppose...55
No opinion...13

High-School Graduate

Favor 41%
Oppose...47
No opinion...12

Less Than High-School Graduate

Favor 31%
Oppose...47
No opinion...22

By Region

East

Favor 32%
Oppose...54
No opinion...14

Midwest

Favor 35%
Oppose...50
No opinion...15

South

Favor 40%
Oppose...49
No opinion...11

West

Favor 32%
Oppose...59
No opinion... 9

By Age

18–29 Years

Favor 41%
Oppose...53
No opinion... 6

30–49 Years

Favor 39%
Oppose...50
No opinion...11

50 Years and Over

Favor 28%
Oppose...56
No opinion...16

By Politics

Republicans

Favor 53%
Oppose...37
No opinion...10

Democrats

Favor 14%
Oppose...73
No opinion...13

Independents

Favor 35%
Oppose...51
No opinion...14

Also asked of the aware group: If Tower is confirmed, he has sworn not to drink any alcohol while serving as secretary of defense. Was this pledge a major reason to favor his confirmation, or not?

Yes...23%
No...74
No opinion... 3

By Politics

Republicans

Yes...23%
No...75
No opinion... 2

Democrats

Yes...33%
No..58
No opinion......................................9

Independents

Yes...21%
No..77
No opinion......................................2

Also asked of the aware group: Do you oppose Tower's confirmation mostly because of his reported drinking problem, his reported womanizing, his positions on defense issues, or his reported dealings with defense contractors?

Drinking problem...............................57%
Dealings with contractors......................55
Womanizing.....................................32
Positions on defense issues....................24
Other (volunteered)............................7
No opinion......................................2
$\qquad\qquad\qquad\qquad\quad$177%*

*Total adds to over 100% due to multiple responses.

Also asked of the aware group: In general, do you think the Senate's inquiry into Tower's personal life has been fair or unfair?

Fair...52%
Unfair...43
No opinion......................................5

By Politics

Republicans

Fair...42%
Unfair...54
No opinion......................................4

Democrats

Fair...64%
Unfair...31
No opinion......................................5

Independents

Fair...51%
Unfair...43
No opinion......................................6

Also asked of the aware group: Do you think it is a good thing for the Senate to investigate the personal lives of cabinet nominees, or do you think the personal lives of cabinet nominees should be off limits to Senate investigations?

Good thing.....................................72%
Off limits.....................................23
No opinion......................................5

By Politics

Republicans

Good thing.....................................68%
Off limits.....................................26
No opinion......................................6

Democrats

Good thing.....................................78%
Off limits.....................................19
No opinion......................................3

Independents

Good thing.....................................71%
Off limits.....................................24
No opinion......................................5

Note: Opposition to John Tower's confirmation as secretary of defense outweighs support by a 3-to-2 ratio. The new survey, in which 53% oppose and 35% favor Tower's confirmation, reveals growing opposition to the nomination in only a few days. In a *Washington Post*-ABC News Poll conducted on February 27, 52% said that the Senate should vote to confirm Tower while 43% disagreed.

As expected, public opinion on the confirmation breaks sharply along political lines. However, at least one third of self-described Republicans (37%) oppose Tower's confirmation, while 53% are in favor. Democrats vote against confirmation by a 5-to-1 ratio, 73% to 14%. Also, the views of men and women diverge sharply. Men are evenly split, with 47% opposing and 44% favoring Tower's confirmation. Women are overwhelmingly opposed, by a 59%-to-26% margin.

About one fourth (23%) of those favoring confirmation say Tower's pledge of abstinence was a major reason to back the nominee, while

74% disagree. This vow to refrain from drinking while serving as defense secretary notwithstanding, those opposing Tower's confirmation in the Gallup Poll cite his reported drinking problem (57%) and dealings with defense contractors (55%) as reasons for their decision. Substantial numbers also mention allegations of his womanizing (32%) and his positions on defense-related issues (24%).

A slim majority believes that the Senate's inquiry into Tower's personal life has been generally fair (52%) rather than unfair (43%), with opinion on this issue colored by political partisanship. Democrats come down heavily on the side of fairness, 64% to 31%, while Republicans hold the opposite point of view, 54% unfair to 42% fair. Nevertheless, large majorities of all political persuasions think it is appropriate, in principle, for the Senate to investigate the personal lives of cabinet nominees, with far fewer believing that they should be off limits to Senate investigators.

MARCH 5
GROUPS NOT WANTED AS NEIGHBORS

Interviewing Date: 1/24–26/89
Survey #AI 877

I am going to read you a list of various groups of people. As I read each one, please tell me whether you would or would not like to have them as neighbors:

Catholics?

Would...94%
Would not..3
Don't know..3

By Sex
Male

Would...94%
Would not..2
Don't know..4

Female

Would...94%
Would not..3
Don't know..3

By Ethnic Background
White

Would...94%
Would not..3
Don't know..3

Nonwhite

Would...94%
Would not..2
Don't know..4

Black

Would...93%
Would not..2
Don't know..5

By Education
College Graduate

Would...97%
Would not..1
Don't know..2

College Incomplete

Would...95%
Would not..2
Don't know..3

High-School Graduate

Would...95%
Would not..2
Don't know..3

Less Than High-School Graduate

Would...89%
Would not..6
Don't know..5

By Region
East

Would...96%
Would not..1
Don't know..3

Midwest

Would...94%
Would not..2
Don't know..4

South

Would....................................92%
Would not...............................5
Don't know..............................3

West

Would....................................96%
Would not...............................1
Don't know..............................3

By Age

18-29 Years

Would....................................95%
Would not...............................4
Don't know..............................1

30-49 Years

Would....................................93%
Would not...............................3
Don't know..............................4

50 Years and Over

Would....................................95%
Would not...............................1
Don't know..............................4

By Household Income

$40,000 and Over

Would....................................96%
Would not...............................2
Don't know..............................2

$25,000-$39,999

Would....................................94%
Would not...............................2
Don't know..............................4

$15,000-$24,999

Would....................................96%
Would not...............................2
Don't know..............................2

Under $15,000

Would....................................93%
Would not...............................5
Don't know..............................2

By Religion

Protestants

Would....................................94%
Would not...............................3
Don't know..............................3

Catholics

Would....................................96%
Would not...............................1
Don't know..............................3

Evangelicals

Would....................................93%
Would not...............................3
Don't know..............................4

Non-Evangelicals

Would....................................96%
Would not...............................2
Don't know..............................2

Selected National Trend

	Would not welcome as neighbors*
1987	1%
1981	1

*In the 1987 and 1981 surveys, respondents were handed lists of groups and asked to name any whom they would not like to have as neighbors.

Protestants?

Would....................................92%
Would not...............................5
Don't know..............................3

By Sex

Male

Would....................................92%
Would not...............................4
Don't know..............................4

Female

Would....................................92%
Would not...............................5
Don't know..............................3

By Ethnic Background

White

Would...94%
Would not...3
Don't know..3

Nonwhite

Would...82%
Would not...12
Don't know..6

Black

Would...80%
Would not...13
Don't know..7

By Education

College Graduate

Would...96%
Would not...1
Don't know..3

College Incomplete

Would...96%
Would not...1
Don't know..3

High-School Graduate

Would...91%
Would not...6
Don't know..3

Less Than High-School Graduate

Would...84%
Would not...9
Don't know..7

By Region

East

Would...95%
Would not...3
Don't know..2

Midwest

Would...96%
Would not...1
Don't know..3

South

Would...87%
Would not...8
Don't know..5

West

Would...91%
Would not...6
Don't know..3

By Age

18–29 Years

Would...90%
Would not...8
Don't know..2

30–49 Years

Would...92%
Would not...4
Don't know..4

50 Years and Over

Would...94%
Would not...2
Don't know..4

By Household Income

$40,000 and Over

Would...96%
Would not...2
Don't know..2

$25,000–$39,999

Would...94%
Would not...2
Don't know..4

$15,000–$24,999

Would...93%
Would not...5
Don't know..2

Under $15,000

Would...88%
Would not...8
Don't know..4

By Religion

Protestants

Would	92%
Would not	4
Don't know	4

Catholics

Would	93%
Would not	5
Don't know	2

Evangelicals

Would	89%
Would not	6
Don't know	5

Non-Evangelicals

Would	94%
Would not	4
Don't know	2

Selected National Trend

	Would not welcome as neighbors
1987	2%
1981	1

Jews?

Would	91%
Would not	5
Don't know	4

By Sex

Male

Would	91%
Would not	5
Don't know	4

Female

Would	92%
Would not	5
Don't know	3

By Ethnic Background

White

Would	92%
Would not	4
Don't know	4

Nonwhite

Would	87%
Would not	8
Don't know	5

Black

Would	86%
Would not	8
Don't know	6

By Education

College Graduate

Would	95%
Would not	2
Don't know	3

College Incomplete

Would	95%
Would not	2
Don't know	3

High-School Graduate

Would	90%
Would not	7
Don't know	3

Less Than High-School Graduate

Would	87%
Would not	6
Don't know	7

By Region

East

Would	94%
Would not	3
Don't know	3

Midwest

Would	92%
Would not	4
Don't know	4

South

Would	89%
Would not	8
Don't know	3

West

Would..91%
Would not..4
Don't know...5

By Age

18–29 Years

Would..91%
Would not..8
Don't know...1

30–49 Years

Would..91%
Would not..5
Don't know...4

50 Years and Over

Would..94%
Would not..2
Don't know...4

By Household Income

$40,000 and Over

Would..97%
Would not..2
Don't know...1

$25,000–$39,999

Would..92%
Would not..4
Don't know...4

$15,000–$24,999

Would..94%
Would not..4
Don't know...2

Under $15,000

Would..88%
Would not..7
Don't know...5

By Religion

Protestants

Would..92%
Would not..5
Don't know...3

Catholics

Would..91%
Would not..6
Don't know...3

Evangelicals

Would..89%
Would not..7
Don't know...4

Non-Evangelicals

Would..94%
Would not..3
Don't know...3

Selected National Trend

*Would not welcome
as neighbors*

1987..3%
1981..2

Blacks?

Would..83%
Would not...12
Don't know...5

By Sex

Male

Would..83%
Would not...13
Don't know...4

Female

Would..84%
Would not...11
Don't know...5

By Ethnic Background

White

Would..82%
Would not...13
Don't know...5

Nonwhite

Would......................................94%
Would not....................................2
Don't know..................................4

Black

Would......................................95%
Would not....................................2
Don't know..................................3

By Education

College Graduate

Would......................................89%
Would not....................................8
Don't know..................................3

College Incomplete

Would......................................82%
Would not....................................13
Don't know..................................5

High-School Graduate

Would......................................84%
Would not....................................12
Don't know..................................4

Less Than High-School Graduate

Would......................................80%
Would not....................................13
Don't know..................................7

By Region

East

Would......................................86%
Would not....................................10
Don't know..................................4

Midwest

Would......................................84%
Would not....................................9
Don't know..................................7

South

Would......................................77%
Would not....................................19
Don't know..................................4

West

Would......................................89%
Would not....................................7
Don't know..................................4

By Age

18–29 Years

Would......................................88%
Would not....................................10
Don't know..................................2

30–49 Years

Would......................................86%
Would not....................................9
Don't know..................................5

50 Years and Over

Would......................................79%
Would not....................................15
Don't know..................................6

By Household Income

$40,000 and Over

Would......................................85%
Would not....................................12
Don't know..................................3

$25,000–$39,999

Would......................................81%
Would not....................................11
Don't know..................................8

$15,000–$24,999

Would......................................86%
Would not....................................11
Don't know..................................3

Under $15,000

Would......................................83%
Would not....................................15
Don't know..................................2

By Religion

Protestants

Would......................................84%
Would not....................................12
Don't know..................................4

Catholics

Would...83%
Would not......................................12
Don't know......................................5

Evangelicals

Would...80%
Would not......................................14
Don't know......................................6

Non-Evangelicals

Would...86%
Would not......................................10
Don't know......................................4

Koreans?

Would...79%
Would not......................................14
Don't know......................................7

By Sex

Male

Would...80%
Would not......................................15
Don't know......................................5

Female

Would...78%
Would not......................................14
Don't know......................................8

By Ethnic Background

White

Would...79%
Would not......................................14
Don't know......................................7

Nonwhite

Would...75%
Would not......................................17
Don't know......................................8

Black

Would...72%
Would not......................................18
Don't know......................................10

By Education

College Graduate

Would...88%
Would not......................................7
Don't know......................................5

College Incomplete

Would...83%
Would not......................................11
Don't know......................................6

High-School Graduate

Would...81%
Would not......................................15
Don't know......................................4

Less Than High-School Graduate

Would...59%
Would not......................................26
Don't know......................................15

By Region

East

Would...82%
Would not......................................12
Don't know......................................6

Midwest

Would...83%
Would not......................................9
Don't know......................................8

South

Would...74%
Would not......................................19
Don't know......................................7

West

Would...76%
Would not......................................18
Don't know......................................6

By Age

18–29 Years

Would...77%
Would not......................................21
Don't know......................................2

30–49 Years

Would..84%
Would not...10
Don't know...6

50 Years and Over

Would..75%
Would not...14
Don't know..11

By Household Income

$40,000 and Over

Would..87%
Would not..9
Don't know...4

$25,000–$39,999

Would..82%
Would not...11
Don't know...7

$15,000–$24,999

Would..75%
Would not...19
Don't know...6

Under $15,000

Would..72%
Would not...20
Don't know...8

By Religion

Protestants

Would..78%
Would not...15
Don't know...7

Catholics

Would..80%
Would not...15
Don't know...5

Evangelicals

Would..76%
Would not...16
Don't know...8

Non-Evangelicals

Would..81%
Would not...14
Don't know...5

Hispanics?

Would..78%
Would not...16
Don't know...6

By Sex

Male

Would..78%
Would not...17
Don't know...5

Female

Would..79%
Would not...15
Don't know...6

By Ethnic Background

White

Would..78%
Would not...16
Don't know...6

Nonwhite

Would..80%
Would not...14
Don't know...6

Black

Would..74%
Would not...18
Don't know...8

By Education

College Graduate

Would..87%
Would not...11
Don't know...2

College Incomplete

Would	80%
Would not	13
Don't know	7

High-School Graduate

Would	78%
Would not	18
Don't know	4

Less Than High-School Graduate

Would	66%
Would not	21
Don't know	13

By Region

East

Would	78%
Would not	17
Don't know	5

Midwest

Would	80%
Would not	12
Don't know	8

South

Would	72%
Would not	22
Don't know	6

West

Would	86%
Would not	11
Don't know	3

By Age

18–29 Years

Would	81%
Would not	17
Don't know	2

30–49 Years

Would	81%
Would not	14
Don't know	5

50 Years and Over

Would	75%
Would not	17
Don't know	8

By Household Income

$40,000 and Over

Would	82%
Would not	15
Don't know	3

$25,000–$39,999

Would	81%
Would not	14
Don't know	5

$15,000–$24,999

Would	77%
Would not	16
Don't know	7

Under $15,000

Would	77%
Would not	17
Don't know	6

By Religion

Protestants

Would	77%
Would not	16
Don't know	7

Catholics

Would	81%
Would not	15
Don't know	4

Evangelicals

Would	74%
Would not	19
Don't know	7

Non-Evangelicals

Would	82%
Would not	14
Don't know	4

Selected National Trend

	Would not welcome as neighbors
1987	9%
1981	18

Indians or Pakistanis?

Would...78%
Would not.......................................15
Don't know.......................................7

By Sex

Male

Would...77%
Would not.......................................17
Don't know.......................................6

Female

Would...78%
Would not.......................................14
Don't know.......................................8

By Ethnic Background

White

Would...77%
Would not.......................................16
Don't know.......................................7

Nonwhite

Would...83%
Would not.......................................12
Don't know.......................................5

Black

Would...81%
Would not.......................................12
Don't know.......................................7

By Education

College Graduate

Would...84%
Would not.......................................10
Don't know.......................................6

College Incomplete

Would...80%
Would not.......................................15
Don't know.......................................5

High-School Graduate

Would...78%
Would not.......................................17
Don't know.......................................5

Less Than High-School Graduate

Would...68%
Would not.......................................17
Don't know.......................................15

By Region

East

Would...79%
Would not.......................................16
Don't know.......................................5

Midwest

Would...78%
Would not.......................................13
Don't know.......................................9

South

Would...73%
Would not.......................................17
Don't know.......................................10

West

Would...82%
Would not.......................................14
Don't know.......................................4

By Age

18–29 Years

Would...79%
Would not.......................................18
Don't know.......................................3

30–49 Years

Would...80%
Would not.......................................13
Don't know.......................................7

50 Years and Over

Would 74%
Would not 16
Don't know 10

By Household Income

$40,000 and Over

Would 79%
Would not 16
Don't know 5

$25,000-$39,999

Would 81%
Would not 12
Don't know 7

$15,000-$24,999

Would 77%
Would not 18
Don't know 5

Under $15,000

Would 74%
Would not 18
Don't know 8

By Religion

Protestants

Would 77%
Would not 15
Don't know 8

Catholics

Would 80%
Would not 15
Don't know 5

Evangelicals

Would 76%
Would not 15
Don't know 9

Non-Evangelicals

Would 79%
Would not 16
Don't know 5

Vietnamese?

Would 75%
Would not 18
Don't know 7

By Sex

Male

Would 75%
Would not 19
Don't know 6

Female

Would 76%
Would not 16
Don't know 8

By Ethnic Background

White

Would 76%
Would not 17
Don't know 7

Nonwhite

Would 72%
Would not 19
Don't know 9

Black

Would 70%
Would not 20
Don't know 10

By Education

College Graduate

Would 87%
Would not 9
Don't know 4

College Incomplete

Would 79%
Would not 14
Don't know 7

High-School Graduate

Would..75%
Would not..21
Don't know.. 4

Less Than High-School Graduate

Would..60%
Would not..25
Don't know..15

By Region

East

Would..80%
Would not..15
Don't know.. 5

Midwest

Would..78%
Would not..13
Don't know.. 9

South

Would..68%
Would not..24
Don't know.. 8

West

Would..77%
Would not..18
Don't know.. 5

By Age

18–29 Years

Would..75%
Would not..23
Don't know.. 2

30–49 Years

Would..79%
Would not..16
Don't know.. 5

50 Years and Over

Would..72%
Would not..17
Don't know..11

By Household Income

$40,000 and Over

Would..81%
Would not..14
Don't know.. 5

$25,000–$39,999

Would..78%
Would not..15
Don't know.. 7

$15,000–$24,999

Would..71%
Would not..22
Don't know.. 7

Under $15,000

Would..70%
Would not..23
Don't know.. 7

By Religion

Protestants

Would..73%
Would not..19
Don't know.. 8

Catholics

Would..78%
Would not..16
Don't know.. 6

Evangelicals

Would..73%
Would not..19
Don't know.. 8

Non-Evangelicals

Would..78%
Would not..17
Don't know.. 5

Unmarried people living together?

Would..71%
Would not..23
Don't know.. 6

By Sex

Male

Would..............................72%
Would not.........................20
Don't know......................... 8

Female

Would..............................69%
Would not.........................25
Don't know......................... 6

By Ethnic Background

White

Would..............................71%
Would not.........................23
Don't know......................... 6

Nonwhite

Would..............................70%
Would not.........................23
Don't know......................... 7

Black

Would..............................68%
Would not.........................24
Don't know......................... 8

By Education

College Graduate

Would..............................81%
Would not.........................13
Don't know......................... 6

College Incomplete

Would..............................74%
Would not.........................19
Don't know......................... 7

High-School Graduate

Would..............................69%
Would not.........................25
Don't know......................... 6

Less Than High-School Graduate

Would..............................58%
Would not.........................33
Don't know......................... 9

By Region

East

Would..............................77%
Would not.........................17
Don't know......................... 6

Midwest

Would..............................74%
Would not.........................16
Don't know......................10

South

Would..............................61%
Would not.........................35
Don't know......................... 4

West

Would..............................73%
Would not.........................20
Don't know......................... 7

By Age

18–29 Years

Would..............................80%
Would not.........................16
Don't know......................... 4

30–49 Years

Would..............................78%
Would not.........................16
Don't know......................... 6

50 Years and Over

Would..............................57%
Would not.........................35
Don't know......................... 8

By Household Income

$40,000 and Over

Would..............................77%
Would not.........................18
Don't know......................... 5

$25,000–$39,999

Would..............................74%
Would not.........................20
Don't know......................... 6

$15,000–$24,999

Would..70%
Would not..24
Don't know..6

Under $15,000

Would..66%
Would not..27
Don't know..7

By Religion
Protestants

Would..65%
Would not..29
Don't know..6

Catholics

Would..79%
Would not..15
Don't know..6

Evangelicals

Would..57%
Would not..36
Don't know..7

Non-Evangelicals

Would..81%
Would not..13
Don't know..6

Selected National Trend

	Would not welcome as neighbors
1987	12%
1981	14

Religious fundamentalists?

Would..58%
Would not..30
Don't know..12

By Sex
Male

Would..61%
Would not..30
Don't know..9

Female

Would..55%
Would not..31
Don't know..14

By Ethnic Background
White

Would..57%
Would not..32
Don't know..11

Nonwhite

Would..64%
Would not..22
Don't know..14

Black

Would..65%
Would not..20
Don't know..15

By Education
College Graduate

Would..67%
Would not..27
Don't know..6

College Incomplete

Would..60%
Would not..30
Don't know..10

High-School Graduate

Would..57%
Would not..33
Don't know..10

Less Than High-School Graduate

Would..47%
Would not..30
Don't know..23

By Region
East

Would..61%
Would not..31
Don't know..8

Midwest

Would..55%
Would not...................................34
Don't know.................................11

South

Would..59%
Would not...................................26
Don't know.................................15

West

Would..56%
Would not...................................31
Don't know.................................13

By Age

18–29 Years

Would..62%
Would not...................................31
Don't know...................................7

30–49 Years

Would..59%
Would not...................................31
Don't know.................................10

50 Years and Over

Would..55%
Would not...................................29
Don't know.................................16

By Household Income

$40,000 and Over

Would..63%
Would not...................................31
Don't know...................................6

$25,000–$39,999

Would..58%
Would not...................................34
Don't know...................................8

$15,000–$24,999

Would..59%
Would not...................................32
Don't know...................................9

Under $15,000

Would..54%
Would not...................................25
Don't know.................................21

By Religion

Protestants

Would..61%
Would not...................................27
Don't know.................................12

Catholics

Would..55%
Would not...................................36
Don't know...................................9

Evangelicals

Would..65%
Would not...................................24
Don't know.................................11

Non-Evangelicals

Would..54%
Would not...................................35
Don't know.................................11

Selected National Trend

*Would not welcome
as neighbors*

1987..13%
1981..11

Members of minority religious sects or cults?

Would..31%
Would not...................................62
Don't know...................................7

By Sex

Male

Would..35%
Would not...................................57
Don't know...................................8

Female

Would..28%
Would not...................................65
Don't know...................................7

By Ethnic Background

White

Would	30%
Would not	63
Don't know	7

Nonwhite

Would	40%
Would not	53
Don't know	7

Black

Would	35%
Would not	57
Don't know	8

By Education

College Graduate

Would	34%
Would not	59
Don't know	7

College Incomplete

Would	34%
Would not	61
Don't know	5

High-School Graduate

Would	28%
Would not	67
Don't know	5

Less Than High-School Graduate

Would	31%
Would not	55
Don't know	14

By Region

East

Would	33%
Would not	62
Don't know	5

Midwest

Would	30%
Would not	62
Don't know	8

South

Would	30%
Would not	62
Don't know	8

West

Would	33%
Would not	60
Don't know	7

By Age

18–29 Years

Would	37%
Would not	60
Don't know	3

30–49 Years

Would	32%
Would not	60
Don't know	8

50 Years and Over

Would	27%
Would not	65
Don't know	8

By Household Income

$40,000 and Over

Would	32%
Would not	62
Don't know	6

$25,000–$39,999

Would	32%
Would not	63
Don't know	5

$15,000–$24,999

Would	30%
Would not	64
Don't know	6

Under $15,000

Would	28%
Would not	63
Don't know	9

By Religion

Protestants

Would.....................................30%
Would not..............................62
Don't know............................ 8

Catholics

Would.....................................31%
Would not..............................65
Don't know............................ 4

Evangelicals

Would.....................................31%
Would not..............................63
Don't know............................ 6

Non-Evangelicals

Would.....................................32%
Would not..............................61
Don't know............................ 7

Selected National Trend

	Would not welcome as neighbors
1987	44%
1981	30

Note: Recent clashes between whites and blacks have underscored the extent of racial tensions in the United States, but a new Gallup Poll also reveals a broad pattern of prejudice against diverse religious and ethnic minorities and persons with unconventional life-styles. Almost two thirds of the public (62%), for example, would not like to have members of minority sects or cults as neighbors, and many would not welcome religious fundamentalists (30%) or unmarried couples (23%). Substantial proportions, moreover, would be inhospitable to members of various ethnic minorities, including Vietnamese (18%), Hispanics (16%), Indians or Pakistanis (15%), Koreans (14%), and blacks (12%).

Intolerance based solely on religious preference is quite rare, however. Relatively few Americans would object to living next door to Jews (5%), Protestants (5%), or Catholics (3%).

Comparison with earlier survey findings suggests that hostility toward religious cults, fundamentalists, and single persons sharing the same living quarters may be growing. In a 1981 poll 30% said that they would not welcome cult members as neighbors, with that figure rising to 44% in 1987 and to 62% at present. Similarly, reported bias against religious fundamentalists increased from 11% in 1981 to 13% in 1987 to the current 30%. And the number who would object to having unmarried couples as neighbors has grown from 14% to 23% since 1981. At the same time, prejudice against other groups measured in one or both of the earlier surveys—Vietnamese, Hispanics, blacks, Jews, Protestants, and Catholics—has not changed significantly.

However, it should be noted that a change in survey methodology may have affected the comparative findings. Participants in the latest poll were asked whether they would or would not like to have members of each group as neighbors. In the earlier surveys they were handed lists of groups and asked to single out any they would not like as neighbors.

MARCH 12
PRESIDENT BUSH

Interviewing Date: 2/28–3/2/89
Survey #AI 878

Do you approve or disapprove of the way George Bush is handling his job as president?

Approve.....................................63%
Disapprove.............................13
No opinion............................24

By Politics

Republicans

Approve.....................................82%
Disapprove............................ 4
No opinion............................14

Democrats

Approve.....................................46%
Disapprove.............................21
No opinion............................33

Independents

Approve...57%
Disapprove.......................................15
No opinion.......................................28

Those Who Support
John Tower's Confirmation

Approve...83%
Disapprove... 3
No opinion.......................................14

Those Who Oppose
John Tower's Confirmation

Approve...52%
Disapprove.......................................23
No opinion.......................................25

Do you approve or disapprove of the job President Bush has done so far in explaining his policies and plans for the future to the American people?

Approve...65%
Disapprove.......................................28
No opinion....................................... 7

By Politics

Republicans

Approve...78%
Disapprove.......................................17
No opinion... 5

Democrats

Approve...58%
Disapprove.......................................33
No opinion... 9

Independents

Approve...58%
Disapprove.......................................34
No opinion... 8

So far, based on what you have heard or read, do you approve or disapprove of President Bush's cabinet appointments?

Approve...55%
Disapprove.......................................29
No opinion.......................................16

By Politics

Republicans

Approve...71%
Disapprove.......................................16
No opinion.......................................13

Democrats

Approve...41%
Disapprove.......................................41
No opinion.......................................18

Independents

Approve...53%
Disapprove.......................................31
No opinion.......................................16

Note: President George Bush continues to enjoy a large measure of public confidence despite the Tower controversy and charges that his administration is adrift. More than six in ten (63%) approve of Bush's performance in office, while only 13% disapprove and 24% are undecided—similar to the job ratings given to Bush's predecessors at comparable points in their tenure. In Gallup's first assessment in late January, 51% approved and 6% disapproved of Bush's job performance, with 43% undecided.

Refuting criticism of the White House as floundering and lacking a clear sense of purpose, Americans of all political stripes commend the new president for the job he has done in communicating his policies and agenda. And although the public opposed Senate confirmation of John Tower to be secretary of defense, a solid majority approves of Bush's cabinet appointments overall.

Asked to rate Bush's success to date in "explaining his policies and plans for the future to the American people," 65% approve and 28% disapprove. Republicans are overwhelmingly positive, 78% to 17%, while majorities of Democrats and independents (58% each) also approve.

The public supports Bush's cabinet appointees by almost a 2-to-1 ratio, 55% to 29%. Democrats are evenly divided between those favoring and opposing Bush's cabinet choices (41% each), while majorities of Republicans (71%) and independents (53%) approve.

The survey findings suggest that the public's confidence in Bush may weather fallout over the Tower nomination. His job performance rating among those favoring confirmation is overwhelmingly positive, 83% to 3%. And even among those opposed to Tower, approval of Bush's overall conduct in office outweighs disapproval by more than a 2-to-1 ratio, 52% to 23%.

MARCH 16
PRESIDENT BUSH

Interviewing Date: 2/28–3/2/89
Survey #AI 878

Now let me ask you about some specific foreign and domestic problems. As I read off each problem, would you tell me whether you approve or disapprove of the way President Bush is handling that problem:

Relations with the Soviet Union?

Approve	70%
Disapprove	10
No opinion	20

By Politics

Republicans

Approve	80%
Disapprove	7
No opinion	13

Democrats

Approve	64%
Disapprove	11
No opinion	25

Independents

Approve	68%
Disapprove	11
No opinion	21

Foreign policy?

Approve	62%
Disapprove	15
No opinion	23

By Politics
Republicans

Approve	76%
Disapprove	10
No opinion	14

Democrats

Approve	48%
Disapprove	20
No opinion	32

Independents

Approve	61%
Disapprove	16
No opinion	23

Economic conditions in this country?

Approve	52%
Disapprove	27
No opinion	21

By Politics
Republicans

Approve	75%
Disapprove	13
No opinion	12

Democrats

Approve	31%
Disapprove	42
No opinion	27

Independents

Approve	47%
Disapprove	27
No opinion	26

The drug epidemic?

Approve	48%
Disapprove	32
No opinion	20

By Politics
Republicans

Approve	58%
Disapprove	27
No opinion	15

Democrats

Approve...38%
Disapprove...35
No opinion...27

Independents

Approve...48%
Disapprove...33
No opinion...19

Situation in the Middle East?

Approve...44%
Disapprove...26
No opinion...30

By   Politics

Republicans

Approve...62%
Disapprove...17
No opinion...21

Democrats

Approve...30%
Disapprove...33
No opinion...37

Independents

Approve...38%
Disapprove...30
No opinion...32

Inflation?

Approve...41%
Disapprove...33
No opinion...26

By   Politics

Republicans

Approve...57%
Disapprove...25
No opinion...18

Democrats

Approve...26%
Disapprove...43
No opinion...31

Independents

Approve...39%
Disapprove...33
No opinion...28

Federal budget deficit?

Approve...40%
Disapprove...36
No opinion...24

By   Politics

Republicans

Approve...58%
Disapprove...25
No opinion...17

Democrats

Approve...26%
Disapprove...46
No opinion...28

Independents

Approve...34%
Disapprove...39
No opinion...27

Situation in Central America?

Approve...37%
Disapprove...33
No opinion...30

By   Politics

Republicans

Approve...53%
Disapprove...23
No opinion...24

Democrats

Approve...25%
Disapprove...40
No opinion...35

Independents

Approve...31%
Disapprove...39
No opinion...40

Bush-Reagan Comparisons
(Percent Approval)

	Bush (Feb–March 1989)	Reagan (July 1988)
Job overall	63%	51%
Soviet relations	70%	77%
Foreign policy	62	54
Economic conditions	52	43
Drug epidemic	48	45
Budget deficit	40	25

Note: Against a backdrop of sharply reduced international tensions, the American people give President George Bush higher marks for his handling of Soviet relations and foreign policy in general than for his other undertakings. Fully seven in ten (70%) currently approve of his conduct of U.S. relations with the Soviet Union, while 10% disapprove and 20% are undecided. A high level of confidence is expressed by Americans of all political persuasions, including 80% of Republicans, 68% of independents, and 64% of Democrats.

In the latest survey, conducted soon after his Asian trip, 62% approve and 15% disapprove of Bush's handling of foreign policy, with 23% undecided. Judgments of the new president's competence in this area have a more partisan cast, with 76% of Republicans, compared to 48% of Democrats, approving.

About one half give Bush a passing grade for his handling of economic conditions (52%) and the drug epidemic (48%), followed by the situation in the Middle East (44%), inflation (41%), the federal budget deficit (40%), and the Central American situation (37%). Statistically equal percentages approve and disapprove of the way Bush is dealing with each of the last two problems.

In its final survey of President Ronald Reagan's accomplishments, the Gallup Poll found three fourths of Americans (77%) approving of his handling of Soviet relations, the largest proportion to have done so throughout his tenure. This perception helped push Reagan's approval rating for foreign policy in general over the halfway mark (to 54%) for the first time since news of the Iran-contra scandal broke.

The same mid-1988 poll probed the public's views about how well candidate Bush would handle these tasks if elected president in November. About one half said that he would do as well as Reagan. Of the remainder the consensus was that Bush would have a hard time measuring up to Reagan, with relatively few thinking that Bush would do a better job.

The current survey suggests that Bush is exceeding public expectations, at least during the honeymoon phase of his new administration. His current approval rating for Soviet relations (70%) is almost as good as Reagan's (77%) in mid-1988. Bush tops Reagan on foreign policy (62% to 54%), the economy (52% to 43%), and the budget deficit (40% to 25%), while both presidents draw almost identical approval ratings for dealing with the drug crisis (48% to 45%).

MARCH 19
FIREARMS

Interviewing Date: 2/28–3/2/89
Survey #AI 878

In general, do you feel that the laws covering the sale of firearms should be made more strict, less strict, or kept as they are now?

More strict	70%
Less strict	6
Kept as they are now	22
No opinion	2

By Sex
Male

More strict	59%
Less strict	8
Kept as they are now	31
No opinion	2

Female

More strict	79%
Less strict	4
Kept as they are now	14
No opinion	3

By Ethnic Background
White

More strict	69%
Less strict	5

Kept as they are now............................24
No opinion..2

Nonwhite

More strict..73%
Less strict..11
Kept as they are now............................12
No opinion..4

Black

More strict..72%
Less strict..11
Kept as they are now............................11
No opinion..6

By Education

College Graduate

More strict..76%
Less strict..3
Kept as they are now............................19
No opinion..2

College Incomplete

More strict..66%
Less strict..7
Kept as they are now............................25
No opinion..2

High-School Graduate

More strict..69%
Less strict..7
Kept as they are now............................22
No opinion..2

Less Than High-School Graduate

More strict..69%
Less strict..4
Kept as they are now............................23
No opinion..4

By Region

East

More strict..71%
Less strict..8
Kept as they are now............................19
No opinion..2

Midwest

More strict..72%
Less strict..6
Kept as they are now............................19
No opinion..3

South

More strict..66%
Less strict..5
Kept as they are now............................27
No opinion..2

West

More strict..71%
Less strict..5
Kept as they are now............................22
No opinion..2

By Age

18–29 Years

More strict..70%
Less strict..11
Kept as they are now............................18
No opinion..1

30–49 Years

More strict..70%
Less strict..5
Kept as they are now............................23
No opinion..2

50 Years and Over

More strict..69%
Less strict..3
Kept as they are now............................23
No opinion..5

Gun Owners Only

More strict..58%
Less strict..7
Kept as they are now............................33
No opinion..2

Nonowners Only

More strict..80%
Less strict..5
Kept as they are now............................12
No opinion..3

Selected National Trend*

	More strict	Less strict	Kept as they are	No opinion
1988	64%	6%	27%	3%
1986	60	8	30	2
1980	59	6	29	6
1975	69	3	24	4

*Prior to 1989 the question asked about the sale of handguns rather than firearms.

Would you favor or oppose federal legislation banning the manufacture, sale, and possession of the following types of weapons: Semiautomatic assault guns, such as the AK-47?

Favor 72%
Oppose...23
No opinion.. 5

By Sex

Male

Favor 70%
Oppose...27
No opinion.. 3

Female

Favor 74%
Oppose...19
No opinion.. 7

By Ethnic Background

White

Favor 73%
Oppose...22
No opinion.. 5

Nonwhite

Favor 68%
Oppose...24
No opinion.. 8

Black

Favor 69%
Oppose...22
No opinion.. 9

By Education

College Graduate

Favor 79%
Oppose...17
No opinion.. 4

College Incomplete

Favor 71%
Oppose...25
No opinion.. 4

High-School Graduate

Favor 71%
Oppose...24
No opinion.. 5

Less Than High-School Graduate

Favor 67%
Oppose...23
No opinion..10

By Region

East

Favor 73%
Oppose...21
No opinion.. 6

Midwest

Favor 72%
Oppose...24
No opinion.. 4

South

Favor 68%
Oppose...25
No opinion.. 7

West

Favor 77%
Oppose...18
No opinion.. 5

By Age

18–29 Years

Favor 66%
Oppose...29
No opinion.. 5

30–49 Years

Favor 77%
Oppose..20
No opinion...3

50 Years and Over

Favor 71%
Oppose..21
No opinion...8

Those Who Say That the Sale of Firearms Should Be Made More Strict

Favor 80%
Oppose..16
No opinion...4

Those Who Say That the Sale of Firearms Should Be Made Less Strict

Favor 56%
Oppose..41
No opinion...3

Those Who Say That the Sale of Firearms Should Be Kept as They Are Now

Favor 55%
Oppose..39
No opinion...6

Cheap handguns known as "Saturday night specials"?

Favor 71%
Oppose..25
No opinion...4

By Sex

Male

Favor 68%
Oppose..30
No opinion...2

Female

Favor 73%
Oppose..21
No opinion...6

By Ethnic Background

White

Favor 71%
Oppose..25
No opinion...4

Nonwhite

Favor 66%
Oppose..26
No opinion...8

Black

Favor 68%
Oppose..26
No opinion...6

By Education

College Graduate

Favor 75%
Oppose..19
No opinion...6

College Incomplete

Favor 73%
Oppose..26
No opinion...1

High-School Graduate

Favor 70%
Oppose..26
No opinion...4

Less Than High-School Graduate

Favor 63%
Oppose..30
No opinion...7

By Region

East

Favor 77%
Oppose..21
No opinion...2

Midwest

Favor 70%
Oppose..27
No opinion...3

South

Favor 67%
Oppose 29
No opinion 4

West

Favor 68%
Oppose 24
No opinion 8

By Age

18–29 Years

Favor 69%
Oppose 29
No opinion 2

30–49 Years

Favor 74%
Oppose 24
No opinion 2

50 Years and Over

Favor 66%
Oppose 26
No opinion 8

Those Who Say That the Sale of Firearms Should Be Made More Strict

Favor 80%
Oppose 16
No opinion 4

Those Who Say That the Sale of Firearms Should Be Made Less Strict

Favor 50%
Oppose 45
No opinion 5

Those Who Say That the Sale of Firearms Should Be Kept as They Are Now

Favor 51%
Oppose 46
No opinion 3

Plastic guns invisible to metal detectors?

Favor 75%
Oppose 20
No opinion 5

By Sex

Male

Favor 74%
Oppose 22
No opinion 4

Female

Favor 75%
Oppose 18
No opinion 7

By Ethnic Background

White

Favor 76%
Oppose 19
No opinion 5

Nonwhite

Favor 66%
Oppose 28
No opinion 6

Black

Favor 68%
Oppose 26
No opinion 6

By Education

College Graduate

Favor 84%
Oppose 12
No opinion 4

College Incomplete

Favor 74%
Oppose 23
No opinion 3

High-School Graduate

Favor 73%
Oppose 21
No opinion 6

Less Than High-School Graduate

Favor 68%
Oppose 24
No opinion.. 8

By Region

East

Favor 75%
Oppose 21
No opinion.. 4

Midwest

Favor 76%
Oppose 20
No opinion.. 4

South

Favor 71%
Oppose 24
No opinion.. 5

West

Favor 80%
Oppose 13
No opinion.. 7

By Age

18–29 Years

Favor 72%
Oppose 26
No opinion.. 2

30–49 Years

Favor 80%
Oppose 17
No opinion.. 3

50 Years and Over

Favor 71%
Oppose 20
No opinion.. 9

Those Who Say That the Sale of Firearms Should Be Made More Strict

Favor 80%
Oppose 16
No opinion.. 4

Those Who Say That the Sale of Firearms Should Be Made Less Strict

Favor 67%
Oppose 33
No opinion.. *

Those Who Say That the Sale of Firearms Should Be Kept as They Are Now

Favor 62%
Oppose 29
No opinion.. 9

*Less than 1%

Do you have a gun in the house?

	Yes
National..	47%

By Sex

Male	55%
Female..	41

By Ethnic Background

White...	50%
Nonwhite	31
Black	30

By Education

College graduate...................................	39%
College incomplete...............................	45
High-school graduate............................	50
Less than high-school graduate	60

By Region

East	31%
Midwest...	47
South	61
West	49

By Age

18–29 years.......................................	43%
30–49 years.......................................	49
50 years and over.................................	50

Selected National Trend

1985	.44%
1980	.44
1975	.48
1972	.43
1968	.50
1959	.49

Asked of those who replied in the affirmative: Is it a pistol, shotgun, rifle, or what?

Rifle	.31%
Shotgun	.28
Pistol	.25
Assault gun	1
Other; not sure	2

Selected National Trend

	1985	1975	1972
Rifle	26%	30%	26%
Shotgun	24	31	27
Pistol	22	19	16
Assault gun	*	*	*
Other; not sure	2	1	*

*Not recorded

Asked of gun owners: What is the total number of guns kept in your house?

One	.14%
Two	.10
Three	5
Four or more	.15
Not sure	3

Note: Almost three fourths of the American people favor federal legislation banning the manufacture, sale, and possession of semiautomatic assault guns. In the latest Gallup Poll, 72% favor and 23% oppose laws to ban these so-called Rambo guns. Two thirds or more in all major population groups endorse such legislation. Even those who generally oppose greater restrictions on the sale of firearms support a government ban on assault weapons, 55% to 39%.

Last week the Bush administration, responding to a huge increase in requests for import permits and to charges that these weapons are used extensively by drug traffickers, issued a temporary ban on the importation of AK-47s, Uzis, and similar assault rifles. Controversy over the sale of these weapons has surged since a deranged gunman fired an AK-47 into a California schoolyard in January, killing five children and injuring thirty-one others. The administration's action will block the importation of an estimated 110,000 assault guns for which permits have been sought so far this year, nearly triple the number requested in all of 1988. However, the ban will affect the sale of only a small fraction of these weapons, most of which are manufactured domestically.

The survey also found overwhelming support for federal legislation forbidding the manufacture, sale, and private possession of cheap handguns called "Saturday night specials" (71%) and plastic guns that are invisible to metal detectors (75%). Opponents totaled only 25% and 20%, respectively.

The public has consistently called for tougher gun laws. In the latest poll, 70% say that the laws governing the sale of firearms should be made stricter than they are now, while 22% are content with the current laws; only 6% favor relaxing the present standards. While majorities in all groups favor tougher sales laws, backing is somewhat greater among women (79%) than men (59%), college graduates (76%) than nongraduates (67%), nonsoutherners (71%) than southerners (66%), and nonowners of guns (80%) than owners (58%).

Roughly one half of American households (47%) possesses one or more firearms. This proportion has been remarkably stable over the last thirty years. Currently, 31% own a rifle, 28% a shotgun, 25% a pistol or revolver, and 1% an assault weapon. Moreover, three households in ten (29%) have two or more guns; 15% have four or more.

MARCH 23
THE SATANIC VERSES/U.S. RELATIONS WITH IRAN

Interviewing Date: 2/28–3/2/89
Survey #AI 878

Have you heard or read about the controversy concerning Salman Rushdie's book, The Satanic Verses?

	Yes
National	85%

Asked of the aware group (85% of the sample): Do you think the bookstores made the right decision or the wrong decision by removing the book, The Satanic Verses, from their bookshelves?

Right decision	26%
Wrong decision	64
No opinion	10

By Sex

Male

Right decision	22%
Wrong decision	70
No opinion	8

Female

Right decision	30%
Wrong decision	57
No opinion	13

By Education

College Graduate

Right decision	20%
Wrong decision	75
No opinion	5

College Incomplete

Right decision	25%
Wrong decision	65
No opinion	10

High-School Graduate

Right decision	30%
Wrong decision	59
No opinion	11

Less Than High-School Graduate

Right decision	36%
Wrong decision	46
No opinion	18

By Age

18–29 Years

Right decision	31%
Wrong decision	68
No opinion	1

30–49 Years

Right decision	26%
Wrong decision	65
No opinion	9

50 Years and Over

Right decision	26%
Wrong decision	60
No opinion	14

Also asked of the aware group: The Ayatollah Khomeini, the Iranian leader, has ordered the assassination of Rushdie because he considers the book insulting to the Muslim religion and to the prophet Mohammed. If Salman Rushdie or anyone were to be killed or injured as a result of an assassination attempt, do you think the United States should retaliate against Iran?

Should	41%
Should not	48
No opinion	11

By Sex

Male

Should	52%
Should not	42
No opinion	6

Female

Should	31%
Should not	54
No opinion	15

By Education

College Graduate

Should	37%
Should not	54
No opinion	9

College Incomplete

Should..42%
Should not...50
No opinion...8

High-School Graduate

Should..45%
Should not...43
No opinion...12

Less Than High-School Graduate

Should..40%
Should not...41
No opinion...19

By Age

18-29 Years

Should..44%
Should not...49
No opinion...7

30-49 Years

Should..41%
Should not...49
No opinion...10

50 Years and Over

Should..40%
Should not...47
No opinion...13

Also asked of the aware group: Which of the following types of retaliation, if any, would you support against Iran in that event:

Applying economic sanctions against Iran?

Favor..37%
Oppose..3
Not sure..1
Don't favor retaliation.........................59

Breaking off all diplomatic relations with Iran?

Favor..34%
Oppose..7
Not sure...*
Don't favor retaliation.........................59

Bombing Iranian oil fields or military targets?

Favor..16%
Oppose...23
Not sure..2
Don't favor retaliation.........................59

Encouraging a military coup to remove Khomeini from power?

Favor..28%
Oppose...11
Not sure..2
Don't favor retaliation.........................59

Assassinating the Ayatollah Khomeini?

Favor..13%
Oppose...27
Not sure..1
Don't favor retaliation.........................59

*Less than 1%

Asked of the entire sample: Do you think the Bush administration should try to improve U.S. relations with Iran, or not?

Should..42%
Should not...50
No opinion...8

By Sex

Male

Should..38%
Should not...56
No opinion...6

Female

Should..45%
Should not...45
No opinion...10

By Ethnic Background

White

Should..40%
Should not...52
No opinion...8

Nonwhite

Should..51%
Should not.......................................40
No opinion..9

Black

Should..54%
Should not.......................................37
No opinion..9

By Education

College Graduate

Should..36%
Should not.......................................57
No opinion..7

College Incomplete

Should..48%
Should not.......................................45
No opinion..7

High-School Graduate

Should..39%
Should not.......................................51
No opinion..10

Less Than High-School Graduate

Should..43%
Should not.......................................47
No opinion..10

By Region

East

Should..40%
Should not.......................................51
No opinion..9

Midwest

Should..49%
Should not.......................................44
No opinion..7

South

Should..36%
Should not.......................................56
No opinion..8

West

Should..42%
Should not.......................................50
No opinion..8

By Age

18–29 Years

Should..47%
Should not.......................................48
No opinion..5

30–49 Years

Should..42%
Should not.......................................51
No opinion..7

50 Years and Over

Should..37%
Should not.......................................51
No opinion..12

By Politics

Republicans

Should..39%
Should not.......................................55
No opinion..6

Democrats

Should..43%
Should not.......................................47
No opinion..10

Independents

Should..43%
Should not.......................................48
No opinion..9

Note: American opinion is equivocal about *The Satanic Verses* controversy. While a solid majority of Americans says that bookstores made the wrong decision in removing Salman Rushdie's novel from their shelves, there is little support for a strong U.S. response against Iran should the controversial author be harmed as a consequence of the Ayatollah Khomeini's assassination order.

Among those who have heard or read about the controversy concerning Rushdie, nearly two thirds (64%) think that bookstores made the wrong decision in taking *The Satanic Verses* off their shelves. College graduates (75%) and men (70%) are more likely to protest the decision of stores to remove the novel.

Public opinion of the aware group (85% of the sample) is divided on whether or not the United States should retaliate if Rushdie or anyone else were to be killed or injured as a result of an assassination attempt. Nearly one half (48%) opposes retaliation, while 41% would favor some sort of retaliatory response. Gender differences are the most striking, as a majority of men favor retaliation (52%), compared to only one third of women (31%). Similarly, the less educated are more likely than their counterparts to support it.

Only one third of the public approves of even the mildest forms of retaliation against Iran, including economic sanctions (37%) and the severing of diplomatic relations (34%). Even fewer favor encouraging a military coup to remove Khomeini from power (28%). There is even less support for direct action, as only one in seven favors either bombing the Iranian oil fields (16%) or assassinating Khomeini (13%).

With regard to the more general issue of improving relations with Iran, the public is divided in its views. One half opposes such efforts by the Bush administration (50%), compared to 42% who support them. College graduates (57%), men (56%), and southerners (56%) take the lead in opposing attempts to improve relations with Iran.

MARCH 26
TAX REFORM

Interviewing Date: 1/27–2/5/89
Special Survey*

Do you think the 1986 tax reform bill has made for a fairer distribution of the tax load among all taxpayers, one that's less fair, or hasn't it made much difference from the previous system?

More fair 13%
Less fair 39

*This survey was conducted for *Times Mirror* by the Gallup Organization.

Not much difference 33
No opinion 15

By Education

College Graduate

More fair 20%
Less fair 46
Not much difference 25
No opinion 9

College Incomplete

More fair 20%
Less fair 43
Not much difference 24
No opinion 13

No College

More fair 9%
Less fair 35
Not much difference 38
No opinion 18

By Income

$50,000 and Over

More fair 18%
Less fair 46
Not much difference 23
No opinion 13

$30,000–$49,999

More fair 14%
Less fair 43
Not much difference 30
No opinion 13

Under $30,000

More fair 12%
Less fair 35
Not much difference 37
No opinion 16

Next, I'd like to ask you a few questions about what you think will happen in the next year. First, do you think taxes will increase, decrease, or stay about the same?

Increase 76%
Decrease.. 3
Stay the same 19
No opinion.. 2

By Politics

Republicans

Increase 66%
Decrease.. 3
Stay the same 27
No opinion.. 4

Democrats

Increase 80%
Decrease.. 4
Stay the same 14
No opinion.. 2

Independents

Increase 80%
Decrease.. 2
Stay the same 16
No opinion.. 2

Which one of the following worries you most about the future?

An increase in taxes 42%
An increase in prices 24
You or your spouse may lose your job 14
An increase in interest rates...................11
None... 5
No opinion.. 4

Note: As Americans look to the approach of the April 17 tax deadline with a mixture of fear and loathing, they are expressing more doubts than ever before that the Tax Reform Act of 1986 actually made the system fairer and more concern that taxes actually will increase by the end of the year. According to a *Times Mirror* survey, most respondents (39%) believe that tax reform has made for a less equitable distribution of the tax load, while only 13% say that the system spreads the tax load more fairly. An additional one third (33%) thinks that it has not made much difference.

When the bill was first passed the public was skeptical that it would create a fairer system, but few expected it to be less equitable. A 1986 Gallup Poll found a majority replying that the new tax bill either would be no different (36%) or fairer (27%). Only one fifth said it would be less fair (20%).

In the current survey, tax reform draws bad reviews from citizens of all income levels. It has failed to convince lower-income people that the system is more equitable. Upper-income people, who have lost some tax loopholes, are more likely (46%) than the average citizen to see the new tax code as being less fair.

Despite the Bush administration's continued assurances that there will be no new taxes, fully three quarters (76%) of Americans expect an increase. An additional one fifth (19%) think that taxes will remain at their current level, while only 3% anticipate lower rates. Partisan differences are evident, with Democrats (80%) more likely than Republicans (66%) to believe that taxes will rise.

In a related measure, anxieties about increased taxes again are manifest. Asked about their concerns for the future, more than four in ten (42%) worry most about an increase in taxes. Significantly fewer cite an increase in prices (24%), the loss of their jobs (14%), or an increase in interest rates (11%) as their biggest concern.

MARCH 30
COST OF LIVING

Interviewing Date: 2/28–3/2/89
Survey #AI 878*

I'm going to read you some products and services many families buy. As I read each one, please tell me how the present cost of that item compares with what you were paying a few months ago. If your family doesn't use a particular item or hasn't bought any in the last few months, please tell me. Have the prices you've been paying for (item) gone up a little, gone up a lot, gone down, or stayed about the same as a few months ago?

Cigarettes?

Gone up a lot......................................56%
Gone up a little 21
Gone down... 1

*Based on users, buyers

Stayed the same.................................10
Don't know 12

Prescription drugs?

Gone up a lot....................................35%
Gone up a little 21
Gone down.. 1
Stayed the same................................29
Don't know 14

Clothing?

Gone up a lot....................................26%
Gone up a little 30
Gone down.. 3
Stayed the same................................37
Don't know 4

Fruits, vegetables?

Gone up a lot....................................25%
Gone up a little 42
Gone down.. 2
Stayed the same................................26
Don't know 5

Gas, electricity?

Gone up a lot....................................22%
Gone up a little 29
Gone down.. 3
Stayed the same................................41
Don't know 5

Meats, poultry?

Gone up a lot....................................18%
Gone up a little 34
Gone down.. 3
Stayed the same................................39
Don't know 6

Dairy products?

Gone up a lot....................................11%
Gone up a little 32
Gone down.. 1
Stayed the same................................52
Don't know 4

Gasoline?

Gone up a lot.................................... 6%
Gone up a little 29

Gone down..15
Stayed the same................................47
Don't know 3

Those Who Say Prices Have Risen*
(By Income)

	$40,000 and over	$25,000–$39,999	Under $25,000
Cigarettes	67%	78%	82%
Prescription drugs	46	58	62
Clothing	49	54	59
Fruits, vegetables	61	69	70
Gas, electricity	41	50	57
Meats, poultry	44	54	57
Dairy products	35	40	48
Gasoline	36	31	35

*Includes "up a little" and "up a lot"

Note: Paralleling government reports of rising consumer prices and renewed inflation fears, majorities in a new Gallup Poll say that the prices they are paying for selected products and services have gone up during the last few months. Consumers of most of these items generally view the recent price increases as modest, but cigarette and prescription drug buyers report that they now are paying a lot more than they did a few months ago. For dairy products and gasoline, consumers who think their costs have gone down or stayed about the same slightly outnumber those who think that costs have risen.

Fully three fourths of cigarette buyers (77%) say that the price has gone up recently, with more describing the cost as increasing a lot (56%) rather than a little (21%). Prescription drug buyers also are likely to perceive a substantial (35%) rather than a modest rise (21%) in the prices they pay.

Fruits and vegetables rank second only to cigarettes in consumers' perceptions that their cost has gone up recently (67%), but the prevailing view is that produce prices have risen a little (42%) rather than a lot (25%). Also, more than one half of clothing purchasers (56%) think that they are paying more for apparel than they did a few months ago. These consumers are about evenly divided between those who say that prices have gone up a little (30%) and a lot (26%).

A 51% majority of utility customers think that their costs for gas and electricity have risen a little (29%) or a lot (22%). About one half of meat and poultry buyers (52%) now are paying more than they did a few months ago, but only 18% think that prices have gone up sharply, while 34% see a slight increase.

Dairy products buyers, as noted, are among those least inclined to perceive an overall price increase (43%) and are three times more likely to think that their costs have risen a little (32%) rather than a lot (11%). About one third of gasoline purchasers (35%) thinks that prices have gone up a little (29%) or a lot (6%). In contrast, 47% say that they are paying about the same as they did a few months ago, while 15% think that gas is cheaper now.

As a rule, less educated and less well-to-do consumers are feeling the pinch of price increases more than their college-educated and more affluent counterparts. For example, 67% of cigarette buyers with annual family incomes of $40,000 or more think that their cost has gone up in the last few months; the figure rises to 78% among middle-income consumers and to 82% in the lowest income group.

APRIL 2
CHILD ABUSE

Interviewing Date: 2/28–3/2/89
Survey #AI 878

Do you personally know any children you suspect have been physically or sexually abused?

Here is a very personal question. We are only asking this question in order to get an accurate estimate of the size of the problem. Your answer is strictly confidential. Were you, yourself, ever a victim of child abuse?

	Know possible victim(s)	Personally abused
National	15%	8%

By Sex

	Know possible victim(s)	Personally abused
Male	11%	5%
Female	18	10

By Ethnic Background

	Know possible victim(s)	Personally abused
White	16%	8%
Nonwhite	6	7
Black	3	6

By Education

	Know possible victim(s)	Personally abused
College graduate	18%	7%
College incomplete	13	7
High-school graduate	15	9
Less than high-school graduate	4	7

By Region

	Know possible victim(s)	Personally abused
East	14%	6%
Midwest	15	9
South	12	6
West	19	11

By Age

	Know possible victim(s)	Personally abused
18–29 years	21%	6%
30–49 years	16	12
50 years and over	9	3

By Family Income

	Know possible victim(s)	Personally abused
$40,000 and over	18%	7%
$25,000–$39,999	18	7
$15,000–$24,999	12	11
Under $15,000	12	8

	Know possible victim(s)	Personally abused
Know possible victim(s)	100%	21%
Don't know victim(s)	–	5
Personally abused	41	100
Not abused	13	–

Do you think child abuse is more prevalent today than it was in the past, or do you think the reason there are more reported cases of child abuse is because people are more aware of the problem?

More prevalent today	26%
People more aware	70
Don't know	4

By Age
18–29 Years

More prevalent today	25%
People more aware	74
Don't know	1

30-49 Years

More prevalent today.............................22%
People more aware 75
Don't know.. 3

50 Years and Over

More prevalent today.............................31%
People more aware 63
Don't know.. 6

Those Who Know Possible Victim(s)

More prevalent today.............................36%
People more aware 62
Don't know.. 2

Those Who Don't Know Victim(s)

More prevalent today.............................24%
People more aware 72
Don't know.. 4

Those Who Were Personally Abused

More prevalent today.............................25%
People more aware 74
Don't know.. 1

Those Who Were Not Abused

More prevalent today.............................26%
People more aware 70
Don't know.. 4

Note: Some 25 million Americans, or 15% of the adult population, claim to know children whom they suspect have been physically or sexually abused, while 8 percent say that they themselves were abused as children. The number of reported child abuse incidents has tripled in recent years, and authorities believe that most cases go unreported. Nevertheless, knowledge of victims is no higher now than it was in 1981, when 15% also said they knew of children who had been physically abused.

Although personal knowledge of such victims has not changed, awareness of the scope of these vicious crimes doubtless has been enhanced by highly publicized cases such as the beating death of 6-year-old Lisa Steinberg by her adoptive father. The weight of public opinion, in fact, attributes the larger number of reported child abuse cases to greater public awareness of the problem (70%) than to an increase in actual victimization (26%).

Women are more likely than men by 18% and 11%, respectively, to cite personal knowledge of child abuse victims. Awareness drops sharply by age, with 21% of 18 to 29-year-olds, compared to 16% of 30 to 49-year-olds and 9% of those 50 and older, saying that they know children who they think have been abused. Knowledge of victims is higher among college graduates and persons from upper-income families than among the less educated and less affluent. Differences by geographic region are inconclusive.

More women (10%) than men (5%) claim to have been personally abused as children. Reported victimization also is higher among 30 to 49-year-olds (12%) than among younger (6%) or older (3%) adults. Education and income apparently have little bearing on child abuse, with adults from widely varying walks of life reporting about the same incidence.

Moreover, knowledge of child abuse cases and personal victimization are strongly interrelated. Four in ten of those who say that they were victims (41%) claim to know children who have been abused. In sharp contrast, only 13% of those who were not abused are aware of children whom they suspect are victims.

Large majorities in all population groups believe that the greater number of reported child abuse cases is more a function of growing public awareness than of a broadening of the problem. People who have personal knowledge of abused children, however, are more inclined than those who are not aware of such victims to find that the problem is more prevalent today than in the past, 36% and 24%, respectively.

APRIL 6
RATING THE UNITED STATES AND OTHER NATIONS

Interviewing Date: 2/28–3/2/89
Survey #AI 878

I'd like your overall opinion of some foreign countries. Is your overall opinion of (country) very favorable, mostly favorable, mostly unfavorable, or very unfavorable?

Trend in Attitudes

	Total favorable		Total unfavorable	
	1989	1976	1989	1976
United States	95%	93%	3%	2%
Canada	92	91	3	2
Great Britain	86	87	7	6
China	72	20	13	73
Japan	69	74	23	18
Israel	49	65	38	25
Mexico	62	75	27	17
Soviet Union	62	21	29	72
South Africa	33	54	50	35
South Korea	49	*	33	*
Iran	5	48	89	37

*Not asked

Note: The last decade has witnessed a remarkable shift in Americans' perceptions of many foreign nations. In some cases, countries that were considered foes are now seen as friends, while in others ties to our traditional allies have weakened perceptibly.

The most dramatic shift has occurred in Americans' attitudes toward the Soviet Union. In 1976 only 21% expressed positive views about the USSR, while 72% held negative opinions. Today, tensions between the superpowers have eased to the extent that favorable opinions of the Soviet Union outweigh unfavorable ones by a 2-to-1 ratio, 62% to 29%. (The low point in recent relations occurred in September 1983, after the Soviets shot down a South Korean civilian airliner, killing all 269 persons aboard. The U.S. sentiment at the time ran about 10-to-1 negative.)

Public attitudes toward the People's Republic of China have shown an equally radical but more gradual improvement. In the mid-1960s merely 5% of Americans viewed China in a favorable light, but relations began to thaw following President Richard Nixon's 1972 visit. By 1976, 20% held positive opinions but a majority (73%) still thought unfavorably of China. In the latest survey 72% hold positive and 13% negative opinions.

American attitudes toward Israel, on the other hand, have taken a turn for the worse, spurred by that country's harsh treatment of rioters demanding a Palestinian homeland. Favorable opinions of Israel (49%) continue to outweigh unfavorable ones (38%). However, this is the narrowest division of public opinion in a Gallup trend dating back to 1956. In 1976, 65% were positive and 25% negative.

Americans hold similar attitudes about another U.S. ally, South Korea, with 49% expressing favorable and 33% unfavorable opinions in Gallup's first assessment of this country. However, in the present climate of trade-related friction between the United States and Japan, slightly fewer Americans now have positive opinions of Japan than did so in a 1976 survey, 69% and 74%, respectively.

Relations with Mexico, while still predominantly friendly, have deteriorated slightly over the last decade. Currently, Americans holding favorable opinions outnumber those with unfavorable views, 62% to 27%. By comparison, 75% had positive opinions and 17% negative ones in 1976.

Exacerbated by South Africa's refusal to dismantle its apartheid system of racial separation, American sentiment toward that country has worsened considerably. Attitudes were 54%-to-35% positive in a 1976 survey; today they are 50%-to-33% negative.

Attitudes toward Iran, which were moderately (48% to 37%) positive during the reign of the shah, turned sharply negative following seizure of the U.S. embassy and its occupants in Tehran in 1979. The Ayatollah Khomeini's recent order to assassinate British author Salman Rushdie has done nothing to improve relations. Currently, public opinion of Iran is 89%-to-5% negative.

As in the earlier poll, almost as many Americans hold favorable opinions about Canada (92%) and Great Britain (86%) as they do about the United States (95%).

APRIL 9
TELEVISION PROGRAMS

Interviewing Date: 11/14–12/4/88
Special Survey*

On the average, about how many television programs do you watch with your children each week?

*This survey was conducted for CBN Family Channel by the Gallup Organization.

	Average programs per week
National	7.5

By Sex

Male	6.9
Female	7.9

By Education

Attended college	5.5
No college	9.1

By Age

18–29 years	7.6
30 years and over	7.3

By Family Income

$25,000 and over	6.8
Under $25,000	9.5

By Children's Age

Under 6	7.1
6–12	7.9
13–17	8.0

Asked of parents who watch television with their children (83% of parents with children under 18 living at home): About how often would you say you feel uncomfortable about something in a television program that you are watching with your children? Would you say you frequently, occasionally, seldom, or never feel uncomfortable?

Frequently	25%
Occasionally	33
Seldom	25
Never	17

Asked of those who feel uncomfortable: What would you say is most likely to make you feel uncomfortable?

Sex	46%*
Violence	37
Bad language	17
Other	6
Not sure	2

*Multiple responses were given.

Also asked of those who feel uncomfortable: If you feel uncomfortable about something on a television program you are watching with your children, what, if anything, do you usually do about it?

Switch channel, program	46%
Turn television off	24
Explain to children	11
Ban future viewing	5
Express disapproval	4
Other	6
Nothing; not sure	8

*Multiple responses were given.

Also asked of those who feel uncomfortable: Compared to one year ago, how frequently would you say you feel uncomfortable with the television programs you watch with your children?

Much more frequently	17%
Somewhat more frequently	38
About the same	14
Somewhat less frequently	21
Much less frequently	9
Not sure	1

Note: Six in ten parents who watch television with their children at least occasionally feel uncomfortable about the content of the programs. Sex and violence are the principal causes of distress, which parents react to by switching channels or turning off their sets. A recent Gallup study of television viewing also found a majority of parents saying that objectionable programming is more prevalent now than it was one year ago.

The sensitive issue of program content was given new prominence last month when a front-page article in the *New York Times* described a Michigan housewife's campaign to curb sex and violence on television. Her letters of complaint reportedly convinced some major advertisers to remove their commercials from a popular television show because of its sexually oriented content.

Parents watch an average of 7.5 television shows each week with their children under age 18, the survey reveals. The incidence of parent-child viewing is higher among women (7.9 programs) than men (6.9). Heavier viewing also is reported by parents whose formal education ended at the high-school level (9.1), those with annual family incomes of less than $25,000 (9.5), and parents of school-age children (8.0).

About six parents in ten (58%) either frequently (25%) or occasionally (33%) feel uncomfortable about the contents of the programs that they watch with their children. Only one in six (17%) is never troubled, while 25% seldom are. This discomfort over program content tends to be slightly higher among more frequent viewers: women, the less educated and less affluent, and parents of 6 to 17-year-old children.

Those parents who sometimes feel uncomfortable most often object to sexually explicit or suggestive episodes (46%), violence (37%), and bad language (17%). Their most common reactions to objectionable subject matter are switching to a different program or channel (46%), turning off the set (24%), or explaining to their children what should have been said or done (11%). Others refuse to allow their children to watch the program again (5%) and express their disapproval (4%).

More than one half of parents who are uneasy about the television programs that they watch with their children think that these occurrences are either much more (17%) or somewhat more frequent (38%) than one year ago; 14% reply that they are about the same. Only three in ten believe that there now is somewhat less (21%) or much less (9%) objectionable programming.

APRIL 13
DESIGNATED DRIVER

Interviewing Date: 1/16–2/12/89
Special Survey*

Some U.S. communities are promoting a "designated driver" concept as a way to

*This survey was conducted by the Gallup Organization in conjunction with the Center for Health Communications of the Harvard University School of Public Health. It excludes persons who do not attend parties where alcoholic beverages are served (33% nationally).

prevent highway deaths. At places or in situations where alcohol is served, a person is selected, on a voluntary basis, to be the designated driver. This person refrains from drinking any alcoholic beverages and takes responsibility for driving his or her companions home safely. At social occasions like this, do you and your friends select a "designated driver" all of the time, most of the time, not very often, or never?

All of the time	40%
Most of the time	26
Not very often; never	33
Not sure	1

By Sex
Male

All of the time	31%
Most of the time	27
Not very often; never	40
Not sure	2

Female

All of the time	49%
Most of the time	24
Not very often; never	25
Not sure	2

By Education
College Graduate

All of the time	30%
Most of the time	35
Not very often; never	33
Not sure	2

College Incomplete

All of the time	49%
Most of the time	28
Not very often; never	23
Not sure	*

No College

All of the time	40%
Most of the time	21
Not very often; never	37
Not sure	2

By Education

18-34 Years

All of the time 40%
Most of the time................................30
Not very often; never............................20
Not sure 10

35-54 Years

All of the time 37%
Most of the time................................27
Not very often; never............................36
Not sure .... *

55 Years and Over

All of the time 43%
Most of the time................................16
Not very often; never............................35
Not sure 6

Those Who Saw Television Commercials Six or More Times

All of the time 45%
Most of the time................................26
Not very often; never............................28
Not sure 1

Those Who Saw Television Commercials One to Five Times

All of the time 37%
Most of the time................................27
Not very often; never............................34
Not sure 2

Those Who Have Not Seen Television Commercials

All of the time 36%
Most of the time................................23
Not very often; never............................39
Not sure 2

*Less than 1%

During the last three months, on about how many different occasions, if any, did you happen to see television commercials promoting the "designated driver" concept?

One to five times................................36%
Six or more.......................................31

None...22
Not sure 11

Note: A two-thirds majority of adults claims to have adopted the "designated driver" concept when attending social functions at which alcoholic beverages are served. Under this plan, a volunteer refrains from drinking in order to drive his or her companions safely home.

The designated driver concept has been promoted heavily on television as part of the nationwide effort to curb drunken driving. This public service campaign has gained widespread attention. According to a recent Gallup Poll, 67% have seen one or more of the designated driver messages, up from 54% in a survey taken last fall.

Two thirds of partygoers (66%) say that they designate a driver all or most of the time at social events where alcohol is served. An additional 33% either never follow this practice or do not do so very often. The latest findings are similar to those reported last fall, when 62% said safe drivers were chosen at the parties they attended.

Women (73%) are more likely than men (58%) to adopt the concept. Regular observance also is more common among 18 to 34-year-olds (70%)—the age group with the highest incidence of alcohol-related highway fatalities—than either 35 to 54-year-olds (64%) or those age 55 and older (59%).

Two adults in three (67%) say that they have seen television spots promoting the concept within the last three months, with 31% citing exposure on six or more occasions and 36% from one to five times. Indeed, exposure to the designated driver campaign on television is associated with greater observance of the practice. Among people who have never seen these messages, 59% claim to select a safe driver at all or most of the parties they attend. This figure rises to 64% among those who have seen one to five spots and to 71% among those exposed to six or more.

APRIL 16
TRADE AND PROFESSIONAL ASSOCIATIONS/SPECIAL INTEREST GROUPS

Interviewing Date: 2/28-3/2/89
Survey #AI 878

I'd like your overall opinion of some trade and professional associations and special interest groups. Is your overall opinion of (group)* very favorable, mostly favorable, mostly unfavorable, or very unfavorable:

American Cancer Society?

Very favorable.....................................52%
Mostly favorable.................................41
Mostly unfavorable..............................3
Very unfavorable...................................1
No opinion...3

League of Women Voters?

Very favorable.....................................28%
Mostly favorable.................................57
Mostly unfavorable..............................5
Very unfavorable...................................2
No opinion...8

Planned Parenthood Federation?

Very favorable.....................................30%
Mostly favorable.................................52
Mostly unfavorable..............................7
Very unfavorable...................................4
No opinion...7

National Organization for Women (NOW)?

Very favorable.....................................22%
Mostly favorable.................................49
Mostly unfavorable..............................12
Very unfavorable...................................5
No opinion...12

National Rifle Association (NRA)?

Very favorable.....................................19%
Mostly favorable.................................39
Mostly unfavorable..............................20
Very unfavorable...................................13
No opinion...9

National Right to Life Committee?

Very favorable.....................................23%
Mostly favorable.................................33
Mostly unfavorable..............................20

*Excludes those who say that they have never heard of the organization in question.

Very unfavorable...................................13
No opinion...11

Handgun Control Inc.?

Very favorable.....................................19%
Mostly favorable.................................36
Mostly unfavorable..............................18
Very unfavorable...................................12
No opinion...15

American Civil Liberties Union (ACLU)?

Very favorable.....................................16%
Mostly favorable.................................38
Mostly unfavorable..............................18
Very unfavorable...................................11
No opinion...17

Tobacco Institute?

Very favorable.......................................5%
Mostly favorable.................................21
Mostly unfavorable..............................32
Very unfavorable...................................29
No opinion...13

Note: More than nine in ten Americans have generally favorable opinions of the American Cancer Society, giving it higher ratings than eight other trade associations and special interest groups. In a recent Gallup Poll, 93% rate the Cancer Society positively, followed closely by the League of Women Voters (85%) and the Planned Parenthood Federation (82%). The Cancer Society is the only organization tested for which highly favorable ratings (52%) outnumber moderately favorable ones (41%).

The National Organization for Women (NOW) is the next highest-rated lobbying group, with favorable opinions expressed by 71%. Majorities rate four other groups in positive terms: the National Rifle Association (58%), the National Right to Life Committee (56%), Handgun Control Inc. (55%), and the American Civil Liberties Union (54%).

The only organization to be given more unfavorable (61%) than favorable ratings (26%) is the Tobacco Institute, the lobbyist for the American tobacco industry. Majorities in each region and every socioeconomic group have negative perceptions of the Tobacco Institute. Positive attitudes are slightly more prevalent among the least well educated, more of whom are cigarette smokers, and among residents of the South.

APRIL 20
PRESIDENT BUSH

Interviewing Date: 4/10–16/89
Survey #GO 667-Z

Do you approve or disapprove of the way George Bush is handling his job as president?

Approve...58%
Disapprove...16
No opinion..26

By Politics

Republicans

Approve...81%
Disapprove... 6
No opinion..13

Democrats

Approve...42%
Disapprove...25
No opinion..33

Independents

Approve...51%
Disapprove...18
No opinion..31

Selected National Trend

	Approve	Dis-approve	No opinion
March 10–13.........	56%	16%	28%
February 28–March 2...........	63	13	24
January 24–26.......	51	6	43

Presidential Performance Ratings
(In April of Inaugural Year)

		Approve	Dis-approve	No opinion
Bush	1989	58%	16%	26%
Reagan	1981	67	19	14
Carter	1977	63	18	19

Nixon	1969	61	12	27
Kennedy	1961	78	6	16
Eisenhower	1953	74	10	16

Note: After three months in office George Bush has far more boosters (58%) than detractors (16%). However, one American in four (26%) is unwilling or unable to judge the president's job performance, thus fueling criticism that his administration lacks a clear sense of purpose.

Bush's current job approval rating is lower than those given to Presidents John Kennedy (78% in 1961), Dwight Eisenhower (74% in 1953), Ronald Reagan (67% in 1981), and Jimmy Carter (63% in 1977). It is statistically equivalent to the 61% who approved of President Richard Nixon at the same point in his tenure, in 1969. Nixon, like Bush, had a high (27%) undecided vote. (Presidents Gerald Ford, Lyndon Johnson, and Harry Truman were excluded from this analysis because they took office under unusual circumstances.)

Bush may have developed a "gender gap" similar to President Reagan's. In each of four Gallup surveys this year, Bush's approval rating among women has trailed his standing with men by an average of 8 percentage points. Women are no more likely than men to disapprove of Bush's performance in office, but more of the former than the latter are undecided. During the same period in 1981, 64% of men and 57% of women approved of Reagan's job performance.

APRIL 23
GOVERNMENT SPENDING

Interviewing Date: 1/27–2/5/89
Special Survey*

This card lists seven major areas of government spending. Do you happen to know which two areas account for the largest share of federal spending?

National defense and
Social Security (correct)...................20%

*This survey was conducted for *Times Mirror* by the Gallup Organization.

If you had a say in making up the federal budget this year, for which of the following programs should spending be increased, for which should spending be decreased, and for which should spending be kept the same:

Combating drug problem?

Increased...65%
Same...28
Decreased 4
No opinion...3

Research on AIDS?

Increased...52%
Same...38
Decreased 6
No opinion...4

Programs for the elderly?

Increased...50%
Same...45
Decreased 3
No opinion...2

Social Security?

Increased...46%
Same...47
Decreased 3
No opinion...4

Environmental protection?

Increased...39%
Same...49
Decreased 7
No opinion...5

Scientific research?

Increased...32%
Same...55
Decreased 9
No opinion...4

Military arms, defense?

Increased...11%
Same...49
Decreased 37
No opinion...3

I am going to read you a number of ways in which government revenues could be increased or government expenditures could be cut in order to reduce the federal budget deficit. For each one, tell me if you would strongly favor it, favor it, accept it only as a last resort, or strongly oppose it:

Increase taxes on alcoholic beverages?

Strongly favor.....................................47%
Favor 36
Accept as last resort 9
Strongly oppose 6
No opinion...2

Limit defense spending?

Strongly favor.....................................35%
Favor 39
Accept as last resort 16
Strongly oppose 6
No opinion...4

National lottery?

Strongly favor.....................................34%
Favor 30
Accept as last resort 13
Strongly oppose 17
No opinion...6

National sales tax?

Strongly favor..................................... 8%
Favor 23
Accept as last resort 29
Strongly oppose 34
No opinion...6

Reduce Social Security COLAs?

Strongly favor..................................... 5%
Favor 16
Accept as last resort 30
Strongly oppose 45
No opinion...4

Lower Medicare payments?

Strongly favor..................................... 3%
Favor 10
Accept as last resort 27

Strongly oppose 56
No opinion 4

Tax Social Security benefits as ordinary income?

Strongly favor 2%
Favor 8
Accept as last resort 29
Strongly oppose 56
No opinion 5

As you may know, the federal government has a surplus in the amount of money collected for Social Security. Some people feel that the surplus money should be put aside and reserved exclusively for Social Security payments in the future. Others favor borrowing the surplus money to meet current expenses and help reduce the federal budget deficit. Which view comes closer to your own?

Reserve for future benefits 87%
Use for current expenses 6
No opinion 7

Note: Any attempt to impose increased taxes or a means test on affluent Social Security recipients or to limit Medicare benefits would run into a solid wall of public opposition, although even modest cuts in these programs—the largest in the domestic budget—would make a big dent in the federal deficit. A new Gallup survey for *Times Mirror* finds as much support for an increase in the budget for Social Security (46%) as for maintaining the current spending level (47%) and very little backing (3%) for a decrease. Government programs for the elderly are similarly endorsed: 50% favor an increase, while 45% would keep the status quo and 3% favor cuts. As the population ages and the baby boom generation considers the well-being of its parents, support for the elderly is resolute.

Proposals to trim Social Security and Medicare benefits elicit greater public opposition than other deficit reduction measures studied. Fifty-six percent would strongly oppose raising taxes on Social Security payments to the same rate as taxes on ordinary income; the same percentage expresses strong opposition to limiting further the amount Medicare pays for elderly people's annual health care bills. Almost as many (45%) are adamantly opposed to reducing cost-of-

living increases (COLAs) for people on Social Security. About three in ten would accept cuts in each of these programs, but only as a last resort.

Moreover, only 10% would favor taxing 85% of the Social Security benefits for people with incomes over $18,000, even when informed that this might reduce the federal budget deficit by $40 billion over a five-year period. By comparison, large majorities favor raising such "sin taxes" as those on alcoholic beverages (83%). But even such a broad-based deficit-reduction levy as a 5% national sales tax, backed by 31%, is more palatable than taxing Social Security benefits.

To some extent, public support may be colored by misconceptions about the elderly and the programs that help them. Contrary to fact, the elderly are seen as less affluent than the population at large. However, even people who do not see the elderly as disadvantaged are averse to taxing Social Security benefits.

Awareness of the scope of the government's commitment to Social Security is low. Asked which two of seven major programs account for the largest share of federal spending, only 20% correctly name both national defense and Social Security. In fact, more respondents name international affairs and foreign aid than Social Security.

Borrowing surplus funds from the Social Security trust to help meet current government needs and reduce the budget deficit is roundly opposed. By an 87%-to-6% margin, the public believes that these monies should be set aside and reserved exclusively to provide future Social Security benefits.

APRIL 27
INTERNATIONAL RELATIONS

Interviewing Date: 1/27–2/5/89
Special Survey*

Today, which one of the following countries do you think is the world's leading economic power? In the year 2000, which one do you expect to be the world's leading economic power?

*This survey was conducted for *Times Mirror* by the Gallup Organization.

	Today	In year 2000
Japan	58%	45%
United States	29	33
Common Market countries	4	9
Soviet Union	2	1
No opinion	7	12

For the following countries, please tell me if you believe each country has a fair trade policy or an unfair trade policy with the United States:

Canada?

Fair...72%
Unfair.. 7
No opinion..21

Common Market?

Fair..44%
Unfair...26
No opinion..21

South Korea?

Fair..25%
Unfair...39
No opinion..36

Japan?

Fair..22%
Unfair...63
No opinion..15

How do you feel about tariffs on products from (country) that are sold in the United States? In your opinion, is it in the best interests of the United States to increase tariffs on goods from (country), to keep tariffs about the same, reduce tariffs somewhat, or eliminate tariffs altogether?

Canada?

Increase tariffs...................................... 8%
Keep the same....................................49
Reduce, eliminate tariffs.......................28
No opinion..15

Common Market?

Increase tariffs.....................................23%
Keep the same....................................43

Reduce, eliminate tariffs.......................15
No opinion..19

South Korea?

Increase tariffs.....................................36%
Keep the same....................................30
Reduce, eliminate tariffs.......................13
No opinion..21

Japan?

Increase tariffs.....................................53%
Keep the same....................................21
Reduce, eliminate tariffs.......................14
No opinion..12

Do you think Japan is contributing enough to the defense of the Pacific region, or not? Do you think the countries of Western Europe are contributing enough to their own defense, or not?

	Japan	Western Europe
Contributing enough	13%	23%
Not contributing enough	58	58
No opinion	29	19

Some people feel that since Japan has prospered economically in recent years, it should take on more responsibility for its own defense. Others oppose a greater role for Japan in its own defense because they feel it might become an aggressor nation again. Which view comes closer to your own?

Favor greater role 65%
Oppose greater role.............................24
No opinion 11

Would you favor or oppose the United States asking Western European countries and Japan to take more responsibility for military defense?

Favor 73%
Oppose...15
No opinion..12

Asked of those who favor Western European countries and Japan assuming greater military responsibility (73% of the sample): Would you favor or oppose the

United States asking Western European countries and Japan to take more responsibility for military defense, even if it meant that the United States would no longer continue to be the dominant military power among allied nations?

Favor 42%
Oppose 24
No opinion 7
                                                73%

Note: The present climate of economic austerity and perceptions that the United States has lost its status as the world's leading economic power have led to renewed public demands for trade protectionism and for our allies to assume greater responsibility for their own military defense. Americans now regard Japan (58%), not the United States (29%), as the leading economic power. Although some think that our country will regain its competitive edge by the turn of the century, more expect Japan (45%) than the United States (33%) to be the economic leader.

In a new *Times Mirror* survey, criticism for unfair trade practices falls heaviest on Japan, with 63% saying that its trade policy with the United States is unfair and 22% fair. More criticize (39%) than praise South Korea (25%), but large numbers are undecided (36%). The weight of opinion is that the European Common Market countries' trade policies are more fair (44%) than unfair (26%). Canada is almost immune to criticism, with 72% saying that its policies are fair and 7% unfair.

As expected, public demand for increased tariffs on imports from each country is closely related to perceptions of the fairness of that country's trade practices: 53% call for higher tariffs on Japanese products sold in the United States, 36% on South Korean goods, 23% on Common Market imports, and 8% on Canadian commerce.

As for national security, Americans think that Japan (58%) and the nations of Western Europe (also 58%) are not contributing enough to their own military defense. As a consequence, 73% believe that the United States should ask these countries to take on more of this responsibility.

Even when addressed in the context of its recent prosperity and the possibility that an increased defense capability might lead to a resurgence of Japanese militarism, 65% reply that Japan should contribute more to its defense while 24% think that it should not. However, majority support for asking Western Europe and Japan to assume a larger role in their own defense slips to 42% if doing so "meant that the United States would no longer continue to be the dominant military power among allied nations."

APRIL 30
KNOWLEDGE OF ECONOMIC AFFAIRS—A GALLUP SURVEY

Interviewing Date: 1/27–2/5/89
Special Survey*

A new survey reveals a wide disparity in Americans' knowledge of economic affairs. Most respondents have at least a superficial understanding of topics that have received heavy coverage in the news, such as the federal budget deficit, the savings and loan crisis, the trade deficit, and foreign investment in the United States, but many are uninformed or misinformed about issues that have an important bearing on the nation's economic policies.

More than eight Americans in ten are aware that the United States is running a trade deficit with Japan (83%), but far fewer know that our imports from South Korea (53%), Western Europe (38%), and Canada (16%) exceed our exports to these nations. Not coincidentally, 53% call for higher tariffs on Japanese products sold in the United States, 36% on Korean imports, 23% on Common Market goods, and 8% on Canadian products.

Defense spending is correctly cited by 81% as one of the top two items in the federal budget, but only 27% know that Social Security is one of the two largest budget components. In fact, more respondents name international affairs and foreign aid (50%) than Social Security as accounting for a large share of government spending.

About three fourths (78%) are aware that foreign investment in American companies and

*This survey was conducted for *Times Mirror* by the Gallup Organization.

real estate has increased over the last ten years, but public estimates of the amount of this investment are greatly overstated. Only 4% realize that foreign investors own less than 5% of privately held U.S. land, while 29% cite proportions ranging from 5% to 14%, 44% say 15% or more, and 23% are unable to name any percentage.

Three in four (74%) know that the federal budget deficit is larger now than it was ten years ago, but only 18% are aware that the size of the annual deficit is between $100 and $200 billion. Another 18% think that the government is running from $200 to $300 billion in the red each year, while 28% believe that the deficit is more than $300 billion.

Asked to name which of four types of financial institutions has been in the news recently because of bankruptcy proceedings, 73% correctly cite savings and loan associations.

About one half (53%) are aware that the tax on gasoline in the United States is lower than in Western Europe, but substantially fewer respondents (37%) know that Americans pay a smaller percentage of income tax than Europeans do. A similar proportion (38%) believes Americans pay higher taxes, while 25% think that there is not much difference or do not offer an opinion.

Misconceptions about the current status of the Social Security budget also are widespread. Nearly one half (45%) are aware that the amount collected is greater than the amount distributed as benefits, but nearly as many think that receipts are less than disbursements (28%) or that income and outgo are in balance (16%).

The index of knowledge about economic affairs was created by scoring survey participants on the number of questions that they answered correctly. People who gave nine to fourteen correct responses (24% of the total sample) were considered well informed and rated "high" on the scale. Those giving the right responses to six to eight questions (47% of the total) were rated as moderately well informed or "medium." And those responding correctly to less than six questions (29% of the total) were rated "low" on the scale or poorly informed.

Knowledge of economic affairs, or "economic IQ," varies widely by sex, race, age, income, and, especially, education. More than twice the proportion of men (35%) as women (15%) fall into the high IQ group, and far more

whites (27%) than nonwhites (8%) qualify. Knowledge rises steadily by age, with 13% of people under 30, 26% of 30 to 49-year-olds, and 30% of those 50 and older considered well informed.

Almost one half of college graduates (47%) have a high economic IQ, compared to 24% of those with some college exposure, 20% of high-school graduates, and 14% of those who did not finish high school. Knowledge, however, also declines with income, from 36% in the highest income group to 17% in the lowest.

Slightly more Republicans (30%) than Democrats (21%) are well informed about economic affairs, while independents' IQ (24%) mirrors the public at large. Regional differences are inconclusive.

MAY 1
MARRIAGE AND DIVORCE

Interviewing Date: 12/27–29/88
Survey #GO 89024

An Overview of Marital Discord
(Percentage of Ever-Marrieds Who Have Been Divorced, Separated, or Who Have Considered Divorce)

National..51%

By Sex

Male 49%
Female...53

By Education

College graduate.................................50%
College incomplete...............................57
High-school graduate............................53
Less than high-school graduate 56

By Age

18–34 years.......................................52%
35–54 years.......................................64
55 years and over...............................38

By Household Income

$40,000 and over 52%
$25,000–$39,999.................................55
Under $25,000....................................51

The following questions were asked of those in the sample who are married or widowed:

For how many years have you been (were you) married?

Under 5 years......................................15%
5–9..15
10–14..11
15–19..11
20–24..7
25–29..6
30 or more..35

Did you and your husband/wife live together before you got married?

Yes...19%
No...81

How long did you date your husband/wife before you got married?

Less than 6 months.............................10%
6 months to 1 year.............................14
1 year..22
2 years...21
3–5 years..24
More than 5 years................................7
Don't know...2

Have you and your husband/wife ever talked to a marriage counselor or therapist together?

Yes...9%
No...90
Refused to answer 1

The following questions were asked of those in the sample who at one time or another have been divorced:

Whose idea was it first to get divorced? Was it something that you mainly wanted or was it something that he/she mainly wanted?

Respondent wanted 44%
Spouse wanted 32
Both wanted equally (volunteered)............21
Don't know..3

How suddenly did the marital problems appear that led to your separation? Did you know about these problems when you got married, did you learn about them early in your marriage, after you'd been married for a

while, or did you learn about them just before your separation?

When married 7%
Learned about them early 31
After married for a while 36
Just before separation............................22
Refused to answer 4

As a way of dealing with your marital situation, which of the following, if any, did you or your husband/wife do?*

Sought advice of friends, relatives............27%
Talked to marriage counselor together.......22
Sought individual counseling...................17
Sought advice of minister/priest/rabbi 23
Joined marital support group 5
None of the above (volunteered) 46
Don't know...2

*Multiple responses were given.

Looking back, do you think you and your husband/wife might have solved your problems in your marriage if you did things a little differently, or do you think the problems were too difficult to solve?

Might have solved problems 24%
Too difficult to solve.............................70
Don't know..6

Looking back, do you think you made the right decision by separating, or would things be better for you if your marriage had stayed together?

Right decision.......................................82%
Should have stayed together 12
Don't know...6

What would you say was the principal reason you got a divorce?

Drug or alcohol problems 16%
Marital infidelity..................................17
Physical abuse..5
Disputes about money, family
  or children...10
Basic personality differences or
  incompatibility....................................47
Don't know...5

Note: If you have ever been married the odds are now 50:50 that you have either been divorced, separated, or seriously close to separation. If you are between the ages of 35 and 54, those odds increase to 2 out of 3 because you are part of a generation that ushered in the largest increase in divorce ever recorded. These are among the most disturbing findings of an in-depth Gallup study of marriage and divorce in America.

Gallup studied the experiences and beliefs of a nationally representative sample of 1,200 adults who have been married at some point in their lives. Key findings may be summarized as follows:

• While women and men are equally likely to experience separation and divorce, women are more apt to be unhappy in their marriages and are much more likely to initiate the process of separation that leads to divorce.
• Religion enhances marital stability for adults at all ages. Individuals who claim that religion plays a very important role in their lives are much less likely to have experienced severe marital discord. This is true regardless of the specific religious denomination with which people identify.
• Personality differences and incompatibility are the leading causes of divorce. Specific problems such as drug or alcohol abuse, infidelity, physical mistreatment, or financial disputes are far less often cited as causes.
• Doomed marriages typically reveal themselves within the first few years of marriage, but premarital educational courses do not seem particularly effective in forestalling divorce.
• Trial marriages do not appear to affect rates of marital harmony, but couples who had a long dating period are more likely to have stable marriages now.
• Despite the obvious emotional strain involved in going through a divorce, the overwhelming majority of divorced people believe that they made the right choice and reject the idea that their lives would have been better if they had stayed married. Similarly, spouses who weathered a period of severe discord in their marriages and stayed together also affirm their decision.

According to the U.S. Census Bureau, marriage and divorce rates remained relatively stable in the decades immediately after World War II, but between 1965 and 1975 the annual divorce rate nearly doubled. In fact, the rate of divorce grew faster in that ten-year period than it had in the entire previous forty-five-year history of these measurements. These high rates may be attributed in part to women's newly found independence and to changing social norms.

Today, 58% of American adults are married. One in ten is divorced, 2% are separated, 11% are widowed, and 19% have never married. Of all people who have ever been married, almost three fourths are currently married, 14% are widowed, and 15% are now divorced or separated. Among those currently married, 17% have been married before and 83% are in their first marriages. And among widows and widowers, only 7% were married more than once, while 93% had only one marriage.

About one quarter of adult Americans (23%) has been divorced at least once. Of this group, 54% have remarried and 46% have not. Among those who have been divorced, 78% have been divorced once, 16% twice, and 6% more than twice.

Marriages have been particularly fragile for those persons age 35 to 54. Among this group, the incidence of marital instability is two thirds higher than it is for those age 55 and older. Sixty-four percent of middle-aged people who have ever been married have experienced severe marital discord, compared to only 38% of older people. One ever-married person out of five in the middle years (19%) is now divorced or separated.

Among younger ever-marrieds, 18 to 34-years-olds, somewhat fewer (52%) have ever experienced severe marital discord, and 16% are currently divorced or separated. However, most people in this age group have been married for only a short while. If the pattern of marital discord for young marrieds mirrors that of the preceding generation, as appears likely, our nation will soon reach the point where the dominant experience of adults will have been marital instability.

When religion plays an important role in an individual's life, that person is much less likely than others to have experienced severe marital discord (45% versus 58%). Even taking into account the fact that the most religious are older people whose marriages are more stable in any event, religion has a strong influence on stability. For example, 58% of young people who are not very religious have experienced severe discord compared to only 45% among religious young people.

Although men and women are equally likely to have been divorced or separated, women express greater discontent with their marriages and are much more liable than men to be the initiators of marital breakups. Of the divorced women interviewed, 55% say that it was their idea to separate. Only 44% of divorced men claim responsibility for starting the divorce process.

Basic personality differences, or incompatibility, cited by 47% as the underlying factor in their own divorce, are by far the leading cause of marital breakups. Other reasons include infidelity (17%); drug or alcohol problems (16%); disputes about money, family, or children (10%); and physical abuse (5%).

These problems become apparent early in the relationship. More than one third (38%) who have divorced report that they were aware of the problem at the time of their marriage or soon thereafter. Just over one third (36%) learned about them after they had been married for a while. Only 22% say that the problems became apparent just before their separation.

Interestingly, the modern approaches that have been championed as ways of lowering the divorce rate and increasing marital happiness do not seem to work. Trial marriages and marriage preparation courses, which are most prevalent among younger people, do not appear to affect rates of marital success. When people who have experienced trial marriages or taken such courses are contrasted to those of a comparable age group who have not, no meaningful difference in marital contentment is found. On the other hand, the more traditional longer dating period seems to be more effective. Couples who dated for one year or longer are more likely to be very satisfied with their marriages than those who took the step sooner.

When dissatisfaction becomes over-whelming, about one half of those divorced (52%) took one or more steps to deal with their troubled marriage. Chief among these were seeking the advice of friends and relatives (27%), consulting their religious adviser (23%), and visiting a counselor or therapist with their spouse (22%). Others went through

individual therapy or counseling sessions (17%), and a few (5%) joined marital support groups.

In retrospect, only a small minority of divorced people (24%) think that their marital problems might have been resolved if they had "done things a little differently." Almost three times as many (70%) say that the problems were too difficult to overcome. Those who have not remarried, however, are more likely to have had second thoughts: more than one third in this group think that their marriages could have been saved. Nonetheless, the overwhelming majority of all people who have been divorced (82%) believe that divorce was the right decision for them and reject the idea that their lives would have been better if their marriage had stayed intact.

MAY 10
PRESIDENT BUSH/CURRENT EVENTS IN WASHINGTON

Interviewing Date: 5/4–7/89
Survey #GO 89134

Do you approve or disapprove of the way George Bush is handling his job as president?

Approve...56%
Disapprove......................................22
No opinion......................................22

By Politics
Republicans

Approve...79%
Disapprove...................................... 8
No opinion......................................13

Democrats

Approve...41%
Disapprove......................................33
No opinion......................................26

Independents

Approve...48%
Disapprove......................................25
No opinion......................................27

Selected National Trend

	Approve	Dis-approve	No opinion
April 10–16	58%	16%	26%
March 10–13	56	16	28
February 28–March 2	63	13	24
January 24–26	51	6	43

Is your opinion of George Bush very favorable, mostly favorable, mostly unfavorable, or very unfavorable?

Very favorable	15%
Mostly favorable	55
Mostly unfavorable	17
Very unfavorable	7
No opinion	6

By Politics

Republicans

Very favorable	29%
Mostly favorable	62
Mostly unfavorable	5
Very unfavorable	1
No opinion	3

Democrats

Very favorable	7%
Mostly favorable	47
Mostly unfavorable	29
Very unfavorable	10
No opinion	7

Independents

Very favorable	9%
Mostly favorable	56
Mostly unfavorable	18
Very unfavorable	9
No opinion	18

Selected National Trend

	Very, mostly favorable	Mostly, very unfavorable	No opinion
January 1989	78%	13%	9%
January 1988	52	39	9
September 1987	69	27	4
May 1987	67	26	7

Is your opinion of the Supreme Court very favorable, mostly favorable, mostly unfavorable, or very unfavorable?

Very favorable	11%
Mostly favorable	50
Mostly unfavorable	16
Very unfavorable	5
No opinion	18

By Sex

Male

Very favorable	12%
Mostly favorable	53
Mostly unfavorable	14
Very unfavorable	6
No opinion	15

Female

Very favorable	10%
Mostly favorable	47
Mostly unfavorable	17
Very unfavorable	4
No opinion	22

By Ethnic Background

White

Very favorable	9%
Mostly favorable	52
Mostly unfavorable	15
Very unfavorable	5
No opinion	19

Nonwhite

Very favorable	21%
Mostly favorable	35
Mostly unfavorable	20
Very unfavorable	5
No opinion	19

By Education

College Graduate

Very favorable	7%
Mostly favorable	61
Mostly unfavorable	17
Very unfavorable	4
No opinion	11

College Incomplete

Very favorable..................................16%
Mostly favorable...............................54
Mostly unfavorable..........................14
Very unfavorable...............................3
No opinion...13

High-School Graduate

Very favorable.................................. 9%
Mostly favorable...............................51
Mostly unfavorable..........................16
Very unfavorable...............................5
No opinion...19

Less Than High-School Graduate

Very favorable..................................14%
Mostly favorable...............................30
Mostly unfavorable..........................16
Very unfavorable...............................7
No opinion...33

By Region

East

Very favorable..................................11%
Mostly favorable...............................46
Mostly unfavorable..........................17
Very unfavorable...............................6
No opinion...20

Midwest

Very favorable..................................10%
Mostly favorable...............................55
Mostly unfavorable..........................12
Very unfavorable...............................4
No opinion...19

South

Very favorable..................................11%
Mostly favorable...............................48
Mostly unfavorable..........................19
Very unfavorable...............................5
No opinion...17

West

Very favorable..................................11%
Mostly favorable...............................51
Mostly unfavorable..........................14
Very unfavorable...............................4
No opinion...20

By Age

18–29 Years

Very favorable..................................14%
Mostly favorable...............................56
Mostly unfavorable..........................13
Very unfavorable...............................2
No opinion...15

30–49 Years

Very favorable..................................10%
Mostly favorable...............................56
Mostly unfavorable..........................16
Very unfavorable...............................4
No opinion...14

50 Years and Over

Very favorable..................................10%
Mostly favorable...............................39
Mostly unfavorable..........................18
Very unfavorable...............................7
No opinion...26

By Family Income

$50,000 and Over

Very favorable.................................. 7%
Mostly favorable...............................58
Mostly unfavorable..........................15
Very unfavorable...............................3
No opinion...17

$30,000–$49,999

Very favorable..................................12%
Mostly favorable...............................56
Mostly unfavorable..........................18
Very unfavorable...............................4
No opinion...10

$15,000–$29,999

Very favorable..................................11%
Mostly favorable...............................51
Mostly unfavorable..........................15
Very unfavorable...............................4
No opinion...19

Under $15,000

Very favorable..................................13%
Mostly favorable...............................36
Mostly unfavorable..........................17

Very unfavorable................................8
No opinion......................................26

By Politics

Republicans

Very favorable................................10%
Mostly favorable.............................57
Mostly unfavorable..........................14
Very unfavorable..............................3
No opinion......................................16

Democrats

Very favorable................................12%
Mostly favorable.............................45
Mostly unfavorable..........................18
Very unfavorable..............................6
No opinion......................................19

Independents

Very favorable................................11%
Mostly favorable.............................48
Mostly unfavorable..........................15
Very unfavorable..............................5
No opinion......................................21

Selected National Trend

	Very, mostly favorable	Mostly, very unfavorable	No opinion
January 1988	79%	13%	8%
May 1987	76	17	7

Is your opinion of the Democratic congressional leaders very favorable, mostly favorable, mostly unfavorable, or very unfavorable?

Very favorable................................8%
Mostly favorable.............................39
Mostly unfavorable..........................24
Very unfavorable..............................9
No opinion......................................20

By Politics

Republicans

Very favorable................................4%
Mostly favorable.............................30
Mostly unfavorable..........................36

Very unfavorable..............................13
No opinion......................................17

Democrats

Very favorable................................16%
Mostly favorable.............................54
Mostly unfavorable..........................11
Very unfavorable..............................4
No opinion......................................15

Independents

Very favorable................................5%
Mostly favorable.............................35
Mostly unfavorable..........................25
Very unfavorable..............................9
No opinion......................................26

Is your opinion of the Republican congressional leaders very favorable, mostly favorable, mostly unfavorable, or very unfavorable?

Very favorable................................9%
Mostly favorable.............................45
Mostly unfavorable..........................21
Very unfavorable..............................7
No opinion......................................8

By Politics

Republicans

Very favorable................................16%
Mostly favorable.............................61
Mostly unfavorable..........................11
Very unfavorable..............................1
No opinion......................................11

Democrats

Very favorable................................6%
Mostly favorable.............................35
Mostly unfavorable..........................30
Very unfavorable..............................13
No opinion......................................16

Independents

Very favorable................................4%
Mostly favorable.............................39
Mostly unfavorable..........................23
Very unfavorable..............................8
No opinion......................................26

Is your opinion of Jim Wright very favorable, mostly favorable, mostly unfavorable, or very unfavorable?

Very favorable.....................................3%
Mostly favorable.................................16
Mostly unfavorable.............................27
Very unfavorable.................................14
Never heard of him............................. 9
No opinion...31

By Politics

Republicans

Very favorable..................................... 2%
Mostly favorable.................................15
Mostly unfavorable.............................26
Very unfavorable.................................16
Never heard of him.............................10
No opinion...31

Democrats

Very favorable..................................... 4%
Mostly favorable.................................16
Mostly unfavorable.............................32
Very unfavorable.................................11
Never heard of him............................. 9
No opinion...28

Independents

Very favorable..................................... 2%
Mostly favorable.................................15
Mostly unfavorable.............................22
Very unfavorable.................................14
Never heard of him.............................10
No opinion...37

Based on what you may have seen, heard, or read about the Ethics Committee's investigation of House Speaker Jim Wright, do you think the charges that Wright violated House rules are serious enough to justify his being replaced as speaker, or not?

Serious enough 44%
Not serious enough 25
No opinion; never heard of him..............31

By Sex

Male

Serious enough 47%
Not serious enough 29
No opinion; never heard of him..............24

Female

Serious enough 41%
Not serious enough 22
No opinion; never heard of him..............37

By Ethnic Background

White

Serious enough 45%
Not serious enough 25
No opinion; never heard of him..............30

Nonwhite

Serious enough 39%
Not serious enough 26
No opinion; never heard of him..............35

By Education

College Graduate

Serious enough 54%
Not serious enough`.............................29
No opinion; never heard of him..............17

College Incomplete

Serious enough 48%
Not serious enough 24
No opinion; never heard of him..............28

High-School Graduate

Serious enough 40%
Not serious enough 26
No opinion; never heard of him..............34

Less Than High-School Graduate

Serious enough 37%
Not serious enough 20
No opinion; never heard of him..............43

By Region

East

Serious enough 41%
Not serious enough 27
No opinion; never heard of him..............32

Midwest

Serious enough....................................38%
Not serious enough 27
No opinion; never heard of him..............35

South

Serious enough...................................47%
Not serious enough 23
No opinion; never heard of him..............30

West

Serious enough...................................49%
Not serious enough 23
No opinion; never heard of him..............28

By Age

18-29 Years

Serious enough...................................34%
Not serious enough 26
No opinion; never heard of him..............40

30-49 Years

Serious enough...................................46%
Not serious enough 27
No opinion; never heard of him..............27

50 Years and Over

Serious enough...................................48%
Not serious enough 22
No opinion; never heard of him..............30

By Family Income

$50,000 and Over

Serious enough....................................53%
Not serious enough 25
No opinion; never heard of him..............22

$30,000-$49,999

Serious enough....................................50%
Not serious enough 25
No opinion; never heard of him..............25

$15,000-$29,999

Serious enough................................34%
Not serious enough 26
No opinion; never heard of him..............40

Under $15,000

Serious enough...................................45%
Not serious enough 24
No opinion; never heard of him..............31

By Politics

Republicans

Serious enough....................................50%
Not serious enough 21
No opinion; never heard of him..............29

Democrats

Serious enough...................................39%
Not serious enough 30
No opinion; never heard of him..............31

Independents

Serious enough...................................43%
Not serious enough 24
No opinion; never heard of him..............33

Is your opinion of Oliver North very favorable, mostly favorable, mostly unfavorable, or very unfavorable?

Very favorable.....................................22%
Mostly favorable..................................37
Mostly unfavorable..............................18
Very unfavorable.................................10
No opinion...13

By Sex

Male

Very favorable....................................24%
Mostly favorable..................................38
Mostly unfavorable..............................17
Very unfavorable.................................11
No opinion...10

Female

Very favorable....................................20%
Mostly favorable..................................36

Mostly unfavorable...............................19
Very unfavorable..............................9
No opinion...16

By Ethnic Background

White

Very favorable....................................23%
Mostly favorable.............................39
Mostly unfavorable..........................17
Very unfavorable.............................9
No opinion...12

Nonwhite

Very favorable....................................16%
Mostly favorable.............................25
Mostly unfavorable..........................24
Very unfavorable.............................17
No opinion...18

By Education

College Graduate

Very favorable....................................17%
Mostly favorable.............................35
Mostly unfavorable..........................28
Very unfavorable.............................13
No opinion...7

College Incomplete

Very favorable....................................23%
Mostly favorable.............................37
Mostly unfavorable..........................22
Very unfavorable.............................11
No opinion...7

High-School Graduate

Very favorable....................................23%
Mostly favorable.............................39
Mostly unfavorable..........................14
Very unfavorable.............................10
No opinion...14

Less Than High-School Graduate

Very favorable....................................27%
Mostly favorable.............................35
Mostly unfavorable..........................11
Very unfavorable.............................7
No opinion...20

By Region

East

Very favorable....................................23%
Mostly favorable.............................35
Mostly unfavorable..........................17
Very unfavorable.............................11
No opinion...14

Midwest

Very favorable....................................21%
Mostly favorable.............................38
Mostly unfavorable..........................17
Very unfavorable.............................12
No opinion...12

South

Very favorable....................................24%
Mostly favorable.............................38
Mostly unfavorable..........................17
Very unfavorable.............................7
No opinion...14

West

Very favorable....................................19%
Mostly favorable.............................37
Mostly unfavorable..........................21
Very unfavorable.............................12
No opinion...11

By Age

18–29 Years

Very favorable....................................22%
Mostly favorable.............................34
Mostly unfavorable..........................20
Very unfavorable.............................13
No opinion...11

30–49 Years

Very favorable....................................20%
Mostly favorable.............................40
Mostly unfavorable..........................20
Very unfavorable.............................8
No opinion...12

50 Years and Over

Very favorable....................................25%
Mostly favorable.............................35
Mostly unfavorable..........................15
Very unfavorable.............................11
No opinion...14

By Family Income

$50,000 and Over

Very favorable.....................................21%
Mostly favorable...............................39
Mostly unfavorable...........................22
Very unfavorable................................10
No opinion...8

$30,000-$49,999

Very favorable.....................................20%
Mostly favorable...............................42
Mostly unfavorable...........................20
Very unfavorable................................10
No opinion...8

$15,000-$29,999

Very favorable.....................................21%
Mostly favorable...............................38
Mostly unfavorable...........................15
Very unfavorable................................11
No opinion...15

Under $15,000

Very favorable.....................................23%
Mostly favorable...............................30
Mostly unfavorable...........................18
Very unfavorable................................11
No opinion...18

By Politics

Republicans

Very favorable.....................................25%
Mostly favorable...............................44
Mostly unfavorable...........................13
Very unfavorable................................4
No opinion...14

Democrats

Very favorable.....................................20%
Mostly favorable...............................30
Mostly unfavorable...........................23
Very unfavorable................................17
No opinion...10

Independents

Very favorable.....................................21%
Mostly favorable...............................35
Mostly unfavorable...........................18

Very unfavorable..............................11
No opinion..15

Selected National Trend

	Very, mostly favorable	Mostly, very unfavorable	No opinion
1987			
September	57%	34%	9%
January	39	35	26

As you may know, the jury in the Oliver North trial has found North guilty on some of the charges against him. Based on what you have seen, heard, or read, do you think the jury made the right decision, or not? If not: Do you think North should have been found guilty on more of the charges, or do you think he should have been found not guilty on all of the charges?

Jury made right decision.......................51%
Guilty on more charges 8
Not guilty...28
No opinion...13

By Politics

Republicans

Jury made right decision.......................53%
Guilty on more charges 5
Not guilty...29
No opinion...13

Democrats

Jury made right decision.......................50%
Guilty on more charges 9
Not guilty...29
No opinion...12

Independents

Jury made right decision.......................50%
Guilty on more charges 10
Not guilty...25
No opinion...15

In your opinion, which one of the following phrases best applies to Oliver North and his role in the Iran-contra affair: a hero and a patriot, well-meaning but misguided, or a liar and a criminal?

Hero and patriot 14%
Well-meaning but misguided...................69
Liar and criminal 11
No opinion..6

By Politics

Republicans

Hero and patriot 18%
Well-meaning but misguided...................72
Liar and criminal 5
No opinion..5

Democrats

Hero and patriot 9%
Well-meaning but misguided...................67
Liar and criminal 18
No opinion..6

Independents

Hero and patriot 13%
Well-meaning but misguided...................68
Liar and criminal 11
No opinion..8

Now that the jury has found North guilty on some charges, do you think he should be punished, or do you think he should be pardoned?

Punished 35%
Pardoned 57
No opinion..8

By Politics

Republicans

Punished 25%
Pardoned 66
No opinion..9

Democrats

Punished 39%
Pardoned 54
No opinion..7

Independents

Punished 40%
Pardoned 52
No opinion..8

Note: In increasing numbers, Americans are being turned off by events in Washington. A new Gallup Poll finds that fewer Americans hold favorable opinions of the president, the vice president, Congress, and even the Supreme Court than did so in the recent past. The only public figure whose popularity seems virtually unaffected by this upsurge in anti-Washington sentiment is Oliver North, who may be leaving town for a jail term.

There are signs that George Bush's "honeymoon" period may be ending, at least in terms of public opinion. The president's approval ratings have begun to slip as criticism has risen regarding his ability to communicate his policies and plans for the future.

House Speaker Jim Wright's troubles, stemming from allegations that he violated rules of congressional conduct, appear to have taken a toll on the image of Congress as well. The public regards Congress less favorably today than it has at any point since 1985.

George Bush

A majority of Americans (56%) continues to approve of the way President Bush is handling his job, but he is attracting more criticism than he did a few months ago. Twenty-two percent now disapprove of Bush's job performance, up significantly from the 16% recorded in March and April Gallup surveys. Further suggesting that we are moving beyond the early, uncritical phase in public opinion toward the new president, one in four Americans (24%) now expresses a generally unfavorable opinion of Bush. In late January, immediately after the inauguration, only 13% said that they had a negative opinion of the new chief executive.

The most dramatic indication that the honeymoon may be at an end is the growing perception that Bush has failed to communicate his plans and policies adequately to the American people. Only about one half (52%) now gives Bush positive marks for getting his message across, down from roughly two thirds (65%) in a Gallup Poll conducted in early March. Moreover, Dan Quayle, Bush's controversial choice for vice president, remains as big a political liability as he was during the campaign. In another poll only one third thought that Quayle is qualified to serve as president if it becomes necessary.

Congress and Jim Wright

Under normal circumstances, a Democratic Congress might be expected to benefit politically from some falloff in a Republican president's public standing, but this is not the case today. As the House of Representatives investigates its speaker for alleged ethical misconduct, Congress's image among the public has declined to a four-year low. Democratic congressional leaders, as one might expect, score lower in public esteem (47%) than Republican leaders (54%).

Speaker Wright is an unpopular figure among most of those familiar with his name. Overall opinion of Wright is 2-to-1 negative (41% to 19%), and Democrats are nearly as negative in their views of the speaker as are Republicans. While many Americans are unable or unwilling to express opinions about the Wright affair, those with an opinion tend to think that the charges against him are serious enough to justify his removal as speaker. Opinion among Republicans and independents leans strongly toward this view, while Democratic opinion is more divided. The House investigation of its highest-ranking member only may reinforce the view always held by many Americans that members of Congress have low ethical standards.

The Supreme Court

While the Supreme Court historically has been better regarded than Congress, the Court has not escaped the recent decline in public confidence in Washington institutions. At a time when its reconsideration of the abortion issue has brought it greater news coverage and public attention, 61% have a favorable opinion of the Court while 21% have an unfavorable opinion. The Court continues to be rated better than Congress. However, its current 61% favorability score represents a decline from 79% in January 1988 and 76% in May 1987.

Oliver North

Public affection for Colonel North remains high despite his recent conviction on three criminal counts in connection with his role in the Iran-*contra* affair. The poll finds public opinion of the retired marine to be as favorable now as it was in the summer of 1987, when North's televised testimony before the congressional Iran-*contra* committee helped to make him a folk hero. Favorable opinions of North (59%) continue to outnumber unfavorable ones (28%) by a 2-to-1 margin.

Prior to North's sentencing, a clear majority (57%) say that they would like to see him pardoned rather than punished for his criminal offenses. Sympathy for North is found in all segments of society but especially among Republicans and supporters of George Bush. Even Democrats, however, are inclined to think that North should not have to go to jail.

Despite their sympathy for North, most Americans (51%) believe that the jury made the right decision in finding North guilty on some, but not all, of the criminal counts against him. What seems to have kept most of the public on North's side is the belief that, even though he may have violated the law on occasion while serving in the Reagan White House, he was trying to do what he thought was right.

Few characterize North as a "patriot and a hero" (14%) for his role in the Iran-*contra* affair, but few think of him as a "liar and a criminal" (11%), either. The overwhelming majority (69%) says that North was "well-meaning but misguided."

MAY 17
ENVIRONMENTAL ISSUES

Interviewing Date: 5/4–7/89
Survey #GO 89134

What do you think is the most important problem facing this country today?

Economic problems	34%
Drug abuse	27
Poverty	10
Crime	6
Moral decline	5
Environment, pollution	4
International, foreign aid	4
Education	3
Fear of war	2
Dissatisfaction with government	2
AIDS	1
Other noneconomic problems	8
None; don't know	7
	113%*

*Total adds to more than 100% due to multiple responses.

Would you say you are a strong environmentalist, or not?

Environmentalist 76%
    Strong...41
    Not strong.....................................35
Nonenvironmentalist 20
No opinion..4

By Sex

Male

Environmentalist 77%
    Strong...42
    Not strong.....................................35
Nonenvironmentalist 21
No opinion..2

Female

Environmentalist 75%
    Strong...40
    Not strong.....................................35
Nonenvironmentalist 20
No opinion..5

By Ethnic Background

White

Environmentalist 78%
    Strong...42
    Not strong.....................................36
Nonenvironmentalist 18
No opinion..4

Nonwhite

Environmentalist 61%
    Strong...30
    Not strong.....................................31
Nonenvironmentalist 34
No opinion..5

By Education

College Graduate

Environmentalist 79%
    Strong...43
    Not strong.....................................36
Nonenvironmentalist 19
No opinion..2

College Incomplete

Environmentalist 81%
    Strong...42
    Not strong.....................................39
Nonenvironmentalist 18
No opinion..1

High-School Graduate

Environmentalist 78%
    Strong...41
    Not strong.....................................37
Nonenvironmentalist 19
No opinion..3

Less Than High-School Graduate

Environmentalist 62%
    Strong...38
    Not strong.....................................24
Nonenvironmentalist 27
No opinion...11

By Region

East

Environmentalist 79%
    Strong...44
    Not strong.....................................35
Nonenvironmentalist 20
No opinion..1

Midwest

Environmentalist 76%
    Strong...42
    Not strong.....................................34
Nonenvironmentalist 20
No opinion..4

South

Environmentalist 70%
    Strong...36
    Not strong.....................................34
Nonenvironmentalist 23
No opinion..7

West

Environmentalist 81%
    Strong...43
    Not strong.....................................38
Nonenvironmentalist 16
No opinion..3

By Age

18–29 Years

Environmentalist 69%
    Strong.......................................31
    Not strong...............................38
Nonenvironmentalist 28
No opinion...3

30–49 Years

Environmentalist 79%
    Strong.......................................39
    Not strong...............................40
Nonenvironmentalist 18
No opinion...3

50 Years and Over

Environmentalist 77%
    Strong.......................................49
    Not strong...............................28
Nonenvironmentalist 17
No opinion...6

By Household Income

$50,000 and Over

Environmentalist 79%
    Strong.......................................38
    Not strong...............................41
Nonenvironmentalist 19
No opinion...2

$30,000–$49,999

Environmentalist 86%
    Strong.......................................43
    Not strong...............................43
Nonenvironmentalist 14
No opinion..*

$15,000–$29,999

Environmentalist 73%
    Strong.......................................42
    Not strong...............................31
Nonenvironmentalist 22
No opinion...5

Under $15,000

Environmentalist 70%
    Strong.......................................42
    Not strong...............................28

Nonenvironmentalist 22
No opinion...8

By Politics

Republicans

Environmentalist 75%
    Strong.......................................38
    Not strong...............................37
Nonenvironmentalist 20
No opinion...5

Democrats

Environmentalist 77%
    Strong.......................................43
    Not strong...............................34
Nonenvironmentalist 19
No opinion...4

Independents

Environmentalist 75%
    Strong.......................................41
    Not strong...............................34
Nonenvironmentalist 22
No opinion...3

*Less than 1%

I'm going to read you a list of environmental problems. As I read each one, please tell me if you personally worry about this problem a great deal, a fair amount, only a little, or not at all:

Pollution of rivers, lakes, and reservoirs?

Great deal 72%
Fair amount.......................................19
Only a little 5
Not at all..3
No opinion...1

Contamination of soil and water by toxic waste?

Great deal 69%
Fair amount.......................................21
Only a little 7

Not at all...................................... 3
No opinion....................................... *

Air pollution?

Great deal 63%
Fair amount..............................25
Only a little 8
Not at all................................ 4
No opinion....................................... *

Ocean and beach pollution?

Great deal 60%
Fair amount..............................23
Only a little 11
Not at all................................ 5
No opinion............................... 1

Loss of natural habitat for wildlife?

Great deal 58%
Fair amount..............................27
Only a little 9
Not at all................................ 5
No opinion............................... 1

Contamination of soil and water by radioactivity from nuclear facilities?

Great deal 54%
Fair amount..............................24
Only a little 14
Not at all................................ 7
No opinion............................... 1

Damage to the earth's ozone layer?

Great deal 51%
Fair amount..............................26
Only a little 13
Not at all................................ 8
No opinion............................... 2

Loss of tropical rain forests?

Great deal 42%
Fair amount..............................25
Only a little 18
Not at all................................12
No opinion............................... 3

Acid rain?

Great deal 41%
Fair amount..............................27

Only a little 18
Not at all................................11
No opinion............................... 3

"Greenhouse effect" or global warming?

Great deal 35%
Fair amount..............................28
Only a little 18
Not at all................................12
No opinion............................... 7

*Less than 1%

*Which of the following things, if any, have you or other household members done in recent years to try to improve the quality of the environment?**

Voluntarily recycled newspapers, glass, aluminum, motor oil, other items 78%
Cut household's use of energy by improving insulation or changing heating or air-conditioning system......76
Replaced "gas-guzzling" automobile with more fuel-efficient one 66
Cut household's use of water 65
Contributed to environmental, conservation, or wildlife preservation group 49
Cut down on use of car by carpooling or taking public transportation..........42
Boycotted a company's products because of its record on environment..............29
Did volunteer work for environmental, conservation, or wildlife preservation group 16
None of the above................................ 2

*Multiple responses were given.

As you may know, some consumer and environmental groups are calling for a national boycott of all products made by Exxon Corporation because of the company's record on the environment. Would you, yourself, seriously consider joining a boycott of Exxon's products, or not?

Would seriously consider boycott............41%
Would not consider boycott....................46
Have already done so (volunteered)...........7
Don't know... 6

Would you favor a ban on chlorofluoro-carbons and other chemicals known to damage the ozone layer even if it meant higher prices for air conditioners, refrigerators, and some other consumer products?

Would favor ban.....................................79%
Would not favor ban.............................13
Don't know...8

Note: For the first time in more than a decade, a significant proportion of the public considers environmental issues to be the most important problem facing the nation, an indication of the effect that the Alaska oil spill has had on the public consciousness. According to a new Gallup Poll, three fourths of Americans now think of themselves as environmentalists, and there are signs that the environmental movement may have broadened its base during the last few years.

This public concern tends to center on ecological problems that are tangible and may be directly observed in people's daily lives. Large majorities say that they worry a great deal about pollution of rivers, lakes, and reservoirs (72%); contamination of soil and water by toxic waste (69%); air pollution (63%); and ocean and beach pollution (60%). Majorities also express great concern about the loss of natural habitat for wildlife (58%)—a likely consequence of the Alaska oil spill—and contamination of soil and water by radioactive waste from nuclear facilities (54%).

Other environmental problems elicit lower levels of worry, despite widespread coverage in the media, probably because they are less obvious, more difficult to understand, and may appear to pose less of an immediate personal threat. Damage to the ozone layer, which could expose people to dangerous levels of ultraviolet radiation, is of great personal concern to 51% of respondents. Even fewer worry a great deal about the loss of tropical rain forests (42%) or the effects of acid rain (41%). And only 35% are seriously concerned about the "greenhouse effect," a global warming trend that could cause sea levels to rise and generate severe storms and drought.

Although depletion of the ozone layer ranks low in general concern, the public favors a ban on chlorofluorocarbons and other chemicals

known to damage the ozone layer by an overwhelming 79%-to-13% margin, even if this leads to higher prices for air conditioners, refrigerators, and other consumer products. Depletion of the ozone layer and the global warming trend have become major concerns of the governments of the industrialized nations. Recently the Bush administration announced that the world environment would be high on the agenda at an international conference to be held in May and at an economic summit scheduled for July.

Today, three in four Americans (76%) identify themselves as environmentalists, and about one half that proportion (41%) think of themselves as strong environmentalists. Concern about ecological issues is no longer associated primarily with younger, better-educated people who were in the vanguard of the movement two decades ago. Today, environmentalists comprise a broad-based coalition from diverse social and economic backgrounds. In fact, strong identification with environmentalism now is more common among people age 50 and older (49%) than either 30 to 49-year-olds (39%) or those under 30 (31%). This is a reversal of the pattern observed twenty years ago, when concern about environmental issues was much greater among younger than older Americans.

A *Times Mirror* survey conducted by Gallup two years ago also found environmentalism more prevalent among older than younger adults. The 1987 poll, however, found significantly more men than women and more whites than nonwhites expressing a strong commitment to protecting the environment. Identification with this cause declined among the less affluent and less-well educated. Today, while the racial differences remain, women (40%) are as likely as men (42%) to consider themselves strong environmentalists, and little change in this respect is found among people from different educational and income backgrounds. In terms of politics, environmentalism is generally bipartisan, with Republicans (38%) and Democrats (43%) about equally committed to this issue.

The most obvious achievement of the environmental movement has been the development of a national consensus that acknowledges the seriousness of environmental problems and the public's stated willingness to tackle them. While specific crises such as the Valdez oil spill evoke public outrage, however, environmental problems in general have been overshadowed by other concerns. Asked to name the most important problems facing the nation, 4% of respondents now cite environmental issues; 34%, various economic problems; 27%, the drug crisis; and 10%, poverty and homelessness. Nevertheless, the proportion mentioning the environment is higher now than it has been throughout the 1980s, when it registered at 1% or less.

Most Americans say they are making some effort in their personal lives to protect the environment. Three in four, for example, are voluntarily recycling newspapers and other household waste (78%) or have reduced their consumption of energy by improving home insulation or changing their heating or air-conditioning systems (76%). Two thirds report having replaced a "gas-guzzling" automobile with a more fuel-efficient one (66%) or are reducing their household's use of water (65%).

Almost one half (49%) say that they have made a donation to an environmental, conservation, or wildlife preservation group, while 42% report that they are carpooling or making greater use of public transportation, thus cutting back on their reliance on private automobiles. Three in ten (29%) claim to have boycotted a company's products because of its environmental policies; 16% are doing volunteer work for an environmental, conservation, or wildlife preservation group.

The worst oil disaster in North American waters occurred in March, when an Exxon tanker spilled 240,000 barrels of oil into an Alaska harbor after striking a reef. The resulting oil slick, covering an area the size of Rhode Island, has taken an enormous toll on wildlife. Expressing their outrage over the incident, 41% of Americans say that they seriously would consider joining a boycott of Exxon's products, while 7% claim that they already have done so. Almost as many (46%) are opposed to a boycott.

MAY 31
CIGARETTE SMOKING

Interviewing Date: 5/15–18/89
Survey #GO 89134

Have you, yourself, smoked any cigarettes in the past week?

	Yes
National	27%

By Sex

Male	28%
Female	26

By Education

College graduate	20%
College incomplete	20
High-school graduate	32
Less than high-school graduate	32

By Age

18–29 years	28%
30–49 years	30
50–64 years	31
65 years and over	16

By Household Income

$50,000 and over	22%
$30,000–$49,999	33
$15,000–$29,999	25
Under $15,000	30

Selected National Trend

	Yes, total	Yes, men	Yes, women
1988	32%	34%	30%
1987	30	33	28
1986	31	35	28
1985	35	37	32
1983	38	40	36
1981	35	38	33
1978	36	39	34
1977	38	41	36
1974	40	45	36
1972	43	48	38
1971	42	47	37
1969	40	44	36
1957	42	52	34
1954	45	57	32
1949	44	54	33
1944	41	48	36

Asked of those who replied in the affirmative: About how many cigarettes do you smoke each day?

Less than one pack.................................39%
One pack...39
More than one pack...............................20
Not sure 2

By Sex

Male

Less than one pack.................................36%
One pack...36
More than one pack...............................25
Not sure 3

Female

Less than one pack.................................42%
One pack...43
More than one pack...............................14
Not sure 1

By Education

College

Less than one pack.................................50%
One pack...33
More than one pack...............................17
Not sure .... *

No College

Less than one pack.................................34%
One pack...42
More than one pack...............................21
Not sure 3

By Age

18–29 Years

Less than one pack.................................53%
One pack...37
More than one pack............................... 6
Not sure 4

30–49 Years

Less than one pack.................................34%
One pack...42
More than one pack...............................22
Not sure 2

50 Years and Over

Less than one pack.................................33%
One pack...37

More than one pack...............................29
Not sure 1

By Income

$30,000 and Over

Less than one pack.................................43%
One pack...36
More than one pack...............................20
Not sure 1

Under $30,000

Less than one pack.................................35%
One pack...42
More than one pack...............................21
Not sure 2

*Less than 1%

Selected National Trend

	Less than one pack	One pack	More than one pack	Not sure
1988	40%	38%	20%	2%
1987	48	32	18	2
1981	38	37	24	1
1977	41	31	27	1

Also asked of cigarette smokers: All things considered, would you like to give up smoking, or not?

Yes...63%
No...33
Not sure 4

Selected National Trend

	Yes	No	Not sure
1988	68%	27%	5%
1987	77	20	3
1986	75	22	3
1981	66	30	4
1977	66	29	5

Asked of those who said they would like to give up smoking: Have you ever made a really serious effort to stop smoking, or not?

Yes, have 38%
No, have not 25
Don't want to quit 37

Note: Cigarette smoking has declined to its lowest level since 1944. In a new Gallup audit, 27% of American adults report having smoked cigarettes during the week prior to being interviewed. Until this year smoking had never dropped below the 30% mark. Despite this trend, other survey findings suggest that Surgeon General C. Everett Koop's vision of a "smokeless society" by the year 2000 faces formidable hurdles.

The trend toward lower rates of consumption—the tendency of smokers to consume fewer cigarettes per day—appears to have halted. Between 1977 and 1987 the proportion smoking more than one pack of cigarettes fell from 27% to 18%, while those reporting consumption of less than a pack edged upward, from 38% to 48%. Currently, 39% say that they smoke less than a pack per day; another 39%, one pack; and 20%, more than a pack, almost identical to the figures reported in last year's poll.

Although a majority of smokers say that they would like to kick the habit, the proportion (63%) now hoping to do so is slightly lower than in 1987 (77%). Of the two thirds who would like to quit, a majority claims to have made a serious effort to stop, lending support to Dr. Koop's contention that nicotine can be as addictive as hard drugs. A majority of smokers in all major population groups would like to stop, and most have tried to do so.

Smokers of all ages acknowledge a link between smoking and serious illnesses such as cancer and heart disease. However, despite evidence that exposure to environmental tobacco smoke is a significant cause of lung cancer in healthy nonsmokers, smokers heavily oppose restrictions in public places and a ban on all cigarette advertising.

Smoking reached a peak of 45% in 1954 and then fell gradually over the next thirty years. For the last three years, however, health risks and mounting social and economic pressures failed to deter about one third of the public.

Historically, more men than women have been smokers. In 1954, for example, 57% of men but only 32% of women said that they smoked cigarettes. Since 1977 almost as many women as men have been smokers. And in the current survey, 28% of men and 26% of women say that they smoked within the last week, a statistically inconclusive difference. Although their incidence of smoking is about the same, men tend to smoke more than women. One fourth of male smokers (25%) report daily consumption of more than one pack of cigarettes, while the figure for women is 14%.

Education is the most important factor in determining whether people smoke. At present only 20% of people who attended college are cigarette smokers, compared to 32% among those whose formal education ended at the high-school level. Moreover, one half of the college-educated smokers (50%), compared to one third of the less-well educated (34%), smokes less than one pack per day.

Age is also a factor. The incidence of smoking is about 30% until age 65, when it drops to 16%. However, consumption is much lower among 18 to 29-year-olds—53% claim to smoke less than one pack each day—than among their older counterparts, of whom one third (34%) are light smokers.

The number of teenage smokers remains discouragingly high. In the latest Gallup Youth Survey, 13% of young people age 13 to 17 said that they had smoked in the preceding week, a slight increase from the 10% level recorded in each of the last two years. This survey found that 11% of teenage boys and 14% of girls are smokers.

JUNE 5
GAMBLING

Interviewing Date: 4/4–9/89
Survey #GO 89109

Some states legalize betting so that the state can raise revenues. Would you approve or disapprove of legalizing each of the following types of betting in your state to help raise revenues:

Lotteries for cash prizes?

Approve...78%
Disapprove..21
No opinion... 1

By Sex

Male

Approve...80%
Disapprove..18
No opinion... 2

Female

Approve...76%
Disapprove..23
No opinion..1

Those Who Say Religion Is
Very Important in Their Life

Approve...69%
Disapprove..30
No opinion..1

Those Who Say Religion Is
Fairly Important in Their Life

Approve...89%
Disapprove..9
No opinion..2

Those Who Say Religion Is
Not Very Important in Their Life

Approve...88%
Disapprove..11
No opinion..1

Those Who Smoke Cigarettes

Approve...88%
Disapprove..11
No opinion..1

Those Who Do Not Smoke Cigarettes

Approve...74%
Disapprove..24
No opinion..2

Those Who Occasionally Drink
Alcoholic Beverages

Approve...86%
Disapprove..13
No opinion..1

Those Who Do Not Drink
Alcoholic Beverages

Approve...64%
Disapprove..34
No opinion..2

Bingo for cash prizes?

Approve...75%
Disapprove..23
No opinion..2

By Sex

Male

Approve...74%
Disapprove..24
No opinion..2

Female

Approve...75%
Disapprove..22
No opinion..3

Those Who Say Religion Is
Very Important in Their Life

Approve...67%
Disapprove..31
No opinion..2

Those Who Say Religion Is
Fairly Important in Their Life

Approve...86%
Disapprove..12
No opinion..2

Those Who Say Religion Is
Not Very Important in Their Life

Approve...82%
Disapprove..15
No opinion..3

Those Who Smoke Cigarettes

Approve...85%
Disapprove..14
No opinion..1

Those Who Do Not Smoke Cigarettes

Approve...71%
Disapprove..26
No opinion..3

Those Who Occasionally Drink Alcoholic Beverages

Approve..82%
Disapprove...16
No opinion...2

Those Who Do Not Drink Alcoholic Beverages

Approve..63%
Disapprove...34
No opinion...3

Casino gambling at resort areas?

Approve..55%
Disapprove...42
No opinion...3

By Sex

Male

Approve..57%
Disapprove...39
No opinion...4

Female

Approve..52%
Disapprove...45
No opinion...3

Those Who Say Religion Is Very Important in Their Life

Approve..45%
Disapprove...51
No opinion...4

Those Who Say Religion Is Fairly Important in Their Life

Approve..63%
Disapprove...33
No opinion...4

Those Who Say Religion Is Not Very Important in Their Life

Approve..71%
Disapprove...27
No opinion...2

Those Who Smoke Cigarettes

Approve..62%
Disapprove...35
No opinion...3

Those Who Do Not Smoke Cigarettes

Approve..51%
Disapprove...45
No opinion...4

Those Who Occasionally Drink Alcoholic Beverages

Approve..63%
Disapprove...34
No opinion...3

Those Who Do Not Drink Alcoholic Beverages

Approve..40%
Disapprove...56
No opinion...4

Off-track betting on horse races?

Approve..54%
Disapprove...42
No opinion...4

By Sex

Male

Approve..60%
Disapprove...37
No opinion...3

Female

Approve..48%
Disapprove...46
No opinion...6

Those Who Say Religion Is Very Important in Their Life

Approve..46%
Disapprove...50
No opinion...4

Those Who Say Religion Is Fairly Important in Their Life

Approve...63%
Disapprove.......................................34
No opinion...3

Those Who Say Religion Is Not Very Important in Their Life

Approve...63%
Disapprove.......................................31
No opinion...6

Those Who Smoke Cigarettes

Approve...62%
Disapprove.......................................35
No opinion...3

Those Who Do Not Smoke Cigarettes

Approve...50%
Disapprove.......................................45
No opinion...5

Those Who Occasionally Drink Alcoholic Beverages

Approve...64%
Disapprove.......................................31
No opinion...5

Those Who Do Not Drink Alcoholic Beverages

Approve...37%
Disapprove.......................................60
No opinion...3

Betting on professional sports such as baseball, basketball, or football?

Approve...42%
Disapprove.......................................55
No opinion...3

By Sex

Male

Approve...44%
Disapprove.......................................54
No opinion...2

Female

Approve...41%
Disapprove.......................................57
No opinion...2

Those Who Say Religion Is Very Important in Their Life

Approve...34
Disapprove.......................................61
No opinion...5

Those Who Say Religion Is Fairly Important in Their Life

Approve...49%
Disapprove.......................................49
No opinion...2

Those Who Say Religion Is Not Very Important in Their Life

Approve...52%
Disapprove.......................................44
No opinion...4

Those Who Smoke Cigarettes

Approve...51%
Disapprove.......................................45
No opinion...4

Those Who Do Not Smoke Cigarettes

Approve...38%
Disapprove.......................................58
No opinion...4

Those Who Occasionally Drink Alcoholic Beverages

Approve...46%
Disapprove.......................................50
No opinion...4

Those Who Do Not Drink Alcoholic Beverages

Approve...34%
Disapprove.......................................62
No opinion...4

Jai-alai games at which people can bet?

Approve...41%
Disapprove..41
No opinion..18

By Sex

Male

Approve...46%
Disapprove..38
No opinion..16

Female

Approve...36%
Disapprove..43
No opinion..21

Those Who Say Religion Is Very Important in Their Life

Approve...34%
Disapprove..48
No opinion..18

Those Who Say Religion Is Fairly Important in Their Life

Approve...45%
Disapprove..34
No opinion..21

Those Who Say Religion Is Not Very Important in Their Life

Approve...57%
Disapprove..27
No opinion..16

Those Who Smoke Cigarettes

Approve...48%
Disapprove..34
No opinion..18

Those Who Do Not Smoke Cigarettes

Approve...38%
Disapprove..43
No opinion..19

Those Who Occasionally Drink Alcoholic Beverages

Approve...48%
Disapprove..33
No opinion..19

Those Who Do Not Drink Alcoholic Beverages

Approve...30%
Disapprove..52
No opinion..18

In general, do you think legalized gambling encourages people to gamble more than they can afford?

Yes...62%
No..35
No opinion.. 3

By Sex
Male

Yes...63%
No..35
No opinion.. 2

Female

Yes...62%
No..35
No opinion.. 3

Have you ever played any game for money or prizes, or bet money on the outcome of any event?

	Yes, have
National	68%

By Sex

Male	76%
Female	61

By Age

18–29 years	71%
30–49 years	75
50 years and over	58

By Household Income

$50,000 and over 81%
$30,000–$49,999.............................75
$15,000–$29,999.............................66
Under $15,000...................................58

Those who say religion is
    very important in their life 60%
Those who say religion is
    fairly important in their life..............76
Those who say religion is
    not very important in their life 78

Those who smoke cigarettes...................76%
Those who do not smoke cigarettes 65

Those who occasionally drink
    alcoholic beverages..........................78%
Those who do not drink
    alcoholic beverages..........................51

How much do you, yourself, enjoy making bets? Would you say you enjoy making bets a lot, a little, not too much, or not at all?

A lot 7%
A little..27
Not too much.....................................27
Not at all...38
No opinion... 1

By Sex

Male

A lot 8%
A little..32
Not too much.....................................29
Not at all...31
No opinion.. *

Female

A lot 5%
A little..23
Not too much.....................................25
Not at all...46
No opinion... 1

*Less than 1%

Please tell me whether or not you have done any of the following things in the past twelve months:

Bought a state lottery ticket?

	Yes, have
National	54%

By Sex

Male 59%
Female..49

By Age

18–29 years....................................50%
30–49 years.......................................57
50 years and over...............................51

By Household Income

$50,000 and over 64%
$30,000–$49,999.............................58
$15,000–$29,999.............................53
Under $15,000...................................43

Bet on a professional sports event such as baseball, basketball, or football?

	Yes, have
National	22%

By Sex

Male 33%
Female..12

By Age

18–29 years....................................35%
30–49 years.......................................24
50 years and over...............................11

By Household Income

$50,000 and over 33%
$30,000–$49,999.............................24
$15,000–$29,999.............................21
Under $15,000...................................17

Selected National Trend

1984...17%
1982...15*

*The 1982 results are based on a survey conducted by the Gallup Organization for *Gaming Business Magazine.*

Visited a casino?

	Yes, have
National	20%

By Sex

Male	21%
Female	19

By Age

18–29 years	18%
30–49 years	22
50 years and over	17

By Household Income

$50,000 and over	36%
$30,000–$49,999	21
$15,000–$29,999	15
Under $15,000	11

Selected National Trend

1984...17%
1982...15*

*The 1982 results are based on a survey conducted by the Gallup Organization for *Gaming Business Magazine.*

Bet on a boxing match?

	Yes, have
National	8%

By Sex

Male	13%
Female	3

By Age

18–29 years	13%
30–49 years	7
50 years and over	4

By Household Income

$50,000 and over	6%
$30,000–$49,999	7
$15,000–$29,999	8
Under $15,000	11

Bet on a college sports event such as basketball or football?

	Yes, have
National	14%

By Sex

Male	21%
Female	7

By Age

18–29 years	23%
30–49 years	14
50 years and over	8

By Household Income

$50,000 and over	19%
$30,000–$49,999	14
$15,000–$29,999	14
Under $15,000	13

Played bingo for money?

	Yes, have
National	13%

By Sex

Male	11%
Female	15

By Age

18–29 years	14%
30–49 years	12
50 years and over	13

By Household Income

$50,000 and over 10%
$30,000–$49,999 10
$15,000–$29,999 15
Under $15,000 14

Bet on a dog race?

	Yes, have
National	6%

By Sex

Male 8%
Female 5

By Age

18–29 years 10%
30–49 years 5
50 years and over 5

By Household Income

$50,000 and over 8%
$30,000–$49,999 7
$15,000–$29,999 6
Under $15,000 8

Bet on jai-alai?

	Yes, have
National	3%

By Sex

Male 4%
Female 2

By Age

18–29 years 4%
30–49 years 4
50 years and over 1

By Household Income

$50,000 and over 3%
$30,000–$49,999 2
$15,000–$29,999 4
Under $15,000 2

Played cards for money?

	Yes, have
National	23%

By Sex

Male 32%
Female 14

By Age

18–29 years 35%
30–49 years 23
50 years and over 14

By Household Income

$50,000 and over 30%
$30,000–$49,999 24
$15,000–$29,999 23
Under $15,000 21

Selected National Trend

1950 ....11%
1938 21

Played a slot machine?

	Yes, have
National	19%

By Sex

Male 19%
Female 19

By Age

18–29 years 20%
30–49 years 20
50 years and over 16

By Household Income

$50,000 and over 30%
$30,000–$49,999 21
$15,000–$29,999 16
Under $15,000 11

Selected National Trend

1950 ....9%
1938 23

Played the numbers game?

	Yes, have
National	18%

By Sex

Male 20%
Female 16

By Age

18–29 years..19%
30–49 years..21
50 years and over..............................13

By Household Income

$50,000 and over 22%
$30,000–$49,999..............................17
$15,000–$29,999..............................20
Under $15,000.................................14

Selected National Trend

1950..3%
1938..9

Bet on a horse race?

	Yes, have
National....................................	14%

By Sex

Male 17%
Female 10

By Age

18–29 years..17%
30–49 years..14
50 years and over..............................10

By Household Income

$50,000 and over 25%
$30,000–$49,999..............................13
$15,000–$29,999..............................11
Under $15,000.................................10

Selected National Trend

1950..4%
1938..10

Asked of those who responded in the affirmative: How often—once a week or more often, two to three times a month, once a month, once every few months, or less often—have you:

Bought a state lottery ticket?

Weekly...23%
Monthly..16
Less often..14
Not sure 1
                                                    54%

Bet on pro football during the season?

Weekly... 6%
Monthly..5
Less often..11
Not sure ....*
                                                    22%

Bet on pro basketball during the season?

Weekly... 2%
Monthly..3
Less often..16
Not sure 1
                                                    22%**

Bet on college basketball during the season?

Weekly... 2%
Monthly..3
Less often..8
Not sure 1
                                                    14%**

Played bingo for money?

Weekly... 3%
Monthly..2
Less often..8
Not sure ....*
                                                    13%

Bet on a dog race?

Weekly...*%
Monthly..1
Less often..5
Not sure ....*
                                                    6%

Bet on jai-alai?

Weekly...*%
Monthly 1
Less often.......................................2
Not sure ....*
                                                                    3%

Bet on Major League baseball during the season?

Weekly...1%
Monthly 2
Less often.......................................18
Not sure 1
                                                                  22%**

Visited a casino?

Weekly...1%
Monthly 1
Less often.......................................18
Not sure ....*
                                                                  20%

Bet on a boxing match?

Weekly...*%
Monthly 1
Less often.......................................6
Not sure 1
                                                                    8%

Bet on college football during the season?

Weekly...3%
Monthly 4
Less often.......................................6
Not sure 1
                                                                  14%**

Played cards for money?

Weekly...4%
Monthly 7
Less often.......................................12
Not sure ....*
                                                                  23%

Played a slot machine?

Weekly...*%
Monthly 1
Less often.......................................18
Not sure ....*
                                                                  19%

Played the numbers game?

Weekly...5%
Monthly 5
Less often.......................................7
Not sure 1
                                                                  18%

Bet on a horse race?

Weekly...1%
Monthly 3
Less often.......................................10
Not sure ....*
                                                                  14%

*Less than 1%
**Totals reflect all those who bet on any sport in the category. For example, all pro sports bettors are counted in the total for Major League baseball, although some may limit their betting to pro football.

Summary of Betting Activities

Bet/play something weekly.....................31%
Bet/play something monthly..................18
Less frequent gamblers..........................22
No activity in past twelve months............29

Asked of those who have gambled in the past twelve months: Considering all the money you spent on bets, wagers, or lottery tickets over the past twelve months, as well as your winnings, would you say you are ahead or behind?

Ahead..24%
Behind...58
Broke even 15
Don't know 3

Also asked of those who have gambled in the past twelve months: When you gamble, how satisfied do you usually feel when you win? Would you say you feel extremely satisfied, very satisfied, somewhat satisfied, or not satisfied?

Extremely satisfied 24%
Very satisfied 27
Somewhat satisfied 37

Not satisfied...5
Don't know..7

Also asked of those who have gambled in the past twelve months: When you gamble, how upset do you usually feel when you lose? Would you say you feel extremely upset, very upset, somewhat upset, or not upset?

Extremely upset 4%
Very upset 3
Somewhat upset 30
Not upset...60
Don't know 3

Also asked of those who have gambled in the past twelve months: Thinking about the kinds of bets or wagers you make most often, please tell me the main reason why you like to gamble?*

To have a good time;
  it's enjoyable or for
  recreation/fun......................................39%
It makes the game more
  interesting; I feel more
  a part of the game............................4
For the challenge or
  competition....................................11
To make money;
  to get rich 27
Out of habit...1
For the excitement...............................12
I'm lucky...1
Part of my social life 6
Other...14
Don't know 5

*Multiple responses were given.

Asked of the entire sample: For each of the following events, please tell me how many games, if any, you think are fixed as a result of gambling. Would you say almost all of the games are fixed, most of them, some of them, very few, or none of the games are fixed as a result of gambling:

Pro basketball?

Almost all 3%
Most...4
Some...19

Very few...24
None...32
Don't know 18

Major League baseball?

Almost all 3%
Most...3
Some...17
Very few...25
None...35
Don't know 17

Pro football?

Almost all 3%
Most...6
Some...20
Very few...25
None...31
Don't know 15

Boxing?

Almost all 9%
Most...12
Some...32
Very few...18
None...11
Don't know 18

College sports such as basketball or football?

Almost all 2%
Most...3
Some...18
Very few...28
None...35
Don't know 14

Horse racing?

Almost all 6%
Most...9
Some...32
Very few...20
None...14
Don't know 19

Note: From lotteries to racetracks to casinos, games of chance are attracting more players than they did earlier in the decade, according to a new Gallup Poll. State governments have been a major contributor to the gaming industry's growth, with the number of state lotteries doubling since 1980. Even as the games become legitimized as state-sponsored entertainment, however, the public remains ambivalent about the idea of legalized gambling. Lotteries win broad popular approval, but people are much less eager to expand legal gambling to activities such as sports betting.

Lottery playing may have replaced baseball as the national pastime. With twenty-nine states and the District of Columbia now operating lotteries and with three more states in the process of starting them up, the number of players has risen dramatically. More than one half of all U.S. adults (54%) sometimes buy lottery tickets, up from about one fifth (18%) in 1982. In states that have lotteries, two thirds of adults (66%) at least occasionally buy tickets and close to one third (31%) are weekly players.

However, lotteries are only part of the story. Now that Atlantic City, New Jersey, puts casino gambling within one day's drive of major population centers in the Northeast, annual casino attendance is up sharply. And expanded off-track betting may help horse racing overcome the problem of lagging attendance at the track. More people now than in 1982 say that they have bet on the horses in the past year.

The increase in gambling activity has not been limited to legal games. Sports betting, now legal only in Nevada, also has increased significantly in recent years. Signs that illegal betting has risen along with legal gaming could provide ammunition for gaming industry critics who argue that legalization creates conditions that foster expanded illegal gambling.

Allegations revolving around Cincinnati Reds' manager Pete Rose have called attention to the seamy side of gambling—its association with criminals, the potential for corruption, and the destructive effect it can have on compulsive gamblers and their families. Rose's difficulties may have slowed the momentum of those seeking to expand legal betting to professional and college sports. While public support for some other forms of legalized gambling has increased, opposition to legalized betting on pro sports such as football, basketball, and baseball has held firm.

Gallup polled 1,200 adults recently to find out what games they play, how much they bet, and what they generally think about gambling and its effects on society. The survey demonstrates that America is a nation of gamblers who mostly wager small amounts of money on a whole range of games.

• Participation in games of chance is widespread. Including activities like bingo and the lottery, along with the more serious gambling that takes place in casinos and at racetracks, seven in ten adults (71%) gambled in the past year. Close to one third (31%) plays on a weekly basis. To cite bingo in particular, close to one in seven adults (13%) has played for money in the past year, while 3% are weekly players.

• While most Americans gamble, a majority claim that their gambling activities have a minimal effect on their personal finances. Six in ten (61%) say that their total wins and losses for the year amount to less than $50. The average American who gambles claims never to have lost more than $20 on any single occasion.

• Gambling in general, but especially more serious gambling that often entails specialized knowledge and greater financial risk, continues to be a male-dominated pursuit. A majority of men (58%) plays on at least a monthly basis; fewer than one half of women (41%) are regular gamblers. Of all gamblers who have lost $100 or more in the course of a day's play, four in five are male (79%). Men more often participate in the kinds of activities that attract professional gamblers: card games, racetrack betting, and wagering on sporting events. The majority of women who gamble (57%) limit their participation to the lottery, bingo, and other games of luck.

• Gambling, broadly defined, is popular among people from all walks of life. On the basis of their demographic profile, the minority who never even play bingo, purchase a lottery ticket, or play a friendly game of poker appear to shun gambling mostly on moral grounds. Nongamblers tend to be older, less affluent, more religious, and teetotalers.

• Nongamblers are most numerous in the South, but this seems to result more from lack of opportunity than from lack of interest. Twice as many southerners (44%) as nonsoutherners (22%) say that they have not bet in the past year. However, southerners are as likely to participate in card games, racetrack betting, and sports betting as people in other regions. Most southerners lack easy access to a lottery, since Florida and Kentucky are the only states in the region with lotteries. Nevertheless, the idea of a state lottery wins broad public approval in the South, with 72% of southerners favoring one in their state.

• Westerners, four in ten of whom visit a casino annually, continue to set the pace for gambling in America. Residents of western states tend to get more enjoyment out of placing bets and to wager larger amounts than people who live in the East.

• Americans play a variety of games for many different reasons. including entertainment, the opportunity to make money, and the excitement of taking financial risks. Each category of game attracts a different type of player. The survey provides a statistical portrait of gamblers in America, how often they play, and how much they risk for a variety of gambling activities: bingo, the lottery, card games, pari-mutuel and sports betting, and casino gambling.

JUNE 14
PRESIDENT BUSH/CHINA AND THE SOVIET UNION

Interviewing Date: 6/8–11/89
Survey #GO 89135

Do you approve or disapprove of the way George Bush is handling his job as president?

Approve..70%
Disapprove..14
No opinion...16

Selected National Trend

	Approve	Dis-approve	No opinion
May 4–7	56%	22%	22%
April 10–16	58	16	26
March 10–13	56	16	28
February 28– March 2	63	13	24
January 24–26	51	6	43

Which of the following events is of the most importance to the United States?

Chinese student uprising 48%
Gorbachev's political, economic reforms...........................27
Death of the Ayatollah Khomeini...............7
Solidarity's victory in Polish elections...............................5
None...3
Don't know...10

Do you approve or disapprove of the way President Bush is dealing with the recent events in China?

Approve...67%
Disapprove...19
No opinion...14

Do you think the Bush administration has gone too far or not far enough in expressing American disapproval of the use of military force against the student demonstrators in China, or do you feel the administration's response has been about right?

Gone too far..5%
Not far enough....................................28
About right...60
No opinion..7

As I read you some measures the United States could take to demonstrate its disapproval of the Chinese government's actions against the demonstrators, please tell me whether you favor or oppose each one:

Suspend the sale of U.S. arms to China?

Favor 75%
Oppose..21
No opinion...4

Permit Chinese students now in the United States to remain here after their visas expire?

Favor 71%
Oppose..23
No opinion...6

Restrict American investments in China?

Favor 60%
Oppose...33
No opinion..7

Recall the U.S. ambassador to China?

Favor 42%
Oppose...49
No opinion..9

Break off diplomatic relations with China?

Favor 22%
Oppose...72
No opinion..6

Over the next few years, do you think China will continue to implement free-market economic reforms, or do you think China will revert to a more closed economic system?

Continue free-market reforms..................36%
Revert to closed system.........................43
No opinion..21

Over the next few years, do you think that a more open, multiparty political system will emerge in China, or that the leaders will forcibly resist any democratic reforms?

More open system will emerge................35%
Leaders will resist reforms.....................51
No opinion..14

Do you think a popular uprising or civil war is or is not likely to erupt if the Chinese government continues to resist democratic reforms?

Likely to erupt....................................72%
Not likely to erupt 21
No opinion..7

If a full-scale civil war were to break out, would you favor or oppose the United States sending military aid to the prodemocracy side?

Favor 27%
Oppose...64
No opinion..9

Now, what are your expectations for the Soviet Union? Do you think President Gorbachev's attempts to restructure the Soviet economy are likely to succeed or likely to fail?

Likely to succeed................................65%
Likely to fail......................................21
No opinion..14

If Gorbachev's free-market economic policies fail within the next few years, do you think the Gorbachev regime will be replaced, or not?

Will be replaced 60%
Will not be replaced 29
No opinion..11

Do you think the Soviet Union's new openness and democracy will continue, or that it will return to a more closed society?

Openness will continue.........................66%
Return to closed society 25
No opinion..9

Do you think the Eastern European nations of Poland, East Germany, and Hungary will continue to govern themselves under the Soviet Union's guidance, or that they eventually will seek complete independence from the Soviet Union?

Continue under Soviet guidance...............25%
Seek complete independence..................63
No opinion..12

Do you think that discontent with life in the Soviet Union will result in popular uprisings and civil strife, or will social and economic change come about peacefully?

Popular uprisings and civil strife.............28%
Changes will come about peacefully.........61
No opinion..11

Do you think the current problems in China and Russia are typical of the upheavals that all nations go through, or that they are an indication of the basic weakness of the Communist system?

Typical upheavals...............................26%
Indication of weakness.........................62

Both (volunteered)...............................3
No opinion...9

Note: The American public is reacting to events in China right in line with official Washington policy. While large majorities favor suspending U.S. arms sales and giving political asylum to Chinese students studying here, a solid majority of Americans opposes breaking off diplomatic relations and a plurality opposes recalling the U.S. ambassador from Beijing.

The poll results are good news for President George Bush. Not only does the public side with him on China policy options, but as many as two in three (67%) also express general approval of his handling of the issue. Bush's overall approval rating in the current poll—70%—is up 14 percentage points since the May survey. The upheaval in China may well be a major factor, since presidential ratings generally rise in times of international crisis as the public rallies around the chief executive.

Americans predict continued strife in China over the next few years. By a margin of 51% to 35%, they see the Beijing government as continuing to resist reforms rather than moving toward a more open political system. Further government repression is viewed as a prescription for further unrest. Seven in ten (72%) believe that continued resistance to democratic reforms on the part of the Chinese government will lead to a popular uprising and civil war.

While Americans are generally pessimistic that a government willing to use bloodshed to put down civil unrest will accept political reform, they are more divided about the future of free-market economic reforms in China. Four in ten (43%) say that Beijing will turn away from privatization and revert to a more closed economic system, but almost as many (36%) disagree. One in five (21%) has no opinion.

President Bush receives a strong vote of confidence for his response to the situation in China. Support for Bush is reflected not only in the majority (67%) who give him positive marks for how he has dealt with the situation and in the majority (60%) who say that he has done enough to express disapproval of Beijing's actions without going too far but also in public opinion on specific U.S. policy options toward China.

One option already taken by the Bush administration—suspending the sale of arms to China—receives the highest level of approval (75%) of the five tested in the poll. Ranking second (71%) is an option that Bush has said he would seriously consider: permitting Chinese students now in the United States to remain here after their visas expire.

While some politicians are demanding that the U.S. ambassador be recalled and that diplomatic relations be cut off, Bush has opposed these steps. At least for now, he has the public on his side. Seventy-two percent oppose breaking relations altogether, while a 49% plurality opposes recalling the ambassador. A majority of the public (60%) favors restricting U.S. investments in China—one case where public opinion does not lean toward the position of the Bush administration.

The public thinks that the problems in China are important to U.S. interests, but not important enough to overcome general opposition to our involvement in the internal affairs of other countries. Americans rate the student uprising in China as rivaling or surpassing Mikhail Gorbachev's reforms in its importance to the United States. Most Americans, however, would not be willing to risk military involvement even if the current situation in China developed into a full-scale civil war. Almost two thirds (64%) say that they would oppose military aid in support of the prodemocracy forces in such a situation.

Americans see the events in China as related to the changes now taking place in the Soviet Union and other Communist countries. Unrest in China and the changes in the Soviet Union under Gorbachev are both perceived as having their roots in the weakness of the Communist system. Six in ten (62%) think that the current problems in the two largest Communist countries indicate the failure of communism rather than typify the upheavals that all nations experience from time to time.

Public optimism that Gorbachev's policies of *glasnost* and *perestroika* will continue in the Soviet Union contrast with more pessimistic views about the future of reform in China. Much of the optimism that reform can succeed in the Soviet Union may be riding on the extraordinarily high regard that Americans and others in the West have for the current Soviet leader. Many (60%), however, believe, that he will be replaced if his policies fail to improve the Soviet economy within the next few years.

Close to two thirds (65%) of Americans say that Gorbachev will succeed in restructuring the Soviet economy; a similar proportion (66%) believes that his policies of openness and democratic reform will continue. Moreover, six in ten (61%) think that social and economic changes in the Soviet Union will come about peacefully rather than as a result of popular uprisings against the government.

JUNE 21
CRIME/CRIMINAL JUSTICE SYSTEM

Interviewing Date: 6/8–11/89
Survey #GO 89135

Is there more crime in your area than there was a year ago, or less?

More..53%
Less..18
Same (volunteered)..............................22
Don't know.. 7

By Community Size

Large City

More..57%
Less..13
Same (volunteered)..............................20
Don't know..10

Suburb

More..52%
Less..20
Same (volunteered)..............................20
Don't know.. 8

Small City/Town

More..53%
Less..19
Same (volunteered)..............................22
Don't know.. 6

Rural

More..48%
Less..19

Same (volunteered)..............................27
Don't know.. 6

Selected National Trend

	More	Less	Same	Don't know
January 1989	47%	21%	27%	5%
1983	37	17	36	10
1982	47	17	28	8
1981	54	8	29	9
1977	43	17	32	8
1975	50	12	29	9
1972	51	10	27	12

Is there more crime in the United States than there was a year ago, or less?

More..84%
Less.. 5
Same (volunteered).............................. 5
Don't know.. 6

In your opinion, what factors are most responsible for crime in the United States today?*

	1989	1981
Drugs	58%	13%
Unemployment	14	37
Breakdown of family, society, values	13	19
Courts too lenient	4	20
Punishment too lax	4	13
Television violence	2	3
Other	19	17
Don't know	6	8

*Multiple responses were given.

What is the most important thing that can be done to help reduce crime?*

	1989	1981
Cut drug supply	25%	3%
Harsher punishment	24	38
Teach values, respect for law	12	13
Reduce unemployment	10	22
More police	5	11
Try cases faster	2	6
Other	21	13
Don't know	14	11

*Multiple responses were given.

How much confidence do you have in the ability of the police to protect you from violent crime: a great deal, quite a bit, not very much, or none at all?

Great deal 14%
Quite a bit 34
Not very much 42
None at all 8
Don't know 2

By Community Size

Large City

Great deal 18%
Quite a bit 22
Not very much 52
None at all 6
Don't know 2

Suburb

Great deal 14%
Quite a bit 36
Not very much 43
None at all 6
Don't know 1

Small City/Town

Great deal 14%
Quite a bit 38
Not very much 39
None at all 8
Don't know 1

Rural

Great deal 12%
Quite a bit 35
Not very much 38
None at all 12
Don't know 3

Selected National Trend

	Great deal, quite a bit	Very much, none at all	Don't know
1985	52%	45%	3%
1981	49	50	1

How much confidence do you have in the ability of the courts to convict and properly sentence criminals: a great deal, quite a bit, not very much, or none at all?

Great deal 5%
Quite a bit 20
Not very much 59
None at all 14
Don't know 2

By Community Size

Large City

Great deal 5%
Quite a bit 23
Not very much 56
None at all 14
Don't know 2

Suburb

Great deal 6%
Quite a bit 17
Not very much 61
None at all 16
Don't know .... *

Small City/Town

Great deal 6%
Quite a bit 19
Not very much 59
None at all 13
Don't know 3

Rural

Great deal 2%
Quite a bit 22
Not very much 59
None at all 16
Don't know 1

*Less than 1%

Selected National Trend

	Great deal, quite a bit	Not very much, none at all	Don't know
1985	30%	66%	4%
1981	28	70	2

In general, do you think the courts in your area deal too harshly or not harshly enough with criminals?

Too harshly 3%
Not harshly enough..............................83
About right (volunteered).......................8
Don't know 6

By Community Size

Large City

Too harshly 2%
Not harshly enough..............................83
About right (volunteered).......................6
Don't know 9

Suburb

Too harshly 2%
Not harshly enough..............................89
About right (volunteered).......................6
Don't know 3

Small City/Town

Too harshly 3%
Not harshly enough..............................80
About right (volunteered).......................9
Don't know 8

Rural

Too harshly 2%
Not harshly enough..............................83
About right (volunteered).......................11
Don't know 4

Selected National Trend

	Too harshly	Not harshly enough	About right	Don't know
1969	2%	75%	13%	10%
1968	2	63	19	16

Which are you more worried about: that some criminals are being let off too easily, or that the constitutional rights of some people accused of committing a crime are not being upheld?

Criminals let off too easily 79%
Constitutional rights not upheld..............16
Don't know 5

By Community Size

Large City

Criminals let off too easily 76%
Constitutional rights not upheld..............17
Don't know 7

Suburb

Criminals let off too easily 84%
Constitutional rights not upheld..............13
Don't know 3

Small City/Town

Criminals let off too easily 78%
Constitutional rights not upheld..............17
Don't know 5

Rural

Criminals let off too easily 79%
Constitutional rights not upheld..............19
Don't know 2

For each of the following, please tell me whether you favor or oppose each as a way of dealing with crime in the United States. First, do you strongly favor, favor, oppose, or strongly oppose:

Making it more difficult for those convicted of violent crimes like murder and rape to be paroled?

Strongly favor......................................54%
Favor 28
Oppose.. 8
Strongly oppose 8
Don't know 2

Not allowing those accused of violent crimes like murder and rape to get out on bail while awaiting trial?

Strongly favor......................................42%
Favor 26
Oppose..17
Strongly oppose 12
Don't know 3

Enacting tougher gun control laws?

Strongly favor......................................28%
Favor 32
Oppose..23

Strongly oppose 11
Don't know 6

Prohibiting plea bargaining—where the defendant agrees to plead guilty to a reduced charge?

Strongly favor 16%
Favor 27
Oppose...33
Strongly oppose 17
Don't know 7

Allowing the police to search a home without a warrant?

Strongly favor 6%
Favor 12
Oppose...43
Strongly oppose 36
Don't know 3

In dealing with those who are in prison, do you think it is more important to punish them for their crimes, or more important to get them started on the right road?

Punish them.......................................38%
Start them on right road.........................48
Don't know 14

To lower the crime rate in the United States, some people think additional money and effort should go to attacking the social and economic problems that lead to crime, through better education and job training. Others feel more money and effort should go to deterring crime by improving law enforcement with more prisons, police, and judges. Which comes closer to your view?

Attack social problems 61%
Improve law enforcement......................32
Don't know 7

Note: Fueled by perceptions of a drug-related crime epidemic, Americans are venting their frustration with what they see as an impotent, ineffective criminal justice system by demanding swifter, surer, and harsher punishment for convicted criminals. And while the public is not willing to suspend civil liberties, a just-completed Gallup Poll finds far more concern about criminals being let off too

easily (79%) than about the possible abuse of defendants' constitutional rights (16%).

The courts bear the brunt of the public's criticism. About three in four respondents (73%) say that they have little or no confidence in the courts' ability to convict and properly sentence criminals; furthermore, the vast majority (83%) thinks that the courts in their area deal too leniently with wrongdoers. While this view has prevailed for at least the last two decades, the proportion advocating tougher treatment of criminals has climbed from 63% in 1968 to 75% in the following year to the present 83%.

The police also come in for their share of the blame. Public opinion is evenly divided between those expressing a great deal or quite a bit of confidence (48%) in the police's ability to protect them from violent crime and those with not very much confidence or none at all (50%), consistent with the results of earlier surveys.

The public's get-tough attitude toward law enforcement comes at a time when the overwhelming majority (84%) believes that the national crime rate has risen during the past year and when 53% think that there is more crime in their neighborhood today than there was one year ago. In fact, according to the Department of Justice's National Crime Survey, one household in four experienced a violent crime or theft in 1988, the same incidence as in the previous three years and substantially below the crime rate recorded in the department's first survey in 1975, when one home in three was the target of a violent crime.

In sharp contrast to 1981, when the public was first asked to name the factors most responsible for crime in the United States, 58% now cite drugs, thus dwarfing such factors as unemployment (14%) and the breakdown of respect for family and social values (13%). In the earlier poll, conducted during the 1981–82 recession, drugs (13%) were overshadowed by unemployment (37%), too lenient courts (20%), and a breakdown of family values (19%).

Responses to a companion question show a similar shift in the public's priorities for reducing crime. Currently, the leading remedies are reducing the drug supply (25%), meting out harsher punishment for criminals (24%), instilling social values and respect for the law (12%), and cutting unemployment (10%). In

1981 the emphasis was on harsher penalties (38%), creating jobs (22%), teaching values (13%), and adding more police (11%); cutting the drug trade was mentioned by only 3%.

In addition to demanding swifter and tougher punishment for convicted criminals, the public backs several court reforms that would help stem "revolving door" justice. Eight in ten (82%) favor making it more difficult for people convicted of violent crimes to obtain paroles, with most (54%) strongly favoring such a move. Two in three (68%) would deny bail to defendants accused of violent crimes while awaiting trial. Prohibiting plea bargaining—permitting defendants to plead guilty to lesser crimes in exchange for lighter sentences—meets with slightly more opposition (50%) than approval (43%). Opposition to granting police the right to search homes without warrants far outweighs support, 79% to 18%. In addition, by almost a 2-to-1 margin (60% to 34%), the public favors tougher gun control laws as a crime prevention measure.

Americans continue to accept the principle that the prisons' most important role should be to rehabilitate inmates (48%) rather than to punish them (38%), but in 1982 substantially more subscribed to the rehabilitation theory and fewer to punishment, 59% to 30%. Public attitudes toward criminal justice clearly have swung toward more stringent law enforcement. Nevertheless, the 2-to-1 weight of public opinion is that reducing crime can be accomplished more effectively by addressing the social and economic problems that lead to crime through education and job training, rather than by building more prisons and hiring more police and judges.

JUNE 28
COST OF LIVING/PERSONAL FINANCES

Interviewing Date: 6/15–18/89
Survey #GO 89135-2

How often do you worry that your total family income will not be enough to meet your family's expenses and bills—all of the time, most of the time, some of the time, or almost never?

All or most of the time..........................26%
Some of the time 35
Almost never....................................38
No opinion.......................................1

By Sex

Male

All or most of the time..........................21%
Some of the time 35
Almost never....................................43
No opinion.......................................1

Female

All or most of the time..........................30%
Some of the time 34
Almost never....................................35
No opinion.......................................1

By Ethnic Background

White

All or most of the time..........................24%
Some of the time 35
Almost never....................................40
No opinion.......................................1

Black

All or most of the time..........................42%
Some of the time 31
Almost never....................................25
No opinion.......................................2

By Education

College Graduate

All or most of the time..........................14%
Some of the time 36
Almost never....................................50
No opinion.......................................*

College Incomplete

All or most of the time..........................24%
Some of the time 36
Almost never....................................39
No opinion.......................................1

High-School Graduate

All or most of the time..........................28%
Some of the time 38
Almost never....................................34
No opinion.......................................*

Less Than High-School Graduate

All or most of the time..........................37%
Some of the time 25
Almost never....................................34
No opinion.......................................4

By Age

18-29 Years

All or most of the time..........................24%
Some of the time 39
Almost never....................................36
No opinion.......................................1

30-49 Years

All or most of the time..........................30%
Some of the time 36
Almost never....................................33
No opinion.......................................1

50-64 Years

All or most of the time..........................25%
Some of the time 31
Almost never....................................43
No opinion.......................................1

65 Years and Over

All or most of the time..........................19%
Some of the time 29
Almost never....................................49
No opinion.......................................3

By Household Income

$50,000 and Over

All or most of the time..........................10%
Some of the time 32
Almost never....................................57
No opinion.......................................1

$30,000-$49,999

All or most of the time..........................19%
Some of the time 37

Almost never....................................43
No opinion.......................................1

$15,000-$29,999

All or most of the time..........................39%
Some of the time 28
Almost never....................................25
No opinion.......................................8

Under $15,000

All or most of the time..........................45%
Some of the time 28
Almost never....................................25
No opinion.......................................2

*Less than 1%

Selected National Trend

	All or most of the time	Some of the time	Almost never	Not sure
1987	31%	38%	30%	1%
1984	35	30	34	1
1974	25	36	38	1

Have there been times during the last year when you did not have enough money to buy food your family needed?

Yes
National...13%

By Sex

Male 9%
Female...16

By Ethnic Background

White...10%
Black 36

By Education

College graduate..................................3%
College incomplete...............................11
High-school graduate............................13
Less than high-school graduate 25

By Age

18–29 years	17%
30–49 years	15
50–64 years	8
65 years and over	7

By Household Income

$50,000 and over	1%
$30,000–$49,999	5
$15,000–$29,999	12
Under $15,000	33

Selected National Trend

1987	16%
1984	20
1974	14

Have there been times during the last year when you did not have enough money to buy clothing your family needed?

	Yes
National	17%

By Sex

Male	12%
Female	21

By Ethnic Background

White	14%
Black	37

By Education

College graduate	6%
College incomplete	16
High-school graduate	18
Less than high-school graduate	28

By Age

18–29 years	18%
30–49 years	21
50–64 years	14
65 years and over	8

By Household Income

$50,000 and over	1%
$30,000–$49,999	7
$15,000–$29,999	21
Under $15,000	37

Selected National Trend

1987	19%
1984	26
1974	19

Have there been times during the last year when you did not have enough money to pay for medical or health care?

	Yes
National	21%

By Sex

Male	18%
Female	23

By Ethnic Background

White	19%
Black	41

By Education

College graduate	9%
College incomplete	17
High-school graduate	22
Less than high-school graduate	37

By Age

18–29 years	25%
30–49 years	22
50–64 years	15
65 years and over	19

By Household Income

$50,000 and over	4%
$30,000–$49,999	9
$15,000–$29,999	24
Under $15,000	46

Selected National Trend

1987	21%
1984	25
1974	15

People Unable to Buy One or More of Three Items Listed

	Yes to food, clothing, or medical care
National	28%

By Sex

Male	22%
Female	32

By Ethnic Background

White	25%
Black	51

By Education

College graduate	13%
College incomplete	24
High-school graduate	28
Less than high-school graduate	47

By Age

18–29 years	33%
30–49 years	29
50–64 years	23
65 years and over	23

By Household Income

$50,000 and over	5%
$30,000–$49,999	12
$15,000–$29,999	34
Under $15,000	58

Selected National Trend

	Better	Worse	Same	No opinion
1989				
January	61%	13%	19%	7%
1988				
September–October	67	9	17	7
May	63	9	17	11
January	58	14	18	10
1987				
August–September	56	16	20	8
March	59	17	18	6
January	51	16	26	7

The following are "super optimists," those who claim to be better off now than they were one year ago and expect to be still better off next year:

	Super optimists
National	33%

By Sex

Male	34%
Female	32

By Ethnic Background

White	33%
Black	31

By Education

College graduate	36%
College incomplete	41
High-school graduate	35
Less than high-school graduate	17

We are interested in how people's financial situation may have changed. Would you say that you are financially better off now than you were a year ago, or are you financially worse off now?

Better	42%
Worse	25
Same (volunteered)	31
No opinion	2

Selected National Trend

	Better	Worse	Same	No opinion
1989				
January	44%	26%	28%	2%
1988				
September–October	53	33	23	1
May	47	24	28	1
January	41	28	29	2
1987				
August–September	43	29	27	1
March	46	30	23	1
January	39	28	33	*

*Less than 1%

Now, looking ahead, do you expect that at this time next year you will be financially better off than now, or worse off than now?

Better	58%
Worse	13
Same (volunteered)	20
No opinion	9

By Age

18–29 years	51%
30–49 years	39
50–64 years	20
65 years and over	9

By Household Income

$50,000 and over	45%
$30,000–$49,999	40
$15,000–$29,999	35
Under $15,000	17

The following is the trend in "super optimists," those who claim to be better off now than they were one year ago and expect to be still better off next year:

Selected National Trend

	Super optimists
1989	
January	37%
1988	
September–October	44
May	38
January	32
1987	
August–September	34
March	36
January	29

Note: Seven years of prosperity have reinforced Americans' optimism that the good times will continue, with six in ten (58%) expecting to be better off financially at this time next year. Throughout the recovery, however, a core group of about one fourth of respondents has experienced times when they did not have enough money to buy food, clothing, or medical care for their families. Blacks and people in the lowest education and income categories have been particularly hard hit, with about one half in each of these population groups suffering financial hardship.

Moreover, 26% of participants in a new Gallup Poll say that they worry all or most of the time that their family income will not be enough to meet expenses. This figure is almost identical to the 25% reported in Gallup's first assessment in 1974 and slightly below the 35% recorded in 1984, when the effects of the 1981–82 recession still were being felt. Slightly more Americans now say that they could not afford medical care (21%) than the clothing (17%) or food (13%) needed by their families, with 28% citing the inability to pay for one or more of these items during the last year. The latest findings are similar to those reported in earlier surveys.

As expected, the greatest disparities in financial hardship are based on family income, education, and race. Only 5% of persons with annual family earnings of $50,000 or more, for example, were unable to buy one or more of the three items listed, compared to almost six in ten (58%) of those with incomes of less than $15,000 per year. Similarly, the rate of hardship rises from 13% among college graduates to 47% among those whose formal education ended before graduation from high school. And twice the proportion of blacks (51%) as whites (25%) say that there were times when they could not afford one or more of the items listed. Although the differences are less extreme, more women (32%) than men (22%) experienced financial need during the last twelve months. The hardship rate also was higher among adults under age 30 (33%) than those 50 and older (23%).

In the latest audit of consumers' financial outlook, 58% expect to be better off one year from now, 20% think that their situation will not change much, and 13% predict a downturn. The latest figures represent a slight decrease in optimism since last fall, when 67% thought their finances would improve, 17% remain the same, and 9% grow worse. Those findings marked the high point in consumer buoyancy since 1976, when Gallup began monitoring the public's financial mood. The low point in this barometer occurred in mid-1979—a period of double-digit inflation—when more Americans thought that they would be worse off (37%) than better off (30%) one year hence.

Responses to a companion question also show a marginal decline in consumers' perceptions of their current financial status vis-à-vis one year ago. At present 42% say that they are better off, 31% the same, and 25% worse off than at this time last year. Last fall, optimists reached a peak in this trend, with 53% perceiving an improvement, 23% no change, and 23% a decline from the same period one year earlier. The low points were recorded in July 1979, August 1982, and March 1983, when almost twice as many were pessimistic (46%) as optimistic (25%) about their financial status.

The latest results also show a decline in "super optimists," from 44% last fall to 33% at present. Studies have shown that these people—who say they now are better off than in the past and expect to be still more prosperous in the future—are likely to be buyers of big-ticket discretionary items, such as houses, cars, and major appliances, and to be heavy users of credit. The low point in this trend (17%) was recorded in 1982, during the 1981–82 recession.

Super optimism is strongly influenced by demographic factors such as age, education, and family income. Super optimists tend to be younger, better educated, and more affluent than people who do not share this high degree of optimism. Unlike earlier surveys, in which proportionately more men than women and fewer blacks than whites have been super optimists, the current poll found no significant difference by gender or race.

JULY 3
FAMILY TIES

Interviewing Date: 5/15–18/89
Survey #GO 89134-2

Asked of those over age 18 with at least one living parent/stepparent: About how often do you usually see your parents/mother/father? Is it every day, once a week or more, once a month or more, several times a year, once a year, less than once a year, or never?

Every day	22%
Once a week or more	32
Once a month or more	16
Several times a year	19
Once a year	7
Less than once a year	3
Never	1

By Sex

Male

Every day	23%
Once a week or more	32
Once a month or more	16
Several times a year	18
Once a year	6
Less than once a year	4
Never	1

Female

Every day	21%
Once a week or more	31
Once a month or more	17
Several times a year	20
Once a year	8
Less than once a year	3
Never	*

*Less than 1%

Asked of those over age 18 with at least one living parent/stepparent: And about how often do you talk to them/her/him on the telephone?

Every day	19%
Once a week or more	49
Once a month or more	18
Several times a year	4
Once a year	*
Less than once a year	*
Never	9
Don't know	1

By Sex

Male

Every day	13%
Once a week or more	50
Once a month or more	20
Several times a year	5
Once a year	*
Less than once a year	1
Never	10
Don't know	1

Female

Every day	24%
Once a week or more	48
Once a month or more	16
Several times a year	2
Once a year	1
Less than once a year	*
Never	8
Don't know	1

*Less than 1%

Asked of those over age 18 with at least one living parent/stepparent: Now I want to ask about the kinds of things your parent(s) may have done for you during the past year. Have they/he/she given you any financial help? Given you any help with child care? Given you any help with errands, housework, or home repairs? Given you any gifts? Told you they loved you? Given you advice on a personal matter?

	Things parents did for adult children
Told you they loved you	86%
Gave gifts	83
Gave personal advice	65
Helped with errands, etc.	42
Gave financial help	40
Helped with children	30

By Sex

Male

Told you they loved you	83%
Gave gifts	79
Gave personal advice	61
Helped with errands, etc.	38
Gave financial help	42
Helped with children	23

Female

Told you they loved you	89%
Gave gifts	87
Gave personal advice	69
Helped with errands, etc.	46
Gave financial help	38
Helped with children	37

By Ethnic Background

White

Told you they loved you	87%
Gave gifts	84
Gave personal advice	65
Helped with errands, etc.	41
Gave financial help	38
Helped with children	27

Black

Told you they loved you	82%
Gave gifts	79
Gave personal advice	68
Helped with errands, etc.	46
Gave financial help	54
Helped with children	40

By Age

18–29 Years

Told you they loved you	92%
Gave gifts	93
Gave personal advice	81
Helped with errands, etc.	57
Gave financial help	65
Helped with children	29

30–49 Years

Told you they loved you	84%
Gave gifts	81
Gave personal advice	61
Helped with errands, etc.	38
Gave financial help	28
Helped with children	35

50 Years and Over

Told you they loved you	77%
Gave gifts	62
Gave personal advice	37
Helped with errands, etc.	13
Gave financial help	20
Helped with children	9

*Multiple responses were given.

Asked of those over age 18 with at least one living parent/stepparent: And how about *the kinds of things you may have done for your parent(s) during the past year?**

Things adult children did for parents

Gave gifts...94%
Told them you loved them......................89
Helped with errands, etc. 76
Gave personal advice............................65
Gave financial help.............................30

By Sex

Male

Gave gifts...92%
Told them you loved them......................87
Helped with errands, etc. 78
Gave personal advice............................60
Gave financial help.............................32

Female

Gave gifts...96%
Told them you loved them......................91
Helped with errands, etc. 73
Gave personal advice............................70
Gave financial help.............................28

By Ethnic Background

White

Gave gifts...94%
Told them you loved them......................90
Helped with errands, etc. 76
Gave personal advice............................66
Gave financial help.............................27

Black

Gave gifts...92%
Told them you loved them......................86
Helped with errands, etc. 74
Gave personal advice............................59
Gave financial help.............................55

By Age

18–29 Years

Gave gifts...96%
Told them you loved them......................91
Helped with errands, etc. 85

Gave personal advice............................69
Gave financial help.............................36

30–49 Years

Gave gifts...92%
Told them you loved them......................87
Helped with errands, etc. 72
Gave personal advice............................65
Gave financial help.............................25

50 Years and Over

Gave gifts...94%
Told them you loved them......................90
Helped with errands, etc. 62
Gave personal advice............................56
Gave financial help.............................36

*Multiple responses were given.

Asked of those over age 18 with at least one living sibling: About how often do you usually see your brother/sister? Is it every day, once a week or more, once a month or more, several times a year, once a year, less than once a year, or never?

Every day 12%
Once a week or more...........................26
Once a month or more........................18
Several times a year...........................24
Once a year 11
Less than once a year........................... 8
Never 1

By Sex

Male

Every day 13%
Once a week or more...........................28
Once a month or more........................19
Several times a year...........................20
Once a year 9
Less than once a year...........................10
Never 1

Female

Every day 11%
Once a week or more...........................25
Once a month or more........................17
Several times a year...........................27
Once a year 13

Less than once a year............................6
Never 1

By Ethnic Background

White

Every day 11%
Once a week or more.........................26
Once a month or more.......................18
Several times a year.........................25
Once a year 11
Less than once a year.........................8
Never 1

Black

Every day 18%
Once a week or more.........................30
Once a month or more.......................18
Several times a year.........................14
Once a year 15
Less than once a year.........................5
Never ....*

By Age

18–29 Years

Every day 26%
Once a week or more.........................32
Once a month or more.......................15
Several times a year.........................17
Once a year 5
Less than once a year.........................5
Never ....*

30–49 Years

Every day 8%
Once a week or more.........................27
Once a month or more.......................22
Several times a year.........................24
Once a year 12
Less than once a year.........................6
Never 1

50 Years and Over

Every day 8%
Once a week or more.........................22
Once a month or more.......................15
Several times a year.........................28
Once a year 13

Less than once a year..........................12
Never 2

*Less than 1%

Asked of those over age 18 with at least one living sibling: And about how often do you talk to him/her on the telephone?

Every day 11%
Once a week or more.........................33
Once a month or more.......................29
Several times a year.........................16
Once a year 3
Less than once a year.........................1
Never 6
Don't know......................................1

By Sex

Male

Every day 5%
Once a week or more.........................31
Once a month or more.......................32
Several times a year.........................17
Once a year 4
Less than once a year.........................2
Never 8
Don't know......................................1

Female

Every day 16%
Once a week or more.........................34
Once a month or more.......................26
Several times a year.........................15
Once a year 3
Less than once a year.........................1
Never 5
Don't know......................................*

By Ethnic Background

White

Every day 9%
Once a week or more.........................33
Once a month or more.......................30
Several times a year.........................17
Once a year 3
Less than once a year.........................1
Never 6
Don't know......................................1

Black

Every day 22%
Once a week or more...........................34
Once a month or more..........................20
Several times a year............................13
Once a year 3
Less than once a year 1
Never 7
Don't know ....*

By Age

18–29 Years

Every day 16%
Once a week or more...........................37
Once a month or more..........................28
Several times a year..............................8
Once a year 1
Less than once a year 1
Never 9
Don't know ....*

30–49 Years

Every day 7%
Once a week or more...........................35
Once a month or more..........................30
Several times a year.............................17
Once a year 4
Less than once a year 1
Never 5
Don't know 1

50 Years and Over

Every day 11%
Once a week or more...........................28
Once a month or more..........................29
Several times a year.............................21
Once a year 3
Less than once a year 1
Never 6
Don't know 1

*Less than 1%

Asked of those over age 18 with at least one living parent/stepparent and/or at least one living sibling: Now I'm going to read you some phrases that might describe the kind of relationship you have with your father/mother/brother/sister. For each pair

of words or phrases that I read, please tell me which one best describes your relationship with (relative):

Close or distant?

	Father	Mother	Sibling(s)
Close	69%	90%	85%
Distant	24	8	12
Neither (volunteered)	7	2	3
Don't know	*	*	*

*Less than 1%

Tense or easygoing?

	Father	Mother	Sibling(s)
Tense	21%	12%	10%
Easygoing	74	85	87
Neither (volunteered)	3	3	2
Don't know	2	*	1

*Less than 1%

Fun or boring?

	Father	Mother	Sibling(s)
Fun	72%	87%	87%
Boring	18	7	8
Neither (volunteered)	8	5	4
Don't know	2	1	1

Warm and affectionate or cold and restrained?

	Father	Mother	Sibling(s)
Warm and affectionate	70%	91%	87%
Cold and restrained	20	5	8
Neither (volunteered)	9	3	5
Don't know	1	1	*

*Less than 1%

Asked of those over age 18 with at least one living grandparent: How close is your relationship with your grandmother/ grandfather? Would you say your relationship is very close, somewhat close, somewhat distant, or very distant?

Very close 30%
Somewhat close 48
Somewhat distant 16
Very distant 5
Neither close nor distant
    (volunteered).................................. 1

By Sex

Male

Very close 29%
Somewhat close 46
Somewhat distant 20
Very distant 4
Neither close nor distant
    (volunteered).................................. 1

Female

Very close 31%
Somewhat close 50
Somewhat distant 12
Very distant 6
Neither close nor distant
    (volunteered).................................. 1

By Ethnic Background

White

Very close 27%
Somewhat close 50
Somewhat distant 17
Very distant 5
Neither close nor distant
    (volunteered).................................. 1

Black

Very close 50%
Somewhat close 42
Somewhat distant 4
Very distant 4
Neither close nor distant
    (volunteered)................................. *

By Age**

18–29 Years

Very close 27%
Somewhat close 51
Somewhat distant 17

Very distant 4
Neither close nor distant
    (volunteered).................................. 1

30–49 Years

Very close 33%
Somewhat close 44
Somewhat distant 15
Very distant 7
Neither close nor distant
    (volunteered).................................. 1

*Less than 1%
**The "50 Years and Over" category was omitted because the sample of respondents was too small.

Asked of those over age 18 with at least one living grandparent: About how often do you usually see your grandmother/grandfather?

Every day 5%
Once a week or more..........................18
Once a month or more.........................21
Several times a year...........................24
Once a year 15
Less than once a year..........................16
Never 1

By Sex

Male

Every day 5%
Once a week or more..........................20
Once a month or more.........................22
Several times a year...........................22
Once a year 13
Less than once a year..........................16
Never 2

Female

Every day 4%
Once a week or more..........................17
Once a month or more.........................20
Several times a year...........................26
Once a year 17
Less than once a year..........................15
Never 1

By Ethnic Background

White

Every day	4%
Once a week or more	16
Once a month or more	20
Several times a year	27
Once a year	16
Less than once a year	16
Never	1

Black

Every day	8%
Once a week or more	38
Once a month or more	20
Several times a year	12
Once a year	10
Less than once a year	8
Never	4

By Age*

18–29 Years

Every day	5%
Once a week or more	21
Once a month or more	25
Several times a year	23
Once a year	11
Less than once a year	14
Never	1

30–49 Years

Every day	4%
Once a week or more	14
Once a month or more	14
Several times a year	26
Once a year	21
Less than once a year	19
Never	2

*The "50 Years and Over" category was omitted because the sample of respondents was too small.

Asked of those over age 18 with at least one living grandparent: And about how often do you talk to her/him on the telephone?

Every day	2%
Once a week or more	19
Once a month or more	25
Several times a year	20
Once a year	9
Less than once a year	6
Never	19

*Asked of those over age 18: During the last year, that is, since May 1988, have you been to a wedding, funeral, or religious ceremony for a relative? Been to a large family get-together for a holiday or other social occasion? Given a birthday gift to a relative, other than a parent?**

	Those who have
Given birthday gift	77%
Attended family get-together	70
Attended family wedding, etc.	57

*Multiple responses were given.

*Asked of those over age 18: How far back, in terms of generations, does your knowledge or awareness of your family go? For example, do you know the names, occupations, or anything else definite about your (relative)?**

	Knowledge of family goes back to
Grandparents	82%
Great-grandparents	46
Great-great-grandparents	19
Further than that	13

By Sex

Male

Grandparents	82%
Great-grandparents	47
Great-great-grandparents	20
Further than that	15

Female

Grandparents	82%
Great-grandparents	46
Great-great-grandparents	18
Further than that	12

By Ethnic Background

White

Grandparents	85%
Great-grandparents	49

*Multiple responses were given.

Great-great-grandparents 21
Further than that................................14

Black

Grandparents.....................................59%
Great-grandparents..............................33
Great-great-grandparents 8
Further than that................................ 4

By Age

18–29 Years

Grandparents.....................................85%
Great-grandparents..............................49
Great-great-grandparents 20
Further than that................................13

30–49 Years

Grandparents.....................................85%
Great-grandparents..............................55
Great-great-grandparents 24
Further than that................................15

50 Years and Over

Grandparents.....................................77%
Great-grandparents..............................36
Great-great-grandparents 13
Further than that................................11

Note: Challenging those who believe that the American family is in decline, a new Gallup Poll shows that family ties still bind across the nation. Changing life-styles, distance, divorce, and the demands of life in the 1980s do not prevent most Americans from staying connected to their extended families—parents and grandparents, brothers and sisters, uncles and aunts.

Gallup interviewed adults across the United States to find out how far people live from their extended families, how often they visit and talk with their relatives, and how well they get along with different family members. The poll finds that both men and women tend to stay in touch with their extended families over the course of their lifetimes, but the emotional bond to family is stronger and more enduring for women than it is for men. These are among the key findings:

• Despite the mobility of the population, most adult children live fairly close to their parents. Two thirds (67%) of adults with at least one living parent reside within an hour's driving distance of a parent, including one in seven respondents (13%) who lives in the same household with a mother or father.

• People of all ages and circumstances look to their kinfolk as an important source of financial aid and help with day-to-day problems. These practical concerns, however, are not the only reason Americans stay in contact with their relatives. With few exceptions, people enjoy being with family members and wish that they had more time to spend with them.

• Women continue to act as the glue that holds extended families together. Of all the kinship bonds studied, the mother-daughter relationship proves to be the strongest one. It is a bond that spans generations. Women with more than one living grandparent over-whelmingly feel closest to their mother's mother. The female-to-female bonding pattern extends to other relationships, including sister-sister and aunt-niece.

• Sons and daughters both report problems more often in getting along with their father than their mother, but much of this can be explained by divorce. Children of divorced parents generally are raised by the mother, and a majority of them do not remain close to the father after the divorce.

• While young men and women feel about equally connected to their extended families, the strength of that bond diminishes somewhat in men as they reach their 30s. Women generally maintain the same feelings toward their blood relatives as they grow older.

• Married people of both sexes tend to say that the couple spends more time with the wife's family than with the husband's.

Easier and more affordable communications and transportation have helped bridge the distance between family members that has resulted from geographic mobility. Even when physically separated by great distances, parents and children (86%), brothers and sisters (73%), and grandparents and grandchildren (46%) keep in touch at least monthly by telephone.

Moreover, the interstate highway system and more affordable air travel allow relatives who live farther apart to see each other without a great sacrifice of money or time. This may explain why as many as seven in ten adults (70%) say that they were able to attend one or more large family social gatherings in the past year. Close to six in ten (57%) have attended a wedding, funeral, or religious ceremony for a relative.

The poll also shows that Mother still holds her revered status in American society. People are more likely to be close to their mother than they are to any other extended-family member. Indeed, as many as 90% say that they have a close relationship with their mother. Similar proportions characterize this relationship as warm and affectionate (91%) and fun (87%), but they are somewhat less unanimous (85%) in regarding their interaction with her as easygoing.

Father-child relationships are much more likely to be troubled. One in four (24%) adult children feels emotionally distant from Dad, and sizable proportions describe their relationship with their father as tense (21%), cold and restrained (20%), and boring (18%).

These adult children and their parents interact in a variety of ways. The exchange of gifts and affection is almost universal. Nine in ten adult children say that they have given their parents gifts (94%) and told them that they loved them (89%) during the past year. Nearly as many say that they received expressions of love (86%) and gifts (83%) from parents. Almost two thirds (65%) add that they have advised Mom or Dad on a personal matter in the past year while the same number (65%) of adult children has taken advice from a parent.

Offering help with errands, housework, or home repairs is more often done by children for their parents (76%) than by parents for their children (42%). Parents, however, are more often the source of financial aid (40%), although three in ten adult children say that they helped a parent financially over the past year.

As for the oldest generation of the three dealt with here, respondents were asked about their relationship with their grandparents. Some 78% considered this relationship to be close, while only 21% found it distant. This interaction may contribute to people's awareness of family history. Thirty-two percent had knowledge of their great-great-grandparents or beyond, and 46% knew something about their great-grandparents. Not surprisingly, 82% were familiar with many facts about their grandparents.

JULY 12
OLIVER NORTH

Interviewing Date: 7/6–9/89
Survey #GO 89136-1

As you may have heard, Oliver North was sentenced for his involvement in the Iran-contra case. Do you think the sentence was fair, the sentence was too harsh, or North got off too easy?

Sentence was fair.................................49%
Sentence was too harsh 20
North got off too easy.........................26
Hadn't heard (volunteered).......................1
Don't know 4

By Politics

Republicans

Sentence was fair.................................56%
Sentence was too harsh 25
North got off too easy.........................15
Hadn't heard (volunteered).......................1
Don't know 3

Democrats

Sentence was fair.................................44%
Sentence was too harsh 17
North got off too easy.........................35
Hadn't heard (volunteered).......................*
Don't know 4

Independents

Sentence was fair.................................46%
Sentence was too harsh 19
North got off too easy.........................29
Hadn't heard (volunteered).......................1
Don't know 5

*Less than 1%

Note: A plurality (49%) of Americans says that Colonel Oliver North was treated fairly by the judge who sentenced him recently for his conviction in the Iran-*contra* case. Given that North will not go to jail and the public generally has been sympathetic toward him, such a response might have been expected. Among those who disagree with the sentence, nearly as many reply that it was too harsh (20%) as think that North was treated too leniently (26%).

Reactions to the North sentencing, as expected, differ along political lines. Republicans (56%) are more likely than Democrats (44%) or independents (46%) to find that the sentence was fair. Similarly, those who approve of George Bush's job performance are more likely than the president's critics to approve of North's sentence (53% versus 31%).

JULY 12
ABORTION

Interviewing Date: 7/6–9/89
Survey #GO 89136-1

Do you approve or disapprove of this week's Supreme Court decision allowing states to pass laws that restrict abortion? Do you feel strongly about this, or not?

Approve...37%
    Strongly...................................28
    Not strongly..............................9
Disapprove.......................................55
    Strongly...................................44
    Not strongly.............................11
No opinion.. 8

By Sex

Male

Approve...41%
    Strongly...................................29
    Not strongly.............................12
Disapprove.......................................51
    Strongly...................................40
    Not strongly.............................11
No opinion.. 8

Female

Approve...34%
    Strongly...................................28
    Not strongly..............................6

Disapprove...58
    Strongly...................................47
    Not strongly.............................11
No opinion.. 8

By Ethnic Background

White

Approve...39%
    Strongly...................................29
    Not strongly.............................10
Disapprove.......................................54
    Strongly...................................43
    Not strongly.............................11
No opinion.. 7

Nonwhite

Approve...30%
    Strongly...................................26
    Not strongly..............................4
Disapprove.......................................60
    Strongly...................................49
    Not strongly.............................11
No opinion..10

By Education

College Graduate

Approve...34%
    Strongly...................................27
    Not strongly..............................7
Disapprove.......................................59
    Strongly...................................47
    Not strongly.............................12
No opinion.. 7

College Incomplete

Approve...40%
    Strongly...................................30
    Not strongly.............................10
Disapprove.......................................55
    Strongly...................................49
    Not strongly..............................6
No opinion.. 5

High-School Graduate

Approve...37%
    Strongly...................................28
    Not strongly..............................9

Disapprove...55
    Strongly................................. 43
    Not strongly........................... 12
No opinion............................. 8

Less Than High-School Graduate

Approve..39%
    Strongly................................. 30
    Not strongly...........................9
Disapprove...50
    Strongly................................. 37
    Not strongly........................... 13
No opinion...11

By Region

East

Approve...34%
    Strongly................................. 24
    Not strongly........................... 10
Disapprove...58
    Strongly................................. 46
    Not strongly........................... 12
No opinion....................................... 8

Midwest

Approve...39%
    Strongly................................. 29
    Not strongly........................... 10
Disapprove...52
    Strongly................................. 39
    Not strongly........................... 13
No opinion.......................................9

South

Approve...40%
    Strongly................................. 32
    Not strongly...........................8
Disapprove...51
    Strongly................................. 42
    Not strongly...........................9
No opinion.......................................9

West

Approve...35%
    Strongly................................. 26
    Not strongly...........................9
Disapprove...59
    Strongly................................. 50
    Not strongly...........................9
No opinion....................................... 6

By Age
18–29 Years

Approve...32%
    Strongly................................. 24
    Not strongly...........................8
Disapprove...64
    Strongly................................. 56
    Not strongly...........................8
No opinion............................. 4

30–49 Years

Approve...41%
    Strongly................................. 32
    Not strongly...........................9
Disapprove...53
    Strongly................................. 42
    Not strongly........................... 11
No opinion....................................... 6

50 Years and Over

Approve...38%
    Strongly................................. 27
    Not strongly........................... 11
Disapprove...50
    Strongly................................. 37
    Not strongly........................... 13
No opinion...12

By Household Income
$50,000 and Over

Approve...34%
    Strongly................................. 28
    Not strongly...........................6
Disapprove...60
    Strongly................................. 52
    Not strongly...........................8
No opinion....................................... 6

$30,000–$49,999

Approve...41%
    Strongly................................. 28
    Not strongly........................... 13
Disapprove...52
    Strongly................................. 42
    Not strongly........................... 10
No opinion....................................... 7

$20,000–$29,999

Approve...41%
    Strongly................................. 32
    Not strongly...........................9

Disapprove.............................55
    Strongly..............................42
    Not strongly.........................13
No opinion............................4

Under $20,000

Approve...............................35%
    Strongly..............................26
    Not strongly..........................9
Disapprove............................55
    Strongly..............................43
    Not strongly.........................12
No opinion...........................10

By Politics

Republicans

Approve...............................46%
    Strongly..............................35
    Not strongly.........................11
Disapprove............................47
    Strongly..............................40
    Not strongly..........................7
No opinion............................7

Democrats

Approve...............................32%
    Strongly..............................23
    Not strongly..........................9
Disapprove............................60
    Strongly..............................46
    Not strongly.........................14
No opinion............................8

Independents

Approve...............................33%
    Strongly..............................26
    Not strongly..........................7
Disapprove............................57
    Strongly..............................46
    Not strongly.........................11
No opinion...........................10

By Religion

Born-Again Protestants

Approve...............................48%
    Strongly..............................40
    Not strongly..........................8

Disapprove.............................44
    Strongly..............................32
    Not strongly.........................12
No opinion............................8

Other Protestants

Approve...............................29%
    Strongly..............................19
    Not strongly.........................10
Disapprove............................62
    Strongly..............................51
    Not strongly.........................11
No opinion............................9

Catholics

Approve...............................42%
    Strongly..............................32
    Not strongly.........................10
Disapprove............................50
    Strongly..............................39
    Not strongly.........................11
No opinion............................8

Those Who Approve of President Bush

Approve...............................43%
    Strongly..............................32
    Not strongly.........................11
Disapprove............................51
    Strongly..............................40
    Not strongly.........................11
No opinion............................6

Those Who Disapprove of President Bush

Approve...............................24%
    Strongly..............................19
    Not strongly..........................5
Disapprove............................67
    Strongly..............................55
    Not strongly.........................12
No opinion............................9

In 1973 the Supreme Court ruled that states cannot place restrictions on a woman's right to an abortion during the first three months of pregnancy. Would you like to see this ruling overturned, or not?

Yes...................................34%
No....................................58
No opinion............................8

By Sex

Male

Yes	35%
No	57
No opinion	8

Female

Yes	34%
No	58
No opinion	8

By Ethnic Background

White

Yes	34%
No	58
No opinion	8

Nonwhite

Yes	39%
No	55
No opinion	6

By Education

College Graduate

Yes	28%
No	66
No opinion	6

College Incomplete

Yes	34%
No	61
No opinion	5

High-School Graduate

Yes	36%
No	56
No opinion	8

Less Than High-School Graduate

Yes	40%
No	50
No opinion	10

By Region

East

Yes	32%
No	60
No opinion	8

Midwest

Yes	36%
No	56
No opinion	8

South

Yes	39%
No	53
No opinion	8

West

Yes	28%
No	66
No opinion	6

By Age

18–29 Years

Yes	30%
No	65
No opinion	5

30–49 Years

Yes	34%
No	61
No opinion	5

50 Years and Over

Yes	38%
No	50
No opinion	12

By Income

$50,000 and Over

Yes	31%
No	63
No opinion	6

$30,000-$49,999

Yes..29%
No...63
No opinion... 8

$20,000-$29,999

Yes..36%
No...61
No opinion... 3

Under $20,000

Yes..40%
No...51
No opinion... 9

By Politics

Republicans

Yes..40%
No...53
No opinion... 7

Democrats

Yes..34%
No...59
No opinion... 7

Independents

Yes..29%
No...61
No opinion..10

By Religion

Born-Again Protestants

Yes..50%
No...41
No opinion... 9

Other Protestants

Yes..24%
No...68
No opinion... 8

Catholics

Yes..38%
No...55
No opinion... 7

Those Who Approve of President Bush

Yes..36%
No...58
No opinion... 6

Those Who Disapprove of President Bush

Yes..34%
No...61
No opinion... 5

Selected National Trend

	Yes	No	No opinion
April 1989*	39%	51%	10%
December 1988	37	58	5
January 1988	37	57	6

*Gallup survey for *Newsweek*

As I read some restrictions on abortions that are being considered in some states, tell me if you would favor or oppose such a restriction in your state:

Not allowing abortions to be performed in public hospitals unless the abortion is required to save a woman's life?

Favor 54%
Oppose...43
No opinion... 3

By Sex

Male

Favor 56%
Oppose...11
No opinion... 3

Female

Favor 52%
Oppose...44
No opinion... 4

In cases where the mother is five months pregnant, requiring a test to see if the fetus might survive outside of the womb before allowing the abortion?

Favor 52%
Oppose 41
No opinion 7

By Sex

Male

Favor 52%
Oppose 42
No opinion 6

Female

Favor 53%
Oppose 40
No opinion 7

Requiring that women under 18 years of age get parental consent before they are allowed to have an abortion?

Favor 67%
Oppose 29
No opinion 4

By Sex

Male

Favor 71%
Oppose 26
No opinion 3

Female

Favor 63%
Oppose 31
No opinion 6

Passing laws and regulations that would make it very difficult for women's clinics that perform abortions to continue to operate?

Favor 36%
Oppose 59
No opinion 5

By Sex

Male

Favor 41%
Oppose 56
No opinion 3

Female

Favor 35%
Oppose 60
No opinion 5

Do you feel that it is likely or unlikely that laws will be passed in your state that will make it difficult for a woman to get an abortion?

Likely 54%
Unlikely 36
No opinion 10

By Sex

Male

Likely 54%
Unlikely 37
No opinion 9

Female

Likely 55%
Unlikely 34
No opinion 11

Which political party better reflects your views on abortion—the Republicans or the Democrats?

Republicans 34%
Democrats 37
Neither (volunteered) 8
Both (volunteered) 1
No opinion 20

By Sex

Male

Republicans 36%
Democrats 35
Neither (volunteered) 11
Both (volunteered) 2
No opinion 16

Female

Republicans 32%
Democrats 38
Neither (volunteered) 5
Both (volunteered) 1
No opinion 24

Republicans

Republicans.......................................66%
Democrats 16
Neither (volunteered)........................ 4
Both (volunteered).............................. 1
No opinion..13

Democrats

Republicans.......................................13%
Democrats 63
Neither (volunteered)........................ 3
Both (volunteered).............................. 2
No opinion..19

Independents

Republicans.......................................24%
Democrats 31
Neither (volunteered)........................16
Both (volunteered).............................. 2
No opinion..27

Do you approve or disapprove of the way George Bush has handled the abortion issue?

Approve...43%
Disapprove..35
No opinion..22

By Sex

Male

Approve...50%
Disapprove..30
No opinion..20

Female

Approve...37%
Disapprove..40
No opinion..23

By Politics

Republicans

Approve...59%
Disapprove..25
No opinion..16

Democrats

Approve...33%
Disapprove..43
No opinion..24

Independents

Approve...38%
Disapprove..37
No opinion..25

As a result of the Court's ruling, are you more likely to do any of the following:

Take a political candidate's position on abortion more into account when deciding which candidate to support?

Yes..61%
No..34
No opinion.. 5

By Sex

Male

Yes..58%
No..39
No opinion.. 3

Female

Yes..64%
No..29
No opinion.. 7

By Politics

Republicans

Yes..65%
No..32
No opinion.. 3

Democrats

Yes..60%
No..35
No opinion.. 5

Independents

Yes..59%
No..34
No opinion.. 7

Contribute money or time to an organization supporting your position on abortion?

Yes......................................44%
No...53
No opinion.............................3

By Sex

Male

Yes......................................39%
No...59
No opinion.............................2

Female

Yes......................................48%
No...48
No opinion.............................4

By Politics

Republicans

Yes......................................41%
No...57
No opinion.............................2

Democrats

Yes......................................47%
No...51
No opinion.............................2

Independents

Yes......................................45%
No...51
No opinion.............................4

Call or write an elected official to register your opinion on abortion?

Yes......................................54%
No...44
No opinion.............................2

By Sex

Male

Yes......................................48%
No...50
No opinion.............................2

Female

Yes......................................59%
No...39
No opinion.............................2

By Politics

Republicans

Yes......................................53%
No...45
No opinion.............................2

Democrats

Yes......................................54%
No...43
No opinion.............................3

Independents

Yes......................................54%
No...44
No opinion.............................2

Take part in a public demonstration in support of your position on abortion?

Yes......................................25%
No...72
No opinion.............................3

By Sex

Male

Yes......................................21%
No...78
No opinion.............................1

Female

Yes......................................29%
No...67
No opinion.............................4

By Politics

Republicans

Yes......................................22%
No...77
No opinion.............................1

Democrats

Yes...28%
No..70
No opinion.......................................2

Independents

Yes...26%
No..70
No opinion.......................................4

Note: The Supreme Court's recent decision allowing states to restrict abortions receives a strong and mostly negative reaction from the public. In a new Gallup Poll, 55 percent disapprove of the decision, while 37 percent approve. Seven in ten (72%) say that they have strong opinions one way or the other about the decision.

Americans remain deeply divided in their attitudes toward the abortion issue. Neither side of the debate can claim to have a majority of the public firmly in its camp. While most respondents oppose a complete reversal of the *Roe v. Wade* decision in 1973 that gave women unrestricted access to abortions in the first three months of pregnancy, most would favor some new restrictions at the state level.

Women are reacting more strongly than men to the Court's decision. Now that the states have greater authority to restrict abortion, six in ten (64%) women say that they will give greater weight to a candidate's position on the issue when they vote. A similar proportion (59%) say that they are now more likely to call or write an elected official to register an opinion on this issue. About one half (48%) of women say that they are more likely to contribute time or money to an organization supporting their own point of view, and three in ten (29%) are more likely to participate in a public demonstration on abortion.

Men are consistently less likely to express these attitudes. A majority (58%) of men, however, does say that the abortion issue is going to be a more important consideration in the voting booth.

Women are anything but united in their beliefs about abortion. Overall, close to one half of the women (46%) are classified as "pro-choice," based on their attitudes toward past and present Court decisions, somewhat above the proportion of men on the pro-choice side of

the issue (40%). Roughly one third of both men (35%) and women (34%) take the antiabortion position of the so-called "right to life" movement that *Roe v. Wade* should be overturned.

Women on both sides of the abortion issue are equally likely to say that the recent Missouri decision will act as an incentive to their getting personally involved with the politics of abortion, with one exception. Those favoring an overturn of *Roe v. Wade* are somewhat more likely than pro-choice women to say that the ruling increases their chances of contributing time or money to an organization supporting their own point of view.

Both sexes are inclined to support some new restrictions on abortion at the state level. The kinds of restrictions upheld by the Court in its decision in the Missouri case, however, are supported by only slim majorities. Requiring that parents be notified when a woman under age 18 is seeking an abortion wins the approval of two thirds (67%) of the public. A *Newsweek* poll completed last week also showed majority support (61%) for a ban on publicly funded abortions.

These kinds of restrictions were not at issue in the recent Missouri case. One type that applies to the Missouri decision—a ban on abortions in public hospitals—is supported by 54%. A similar level of public support (52%) is found for state-mandated fetal viability tests beginning at the fifth month of pregnancy, another component of Missouri law governing abortion. And looking ahead to a case that the Court will consider next fall, a majority (59%) of Americans opposes the general idea of passing laws to make it more difficult for abortion clinics to operate.

Both political parties have divisions within their ranks on abortion. The issue clearly helps the GOP with southerners and Evangelical Protestants, two groups who tend to oppose legal abortions. The degree to which Evangelicals increasingly have favored the Republican party helps to explain why self-described Republicans are more likely than Democrats to favor the overturn of *Roe v. Wade* (40% versus 34%). Yet a sizable proportion of Republicans (36%) opposes any change in the legal status of abortion, including the Court's latest ruling. Upper-income people and college graduates—groups that generally have Republican leanings—tend to be pro-choice.

Overall, the two parties rate about evenly when Americans are asked which one better reflects their views on abortion—37% name the Democrats and 34%, Republican. The issue may give the Democrats a slight advantage among political independents, who generally have less restrictive attitudes toward abortion. Independents favor the Democratic party by a margin of 31% to 24% on this issue.

President George Bush gets a mixed rating from the public on how he has handled this controversy—43% approve, while 35% disapprove. More than one in five (22%) expresses no opinion of Bush's handling of the issue. Opponents of legal abortion tend to approve, while a majority of people with pro-choice attitudes disapproves. Those most pleased with Bush on abortion tend to be male, Republican, and of the Catholic or an Evangelical Protestant faith. Those most likely to criticize him on the issue are female, college educated, more affluent, non-Catholic, non-Evangelical, and Democrat or independent politically.

JULY 19
U.S. SPACE PROGRAM—TWENTY YEARS AFTER LANDING ON THE MOON

Interviewing Date: 7/6–9/89
Survey #GO 89136-1

I am going to ask you several questions about government spending. In answering, please bear in mind that sooner or later all government spending has to be taken care of out of the taxes that you and other Americans pay. As I mention each program, tell me whether the amount of money now being spent for that purpose should be increased, kept at the present level, reduced, or ended altogether:

The U.S. space program?

Increased	27%
Kept same	42
Reduced	22
Ended	4
No opinion	5

Selected National Trend

	1986*	1984*
Increased	26%	21%
Kept same	50	48
Reduced	14	23
Ended	5	5
No opinion	5	3

*The 1986 and 1984 results in this and the following four national trends are taken from Gallup surveys for *Newsweek*.

Federal money to improve the quality of public education?

Increased	72%
Kept same	19
Reduced	5
Ended	1
No opinion	3

Selected National Trend

	1986	1984
Increased	63%	65%
Kept same	26	27
Reduced	7	5
Ended	1	1
No opinion	3	2

Improving medical and health care for Americans generally?

Increased	73%
Kept same	18
Reduced	4
Ended	1
No opinion	4

Selected National Trend

	1986	1984
Increased	64%	63%
Kept same	27	28
Reduced	5	5
Ended	1	1
No opinion	3	3

Providing food programs for low-income families?

Increased	51%
Kept same	35

Reduced..9
Ended..1
No opinion..4

Selected National Trend

	1986	1984
Increased	46%	48%
Kept same	35	37
Reduced	11	12
Ended	3	1
No opinion	5	2

Total spending for defense and military purposes?

Increased..17%
Kept same...39
Reduced..38
Ended..2
No opinion..4

Selected National Trend

	1986	1984
Increased	21%	18%
Kept same	41	43
Reduced	31	35
Ended	2	2
No opinion	5	2

Do you happen to recall who spoke the phrase "That's one small step for a man, one giant leap for mankind," and what historic event he was referring to?

Neil Armstrong; moon landing...............59%
Incorrect; don't know...........................41

Do you happen to know who was the first person to walk on the moon?

Neil Armstrong...................................39%
Incorrect; don't know...........................61

How important do you think it is for the United States to be the first country to land a person on Mars? Would you say this is very important, somewhat important, not too important, or not important at all?

Very important...................................19%
Somewhat important............................32
Not too important...............................25
Not important at all.............................23
Don't know.......................................1

Asked of those 25 years and over: In 1969, did you happen to watch on television the first manned moon landing, or not?

Yes...82%
No..15
Don't remember.................................3

By Age

25–29 Years

Yes...61%
No..33
Don't remember.................................6

30 Years and Over

Yes...85%
No..13
Don't remember.................................2

Which country do you think is further ahead in space research—the United States, the Soviet Union, or a European country?

United States..................................52%
Soviet Union...................................34
European country...............................2
Other...2
Don't know.....................................10

Selected National Trend

	1965	1961
United States	47%	38%
Soviet Union	24	38
European country	*	*
Other	*	*
Don't know	29	24

*Less than 1%

Do you think there are people somewhat like ourselves living on other planets in the universe, or not?

Yes...41%
No..48
Don't know.....................................11

Some people feel the U.S. space program should concentrate on unmanned missions like Voyager 2, which will send back information from the planet Neptune.

Others say we should concentrate on maintaining a manned space program like the space shuttle. Which comes closer to your view?

Unmanned missions............................40%
Manned missions 43
Both equal (volunteered)......................9
Don't know.......................................8

Which of the following do you think should be our top priority for the space program?

Basic research on solar
  system and planets..........................30%
Developing zero-gravity
  manufacturing and other
  commercial technologies
  in space.......................................18
Developing space-based
  defense shield................................14
Mining natural resources
  on moon and other planets.................23
Other...2
Don't know......................................13

On the whole, do you feel our investment in space research is worthwhile, or do you think it would be better spent on domestic programs such as health care and education?

Investment is worthwhile.....................43%
Better spent on domestic programs...........52
Don't know.......................................5

By Sex

Male

Investment is worthwhile.....................51%
Better spent on domestic programs...........43
Don't know.......................................6

Female

Investment is worthwhile.....................35%
Better spent on domestic programs...........59
Don't know.......................................6

By Ethnic Background

White

Investment is worthwhile.....................46%
Better spent on domestic programs...........48
Don't know.......................................6

Nonwhite

Investment is worthwhile.....................22%
Better spent on domestic programs...........73
Don't know.......................................5

By Education

College Graduate

Investment is worthwhile.....................58%
Better spent on domestic programs...........39
Don't know.......................................3

College Incomplete

Investment is worthwhile.....................51%
Better spent on domestic programs...........43
Don't know.......................................6

High-School Graduate

Investment is worthwhile.....................38%
Better spent on domestic programs...........56
Don't know.......................................6

Less Than High-School Graduate

Investment is worthwhile.....................26%
Better spent on domestic programs...........66
Don't know.......................................8

College Graduate (Male)

Investment is worthwhile.....................63%
Better spent on domestic programs...........33
Don't know.......................................4

College Graduate (Female)

Investment is worthwhile.....................47%
Better spent on domestic programs...........49
Don't know.......................................4

Less Than College (Male)

Investment is worthwhile.....................42%
Better spent on domestic programs...........51
Don't know.......................................7

Less Than College (Female)

Investment is worthwhile.....................28%
Better spent on domestic programs...........66
Don't know.......................................6

By Region

East

Investment is worthwhile.......................44%
Better spent on domestic programs...........49
Don't know...7

Midwest

Investment is worthwhile.......................43%
Better spent on domestic programs...........54
Don't know...3

South

Investment is worthwhile.......................43%
Better spent on domestic programs...........52
Don't know...5

West

Investment is worthwhile.......................41%
Better spent on domestic programs...........52
Don't know...7

By Age

18–29 Years

Investment is worthwhile.......................43%
Better spent on domestic programs...........55
Don't know...2

30–49 Years

Investment is worthwhile.......................50%
Better spent on domestic programs...........45
Don't know...5

50 Years and Over

Investment is worthwhile.......................35%
Better spent on domestic programs...........57
Don't know...8

By Income

$50,000 and Over

Investment is worthwhile.......................63%
Better spent on domestic programs...........33
Don't know...4

$30,000–$49,999

Investment is worthwhile.......................46%
Better spent on domestic programs...........48
Don't know...6

$20,000–$29,999

Investment is worthwhile.......................43%
Better spent on domestic programs...........52
Don't know...5

Under $20,000

Investment is worthwhile.......................28%
Better spent on domestic programs...........66
Don't know...6

By Politics

Republicans

Investment is worthwhile.......................52%
Better spent on domestic programs...........43
Don't know...5

Democrats

Investment is worthwhile.......................31%
Better spent on domestic programs...........63
Don't know...6

Independents

Investment is worthwhile.......................45%
Better spent on domestic programs...........49
Don't know...6

Note: Twenty years after America first put men on the moon, the public shows only a limited commitment to the U.S. space program. This lukewarm attitude about future space exploration is a consequence of increased awareness of domestic problems, coupled with decreased concern for the U.S.-Soviet rivalry that propelled the space race during the 1960s.

The latest Gallup Poll finds relatively little support for an expanded space program, and even today's scaled-down effort—with a budget about one quarter lower in real terms than it was in 1969—fails to win solid backing from the public at large. Less than one half (43%) of the adult population believes that our country's investment in space research is worthwhile in light of other national priorities.

While support for space spending increased somewhat in the aftermath of the *Challenger* disaster three years ago, as the public rallied to NASA's side during a national tragedy, that trend has been reversed. Currently, about as many Americans would cut NASA's budget or eliminate it altogether (26%) as would increase government spending on space (27%).

Although putting the first man on the moon seemed important two decades ago, most Americans now are not inclined to put a high priority on our sending the first manned probe to Mars. Only one in five (19%) believes that it is very important that the United States make the first manned landing on the red planet. Close to one half (48%) say that reaching Mars first is not very important.

The public is divided over whether manned missions should be the focus of our space program, an issue that has been hotly debated by space experts since the *Challenger* disaster. Four in ten (43%) prefer that manned missions like the shuttle have priority, while a similar proportion (40%) prefers unmanned probes like *Voyager 2*, scheduled to complete its tour of the outer planets when it sends back the first close-up photographs of the planet Neptune.

Today, beating the Soviets in space seems much less critical than it did in the 1960s. Despite NASA's recent troubles, most now see the United States as having the advantage. One half (52%) considers the United States as the world leader in space research, while one third (34%) sees the Soviet Union in the lead.

The space program may be suffering from its association with the Defense Department at a time when four in ten Americans (38%) want to reduce military spending. The poll finds that those who favor defense cuts are twice as likely as other respondents to call for a reduction in NASA's budget.

Those Americans who are most supportive of the space program have a well-defined profile. Most likely to find that our investment in space is worthwhile are men (51%), college graduates (58%), those with household incomes of $50,000 or more (63%), and Republicans (52%). The lack of support for space spending among better-educated women may result from the historic male dominance of the space and aviation field. It was not until 1983 that the United States first sent a woman—Sally Ride—into earth orbit. College-educated women divide down the middle on whether space is a good investment, while college-educated men support NASA.

People who are supportive of the space program are more likely to believe that life forms similar to humans exist elsewhere in the universe and to prefer that manned missions rather than unmanned probes be the focus of the effort. While a plurality of both the overall public and those in favor of funding space programs wants basic research of the planets and the solar system to be NASA's top priority, the biggest backers of space research are more likely to favor the development of new technologies that have commercial applications.

"That's one small step for a man, one giant leap for mankind." Neil Armstrong's words as he became the first human to set foot on the lunar surface have proved to be memorable, but most Americans cannot recall the name of the man who said them. Close to six in ten (59%) correctly associate the "giant leap" quotation with the moon landing or Armstrong, but fewer than one half overall (39%) and a similar proportion (40%) who claims to have watched the moon landing on television in 1969 can specifically remember him as the first man to walk on the moon.

JULY 26
PARTY BETTER FOR PEACE AND PROSPERITY

Interviewing Date: 7/18–21/89
Survey #GO 89136-2

Looking ahead for the next few years, which political party do you think would be more likely to keep the United States out of World War III—the Republican party or the Democratic party?

Republican 45%
Democratic 31
No difference; no opinion 24

Selected National Trend

	Sept. 1988*	Dec. 1987*
Republican party	43%	33%
Democratic party	33	39
No difference; no opinion	24	28

*Asked of registered voters

Which political party—the Republican or the Democratic—do you think will do a better job of keeping the country prosperous?

Republican 51%
Democratic 30
No difference; no opinion......................19

Selected National Trend

	Sept. 1988*	Dec. 1987*
Republican party	52%	41%
Democratic party	34	40
No difference; no opinion	14	19

*Asked of registered voters

In politics, as of today, do you consider yourself a Republican, a Democrat, or an independent?

Selected National Trend*

	Republican	Democrat	Independent
1989			
2d quarter	34%	38%	28%
1st quarter	33	42	25
1988	30	42	28
1987	30	41	29
1986	32	39	29
1985	33	38	29
1984	31	40	29
1983	25	44	31
1982	26	45	29
1981	28	42	30
1980	24	46	30
1979	22	45	33
1976	23	47	30
1975	22	45	33
1972	28	43	29
1968	27	46	27
1964	25	53	22
1960	30	47	23
1954	34	46	20
1950	33	45	22
1946	40	39	21
1937	34	50	16

*Those saying they have no party preference, or who named other parties, are excluded.

Note: Positive feelings among Americans about the state of the U.S. economy and the international situation have helped return the image of the Republican party to the postwar high it enjoyed under Ronald Reagan prior to the Iran-*contra* scandal. Halfway through George Bush's first year as president, the GOP has an advantage over the Democratic party on Gallup barometers of party image. Respondents see the Republicans as better able than the Democrats to keep the country prosperous (51% versus 30%) and to maintain the peace (45% versus 31%).

The GOP is now regarded as highly as it was three years ago, when Reagan was at the peak of his popularity and just before he and his party lost public esteem as a consequence of the Iran-*contra* scandal. Gallup polls in early 1986 found the Republicans to have an edge on the issues of peace and prosperity. This changed dramatically with revelations about arms deals with Iran, followed by the confidence-shaking stock market crash of October 1987. Gallup polls at that time found the Democrats to have overtaken the Republicans as the party better able to keep the nation at peace, but the two parties were even on the prosperity issue. Sentiment shifted back toward the GOP after last year's political conventions, when Bush took the lead in polls over Democratic challenger Michael Dukakis.

Despite the across-the-board advantage that the Republican party enjoys on both issues, more Americans continue to identify themselves as Democrats than as Republicans. Over the last decade, however, the edge has narrowed somewhat. Party-identification figures obtained from those interviewed in Gallup surveys in 1980 showed about one quarter (24%) of the public considering themselves to be Republicans, while close to one half (46%) called themselves Democrats. Comparable data for the second quarter of 1989 shows that the proportion of Republicans has increased to about one third overall (34%), while the proportion of Democrats has decreased to about four adults in ten (38%).

The most hopeful sign for the GOP's future (and most troubling for the Democrats) is the Republican party's appeal to the young. The GOP has a significant advantage among those under 30 years of age on all measures of party strength. With an older generation that remembers the popular Democratic presidents of the past—Franklin D. Roosevelt, John F. Kennedy—being replaced by those who came of age in the Reagan years, the trend is clearly in a Republican direction.

AUGUST 7
WOODSTOCK REMEMBERED—
TWENTY YEARS LATER

Interviewing Date: 6/15–18/89
Survey #GO 89135-2

Which of the following categories best applies to you?

I consider myself a
rock music fan today 32%
I used to be a rock music fan....................20
I never was a rock music fan....................48
Don't know ....*

By Age

18–29 Years

I consider myself a
rock music fan today 58%
I used to be a rock music fan....................18
I never was a rock music fan....................24
Don't know ....*

30–49 Years

I consider myself a
rock music fan today 40%
I used to be a rock music fan....................31
I never was a rock music fan....................29
Don't know ....*

50 Years and Over

I consider myself a
rock music fan today 6%
I used to be a rock music fan...................... 8
I never was a rock music fan....................86
Don't know ....*

*Less than 1%

*Asked of rock fans: Which period of rock music do you enjoy most?**

Music of the 1950s 23%
Music of the 1960s 38

Music of the 1970s 30
Music of the 1980s 20
Don't know 2

By Age

18–24 Years

Music of the 1950s 6%
Music of the 1960s 28
Music of the 1970s 33
Music of the 1980s 47
Don't know 1

25–29 Years

Music of the 1950s 10%
Music of the 1960s 35
Music of the 1970s 43
Music of the 1980s 24
Don't know ....**

30–34 Years

Music of the 1950s 12%
Music of the 1960s 27
Music of the 1970s 49
Music of the 1980s 15
Don't know 4

35–39 Years

Music of the 1950s 18%
Music of the 1960s 51
Music of the 1970s 22
Music of the 1980s 16
Don't know 7

40 Years and Over

Music of the 1950s 49%
Music of the 1960s 47
Music of the 1970s 14
Music of the 1980s 8
Don't know 2

*Multiple responses were given.
**Less than 1%

Do you happen to know the state where Woodstock took place?

Yes, New York....................................33%
Yes, incorrect answer..........................14
No...53

Rock Fans Only

Yes, New York.....................................42%
Yes, incorrect answer...........................13
No...45

*How many people attended Woodstock?**

Under 100,000.................................15%
Between 100,000 and
    500,000 36
Between 500,000 and
    1 million 14
Over 1 million...................................4
Don't know..31

Rock Fans Only

Under 100,000.................................12%
Between 100,000 and
    500,000 43
Between 500,000 and
    1 million 18
Over 1 million...................................6
Don't know..21

*Estimates placed the audience at about 400,000.

Asked of rock fans: Are you a current fan, a former fan, or were you never a fan of the following artists who appeared at Woodstock?

	Current fan	Former* fan
Crosby, Stills, & Nash............	53%	22%
The Who	46	24
Jefferson Airplane	40	27
Santana...............................	34	27
Jimi Hendrix	36	21
Janis Joplin.........................	30	23
Joe Cocker..........................	34	18
Sly & the Family Stone...........	21	24
Grateful Dead......................	29	14
Joan Baez............................	21	19
Arlo Guthrie........................	23	15
The Band............................	15	11
Richie Havens	13	12
John Sebastian	12	13
Country Joe & the Fish............	8	9

*"Never a fan" and "Don't know" responses are omitted.

Also asked of rock fans: What about the creativity of the rock musicians who are performing and making albums? Do you think they are more creative today, were they more creative then, or don't you see much difference?

More creative now 33%
More creative then...............................42
No difference.....................................23
Don't know..2

Asked of those between ages 30–49: During that time, do you feel you had much in common with the young people who attended Woodstock, or do you feel you had little in common with them?

Had much in common...........................25%
Some (volunteered) 6
Had little in common...........................66
No opinion..3

Asked of the entire sample: Does the following word apply more to young people in their teens and twenties today or young people in that same age group twenty years ago:

Idealistic?

Today..38%
Twenty years ago...............................49
Both (volunteered)..............................6
Neither (volunteered)..........................1
No opinion..6

Selfish?

Today..82%
Twenty years ago...............................5
Both (volunteered)..............................7
Neither (volunteered)..........................2
No opinion..4

Materialistic?

Today..79%
Twenty years ago...............................15
Both (volunteered)..............................3
Neither (volunteered)..........................*
No opinion..3

Patriotic?

Today	24%
Twenty years ago	65
Both (volunteered)	4
Neither (volunteered)	2
No opinion	5

Conformist?

Today	42%
Twenty years ago	41
Both (volunteered)	5
Neither (volunteered)	1
No opinion	11

Reckless?

Today	73%
Twenty years ago	14
Both (volunteered)	9
Neither (volunteered)	1
No opinion	3

*Less than 1%

Asked of those between ages 30–49: During the 1960s and 1970s, many young people got involved with alternative life-styles and activities. Regarding the following list, which activities did you participate in?

Got involved in organized protests as part of antiwar movement, civil rights movement, or other social causes	16%
Experimented with LSD or other psychedelic drugs	15
Ever smoked marijuana	42
Regularly smoked marijuana	15
Lived in commune or some form of communal arrangement	5
Took up yoga, transcendental meditation, or an Eastern religion	10
Became vegetarian, organic farmer, or otherwise involved with "back to nature" life-style	12
Dressed like a hippie	27
None of these	44

Asked of those 30 years and older: During those times, did you personally side with those who supported U.S. involvement in Vietnam or with those who opposed U.S. involvement? Did you feel strongly about this issue, or not?

Supported involvement	34%
Strongly	22
Not strongly	12
Opposed involvement	39
Strongly	28
Not strongly	11
No opinion	27

Also asked of those 30 years and older: During those times, did you personally side with those who favored legalized marijuana or with those who opposed legalized marijuana? Did you feel strongly about this issue, or not?

Supported	16%
Strongly	7
Not strongly	9
Opposed	70
Strongly	57
Not strongly	13
No opinion	14

Also asked of those 30 years and older: During those times, did you approve or disapprove of unmarried couples living together? Did you feel strongly about this issue, or not?

Approved	33%
Strongly	17
Not strongly	16
Disapproved	52
Strongly	42
Not strongly	10
No opinion	15

Asked of the entire sample: Do you feel that the following changes that took place in the 1960s were a good thing or a bad thing for our society:

More liberal attitudes toward marijuana and other recreational drugs?

Good	14%
Bad	83
No opinion	3

More openness about sex and the human body?

Good...67%
Bad..28
No opinion.. 5

Greater tolerance of homosexuality as an alternative life-style?

Good...30%
Bad..61
No opinion.. 9

More acceptance of premarital sex?

Good...38%
Bad..54
No opinion.. 8

More willingness to question the authority of government?

Good...84%
Bad..10
No opinion.. 6

Changes in the role of women in society?

Good...82%
Bad..13
No opinion.. 5

Note: As the twentieth anniversary of Woodstock approaches, recollections about the legendary rock music festival and what it symbolized evoke mixed reactions from Americans who lived through those times. A Gallup Poll finds that, while the music endures, the 1960s and its issues remain controversial and divisive, even to those who came of age during that period. Moreover, interviews with the public at large, as well as with some who attended the event itself, suggest that in a society beset by AIDS and crack cocaine, the drug culture and sexual promiscuity of Woodstock seem not only excessive but also downright dangerous.

The survey of a nationally representative sample conducted in early June shows that:

• The public today gives a mixed review to the consequences of the social changes of the 1960s, condemning the era's liberal view of drug use, premarital sex, and homosexuality as

an acceptable life-style. On the other hand, respondents endorse changes in attitude that occurred during that decade regarding the role of women in society, an increased willingness to question authority, and openness about sex and the human body.

• Although we tend to characterize the Sixties generation as being politically and socially rebellious, large majorities of those currently age 30 to 49 say that they did not get involved in antiwar or civil rights movements, smoke marijuana on a regular basis or experiment with psychedelic drugs, or dress like a hippie twenty years ago.

• Overall, people 30 years of age and older are more optimistic about the future of the country and happier about their lives than they were in the Woodstock decade. Forty percent are more politically involved today, and 37% are less involved.

• Yesterday's rebels have become today's middle-aged mainstream Americans who no longer feel as connected to their generation as they once did, but they still stand apart from the rest of the country on some of the issues that they pioneered two decades ago. In particular, they are more likely to see changes in sexual mores that grew out of the 1960s as good for society.

• Nonetheless, people who were young twenty years ago generally are seen as less selfish, less materialistic, and more patriotic than people in their teens and twenties today.

Despite movies, television shows, best-selling albums, and pop-culture legends that have grown up around Woodstock, most people now in their mid-thirties to mid-forties admit that they shared little in those days with young people who attended the historic concert in upstate New York in 1969. Only 25% of those who were in their teens and twenties at the time say that they had a lot in common with festival goers, and as many as 66% say that they shared little with those attending the concert.

More generally, the survey reveals that most people of the generation had only a tenuous connection to the protest and countercultural movements of those times. Dressing hippie-style or experimenting with marijuana was fairly commonplace among people in their teens and twenties. However, only a minority became involved with protests, alternative life-styles, or more regular drug use.

Forty-two percent of those who are now age 30 to 49 tried marijuana at some time in their youth. In contrast, only 15% experimented with LSD or other psychedelic drugs, the same percentage who report having been regular marijuana smokers at one time. Hippie clothing was worn by 27% of the Woodstock generation, but fewer got involved in communal living (5%) or yoga and Eastern or mystical religions (10%). Only 16% actively participated in protests against the Vietnam War or in favor of social causes.

On Vietnam, the Gallup sample of those age 30 and older today shows 34% recalling their opinions as supporting U.S. involvement in the war with 39% opposing, not too different from the recollections of older people nor materially different from Gallup findings in 1969 when opinions of young people concerning the war were recorded.

Only 16% of people in their thirties and older recall supporting the legalization of marijuana, which is about the proportion who used it regularly at that time. A bare third (33%) of this age group report that they approved of unmarrieds living together back in the 1960s. Indeed, middle-aged people who subscribed to the values and attitudes of the protest and countercultural movements seem today as mainstream, happy with their lives, and tuned into politics as those of their generation who were more conventional twenty years ago.

If Woodstock embodied a generation's attitudes about sex, drugs, rock 'n' roll, and rebellion, only the music can be counted as an unqualified asset twenty years later. Were it not for the presence of such rock legends as Jimi Hendrix and Janis Joplin and the continued popularity of groups like Crosby, Stills, and Nash and the Who, most people today might agree with *Newsweek*'s retrospective view that Woodstock was merely "a bunch of naked hippies in the mud."

The three-day outdoor rock concert with more than twenty musical acts was the first of its kind on such a large scale. The size of the crowd that descended on Max Yasgur's farm near Woodstock—usually estimated at about 400,000—went beyond anything that even the promoters had expected. Despite temperatures in the 90s, high humidity, rainstorms, and shortages of food and water, the crowd remained relatively orderly and the music went on.

Two decades later, people remember Hendrix more than any other artist when they think of Woodstock. A victim of a drug overdose only one year after the concert, his stature as a musician has grown with time. Of the major acts, only Crosby, Stills, and Nash, the Who, and Jefferson Airplane today claim more fans overall than does Hendrix. Joplin finishes second to Hendrix, proving that a musician can be remembered without performing in the Woodstock film or appearing on the soundtrack album. Another victim of drug abuse only one year after the event, the blues-influenced rock singer's fans are mostly over age 30 and include equal proportions of men and women.

Crosby, Stills, and Nash, prominently featured in both the movie and soundtrack, have the largest core of devoted followers (53%). If Hendrix summed up the heavy rock sound of the Sixties, then Crosby, Stills, and Nash represent the shift to the more mellow sounds of the Seventies. Their music appeals to men and women about equally. The Who (46%) and Jefferson Airplane (40%) are the two other major bands whose popularity approaches that of Crosby, Stills, and Nash.

The Grateful Dead, the quintessential hippie band, never enjoyed the widespread popularity of some other Woodstock groups. So emblematic of the 1960s, they nonetheless are attracting a sizable following among young rock fans in the 1980s. The Dead are as popular among rock fans under age 25 (39% are current fans) as they are among the 35-to-39 group (35% are current fans).

On the other hand, the folk acts and those associated with protest music—including Joan Baez, Country Joe McDonald, Richie Havens, and Arlo Guthrie—had the staying power of the major rockers. With the exception of Guthrie, the folk and protest singers have as many former fans as current fans, in sharp contrast to Crosby, Stills, and Nash, the Who, Jefferson Airplane, and the Grateful Dead, who have twice as many active as past fans.

AUGUST 16
PRESIDENT BUSH/MIDDLE EAST SITUATION

Interviewing Date: 8/10–13/89
Survey #GO 89137

Do you approve or disapprove of the way George Bush is handling his job as president?

Approve..69%
Disapprove...19
No opinion...12

By Politics

Republicans

Approve..83%
Disapprove... 8
No opinion... 9

Democrats

Approve..59%
Disapprove...27
No opinion...14

Independents

Approve..66%
Disapprove...21
No opinion...13

Selected National Trend

	Approve	Dis-approve	No opinion
1989			
July	66%	19%	15%
June	70	14	16
May	56	22	22
April	58	16	26
January	51	6	43

I'd like your overall opinion of some foreign countries. Is your opinion of (name) very favorable, mostly favorable, mostly unfavorable, or very unfavorable:

China?

Very favorable....................................5%
Mostly favorable.................................26
Mostly unfavorable..............................35
Very unfavorable.................................23
Can't rate..11

Japan?

Very favorable...................................10%
Mostly favorable.................................48
Mostly unfavorable..............................23

Very unfavorable.................................10
Can't rate.. 9

Soviet Union?

Very favorable.................................... 8%
Mostly favorable.................................43
Mostly unfavorable..............................27
Very unfavorable.................................13
Can't rate.. 9

Israel?

Very favorable...................................11%
Mostly favorable.................................34
Mostly unfavorable..............................29
Very unfavorable.................................16
Can't rate..10

Selected National Trend

	Very, mostly favorable	Mostly, very unfavorable	Can't rate
March 1989	49%	38%	13%
1976	65	25	10

Canada?

Very favorable...................................49%
Mostly favorable.................................44
Mostly unfavorable.............................. 1
Very unfavorable................................. 1
Can't rate.. 5

Iran?

Very favorable.................................... 1%
Mostly favorable................................. 4
Mostly unfavorable..............................27
Very unfavorable.................................62
Can't rate.. 6

Selected National Trend

	Very, mostly favorable	Mostly, very unfavorable	Can't rate
March 1989	5%	89%	6%
1976	48	37	15

In the Middle East situation, are your sympathies more with the Israelis or more with the Palestinian Arabs?

Israelis 50%
Palestinian Arabs 14

Both; neither (volunteered)....................15
No opinion.......................................21

Selected National Trend

	Israelis	Palestinian Arabs	Both; neither	No opinion
December				
1988*	46%	24%	16%	14%
May 1986*	43	20	20	17

*Based on informed groups

Some people feel that the Israelis rely too much on military force in dealing with the Palestinian Arabs and others in the region who oppose them. Other people feel that the Israelis have used only as much force as they need to protect themselves. Which comes closer to your view?

Israelis rely too much on
  military force..................................34%
Israelis only protecting
  themselves....................................49
No opinion.......................................17

Do you approve or disapprove of the way George Bush is handling the hostage situation in the Middle East?

Approve..57%
Disapprove.......................................33
No opinion.......................................10

Selected National Trend

	Approve	Disapprove	No opinion
June 1985*	59%	24%	17%
December 1979**	75	16	9

*Gallup survey for *Newsweek*. Rating of Ronald Reagan was taken after the TWA jetliner hijacking.
**Rating of Jimmy Carter on his handling of the Iranian hostage situation.

Are you generally optimistic or pessimistic that efforts now under way to free the American hostages in Lebanon will bring about a hostage release in the near future?

Optimistic.......................................50%
Pessimistic......................................45
No opinion..5

Now that the Ayatollah Khomeini has died and there is a new leader in Iran, do you think there is more of a chance that the American hostages will be released, or do you think that the change in leadership in Iran won't much improve the chances for a hostage release?

More of a chance................................44%
Won't improve chances..........................50
No opinion..6

In terms of U.S. policy in the Middle East today, do you think it's more important to do all we can to free the Americans now being held hostage, or is it more important to deal with the hostage holders in a way that will not encourage future hostage taking and terrorism?

To free hostages................................34%
To not encourage future hostage taking......60
No opinion..6

Do you approve or disapprove of last month's decision by the Israelis to abduct Sheik Obeid?

Approve..24%
Disapprove.......................................51
No opinion.......................................25

Do you, yourself, think Colonel Higgins was killed because the Israelis captured Sheik Obeid, or do you think his captors in Lebanon had planned to kill him all along?

Killed because of capture of sheik.............17%
Planned to kill him all along..................58
Higgins was already dead (volunteered)......13
No opinion.......................................12

If current U.S. efforts to free the remaining hostages fail to win a release soon, do you think the United States should or should not take some type of military action against the hostage holders or the countries supporting them?

Should take military action.....................66%
Should not.......................................26
Don't know..8

*Asked of those who thought the United States should take military action: Which of the following types of military action would you favor?**

Attack suspected terrorist
    bases in Lebanon 46%
Attack military targets
    in countries that have
    supported the hostage takers 39
Other..10
No opinion... 8

*Multiple responses were given.

Note: Recent events in the Middle East may be testing the American public's patience with a U.S. policy of restraint in the face of terrorism. A new Gallup Poll finds that a majority (57%) supports George Bush's handling of the first hostage crisis of his presidency, but there is more disapproval of Bush's performance than was seen for Ronald Reagan or Jimmy Carter when each faced his first hostage crisis. Moreover, only one half (50%) of Americans is optimistic that current efforts now under way to free the hostages in Lebanon will succeed in winning their release any time soon.

The poll also shows that Israel's image in the United States has suffered some damage as a result of its abduction of a Shiite sheik in an attempt to win the release of some Israeli soldiers being held in Lebanon. At the same time, however, American sympathies for the Palestinian Arabs also have declined in the face of terrorism directed at Americans. Most respondents remain sympathetic toward the Israelis in their dispute with the Palestinian Arabs and believe that Israel generally does not use excessive force in dealing with its foes.

The chain of events that started with the Israeli abduction of Sheik Abdul Karim Obeid on July 27, followed by the announcement of the murder of U.S. Marine Colonel William Higgins by his kidnappers in Lebanon a few days later, once again placed a U.S. president in the position of having to deal with terrorists' threats to kill an American hostage if their demands were not met. While Bush's overall approval rating is relatively high (69%) and the public has expressed a high level of confidence in his ability to handle foreign policy, his ratings for dealing with the latest

hostage situation are less favorable than those received by his predecessors. More Americans disapprove of Bush's handling of today's hostage situation (33%) than criticized Reagan for his reaction to the TWA jetliner hostages in 1985 (24%) or Carter for his handling of the Iran hostage crisis shortly after the U.S. embassy in Tehran was seized in late 1979 (16%).

Overall, two thirds of Americans (66%) would support some form of military action against the hostage takers or the countries siding with them if there is not a release soon. Those who favor the military option, however, generally would not go so far as to support strikes against targets in countries, such as Iran and Syria, that have backed hostage taking in the past. Instead, most who favor military retaliation (46%) would limit the strikes to suspected terrorist bases in Lebanon.

One hopeful sign for the Bush administration in terms of its Middle East policy is the public's tendency to take the long view on how to deal with hostage taking. By almost a 2-to-1 margin, Americans say that it is more important to deal with the hostage takers in a way that will discourage future acts of terrorism (60%) than to free those hostages now being held (34%).

While the Iranians sent out some signals indicating that they would like to see a deal worked out to release Americans held in Lebanon, our views of Iran have not changed significantly. Only one in twenty respondents (5%) has a favorable opinion of Iran. A March Gallup Poll found the same result. By a margin of 50% to 44%, the public does not see the death of the Ayatollah Khomeini as increasing the chances that the hostages in Lebanon will be released.

Americans continue to be critical of the Israeli decision to send commandos into Lebanon to abduct Sheik Obeid. The poll finds twice as many respondents disapproving (51%) as approving (24%). Moreover, Israel's favorability ratings have fallen from 49% favorable, 38% unfavorable in March to an even division of 45% favorable, 45% unfavorable today. Israel's foes, however, have not been able to benefit from this situation. By a wide margin Americans continue to sympathize more with the Israelis (50%) than with the Palestinian Arabs (14%) in the Middle East situation.

AUGUST 23
POVERTY IN AMERICA

Interviewing Date: 8/10–13/89
Survey #GO 89137

Do you approve or disapprove of the way George Bush is handling the problems of poverty and homelessness?

Approve..33%
Disapprove.......................................53
No opinion.......................................14

Would you say that the percentage of Americans living below the poverty line is increasing from year to year or decreasing from year to year?

Increasing 83%
Decreasing.......................................11
Staying the same (volunteered)................ 2
No opinion....................................... 4

In your view, have the living conditions of poor people been getting better over the last five years or so, have they been getting worse, or are the living conditions of poor people about what they were five years ago?

Better...17%
Worse..45
Staying the same...............................35
No opinion....................................... 3

Thinking about your own family—both your immediate family living here and your other close relatives like aunts, uncles, cousins, and so on—do you think there is anyone in your family who is living in poverty now?

Yes..24%
No..76
No opinion....................................... *

*Less than 1%

Asked of those who responded that no one in their family is living in poverty: As far as you know, has anyone in your family ever lived in poverty?

Yes...35%
No...65
No opinion....................................... *

*Less than 1%

Do you think poverty will ever be done away with in this country?

Yes... 6%
No...92
No opinion....................................... 2

Selected National Trend

	Yes	No	No opinion
1964	9%	83%	8%
1937	13	83	4

Compared to how you felt about poor people five or so years ago, would you say that you are now more sympathetic or less sympathetic to the problems of poor people today?

More sympathetic..............................71%
Less sympathetic...............................17
No change (volunteered)......................11
No opinion....................................... 1

What about the feelings of your friends and neighbors? Do you think they are now more sympathetic or less sympathetic to the problems of poor people today than five years ago?

More sympathetic..............................53%
Less sympathetic...............................24
No change (volunteered)...................... 7
No opinion.......................................16

In your opinion, which is more often to blame if a person is poor—lack of effort on his own part, or circumstances beyond his control?

Lack of effort...................................38%
Circumstances beyond his control..........42
Both equal (volunteered)......................17
No opinion....................................... 3

Selected National Trend

	Lack of effort	Circum-stances	Equal	No opinion
1984	33%	34%	31%	2%
1964	33	29	2	6

Which do you think is more often to blame if a person is homeless? Do you think it is mainly lack of effort on his own part, or circumstances beyond his control?

Lack of effort	36%
Circumstances beyond his control	47
Both equal (volunteered)	13
No opinion	4

Do you think that most poor people prefer to stay on welfare, or do you think that most poor people would rather earn their own living?

Poor prefer welfare	37%
Poor prefer to earn own living	56
No opinion	7

Which statement do you agree with most: "Welfare benefits give poor people a chance to stand on their own two feet and get started again," or "Welfare benefits make poor people dependent and encourage them to stay poor"?

Give chance to stand on own two feet	25%
Make people dependent	64
Neither; both (volunteered)	10
No opinion	1

Even if the government were willing to spend whatever is necessary to eliminate poverty in the United States, do you think the government knows enough about how to do that, or not?

Yes	24%
No	74
No opinion	2

Which of the following groups do you think has the greatest responsibility for helping the poor: churches, other private charities, the government, the families and relatives of poor people, the poor themselves, or someone else?

Churches	19%
Other private charities	5
Government	36
Families of poor people	12

Poor themselves	18
Someone else	5
No opinion	5

Note: In a country that has enjoyed almost seven years of uninterrupted economic growth, there is a growing public concern about poverty. The latest Gallup Poll reveals that most people think of poverty in America as increasing and see conditions for the poor as getting no better. Few expect a solution to the problem any time soon. Americans also are pessimistic that poverty in this country ever will be eliminated.

George Bush's promise that he will forge a "kinder, gentler nation" stands in sharp contrast to public perceptions of growing poverty in the midst of prosperity. As a consequence, only one third of Americans (33%) approves of the president's handling of the problems of poverty and homelessness, while a majority (53%) disapproves.

The harshness of this rating is underscored by the fact that as many as seven in ten respondents (69%) approve of the overall job that Bush is doing. In the long run, negative evaluations in this area may become a larger problem for him than they were for his predecessor, Ronald Reagan. Bush has promised more, and public feelings about this issue have intensified.

The vast majority of adults polled (83%) believes that the percentage of Americans living below the poverty line is increasing from year to year. This perception is even more widespread than it was midway through the Reagan administration, when a 1984 Gallup Poll found seven in ten (70%) believing poverty to be on the rise. Moreover, a plurality replies that living conditions for the poor have worsened (45%) over the last five years. Only 17% say that poor people are living better today than they were five years ago, and 35% think that the living conditions of the poor have stayed the same.

One quarter of adults (24%) perceive that someone in their immediate family or a close relative is now living in poverty, and 35% of those with no such current experience in their families are aware of past impoverishment among family members. Among minorities, the problem now is even more prevalent. About one third of nonwhites perceive someone among their close relatives as poor. Nonwhites and whites, however, are equally likely to have some direct knowledge of poverty, past or present, in their families.

Americans are divided, as they have been for years, on the question of why someone becomes poor. About four in ten (38%) think that an individual's lack of effort is mostly to blame, while a statistically equivalent percentage (42%) believe that an individual's poverty is caused mainly by circumstances beyond his control. Seventeen percent say that individual and social factors are equally to blame. Gallup surveys in 1964 and 1984 also revealed this division in American attitudes.

Interestingly, the public is slightly less ambivalent about the causes of homelessness than it is about the causes of poverty. Americans are more willing to assign the blame for homelessness to society (47%) than to the individual's lack of effort (36%).

Almost all Americans (92%) continue to believe that poverty will never be done away with in this country. This is an increase in pessimism from 1937 and 1964, when 83% in each of those years thought this way. This pessimism may stem from the fact that most people think that the government is incapable of solving the problem. There is a consensus (74%) that, even if the government were willing to spend whatever is necessary to eliminate poverty, it would not know how to solve this problem.

Indeed, the persistence of poverty is blamed not on the poor themselves but on flawed government programs. A substantial majority (64%) believes that the current welfare system makes people dependent. Only one quarter of the population (25%) says that welfare benefits give poor people a chance to stand on their own feet. Similarly, a majority (56%) of the public believes that poor people prefer to earn their own living, with only one third (37%) holding the opposing view that those people prefer to remain on welfare.

There is no consensus about where the responsibility for the solution to poverty resides. While one third of the public (36%) sees government as primarily responsible, another third (30%) believes that the poor themselves or their families have the greatest responsibility, and one quarter (25%) thinks that the job should be left to churches and other private charities.

AUGUST 30
AIRLINE SAFETY

Interviewing Date: 8/15–18/89
Survey #GO 89137-2

Compared to a few years ago, do you have much more confidence, somewhat more confidence, somewhat less confidence, or much less confidence in the safety and efficiency provided by the airlines?

Much more	5%
Somewhat more	12
Somewhat less	32
Much less	31
Same (volunteered)	14
No opinion	6

Selected National Trend

	Much, some-what more	Somewhat, much less	Same	No opinion
1987	15%	63%	16%	6%
1984*	46	30	14	10

*Gallup survey conducted for *Wall Street Journal*

When you fly, how often, if ever, are you frightened—would you say always, most of the time, sometimes, or never?

	All air travelers	More frequent flyers*
Always	11%	10%
Most of the time	5	4
Sometimes	29	32
Never	54	54
No opinion	1	**

*Those who have taken two or more trips on a commercial airliner in the past twelve months
**Less than 1%

Selected National Trend
All Air Travelers

	Always, most of the time	Some-times	Never	No opinion
August 1987	15%	30%	53%	2%
August 1983*	14	20	65	1

More Frequent Flyers

August 1987	14%	35%	51%	*%
August 1983**	10	20	69	1

*Less than 1%
**Gallup survey conducted for *Newsweek*

Are there any particular types of airplanes that you try to avoid? Which?

	All air travelers	More frequent flyers
Yes, DC-10s	12%	17%
Yes, other	25	25
No	63	58
No opinion	*	*

*Less than 1%

Some people say that last month's crash of a DC-10 in Iowa and the recent "near misses" show that air travel is not very safe today. Others say that even with the recent safety problems, air travel is still basically safe compared with other means of transportation. Which comes closer to your view?

	All air travelers	More frequent flyers
Not very safe	24%	15%
Still basically safe	73	85
No opinion	3	*

*Less than 1%

Note: The perception that air travel in the United States has become less safe is widespread, despite government statistics to the contrary. A poll taken one month after the crash of a United Airlines DC-10 in Sioux City, Iowa, in which more than 100 people died, finds nearly two thirds (63%) of Americans saying that they have lost confidence in the safety and efficiency of the airlines in recent years. Almost one half (45%) who travel by commercial airliner say that they at least sometimes are frightened when they fly.

While news stories on the Sioux City tragedy, along with reports of other aviation accidents and close calls, may have fueled perceptions that air travel is more dangerous than it once was, most people continue to see flying as a relatively safe means of transportation. Nearly three fourths (73%) of respondents say that the Sioux City tragedy does not mean that air travel has become unsafe. More than one in ten (12%) adults who fly, however, say that they try to avoid DC-10s when choosing a flight.

While figures released by the National Transportation Safety Board show recent improvement in the airline industry's safety record, polls show public opinion to be about where it was two summers ago, after another major air disaster—the crash of a Northwest Airlines jet in Detroit—contributed to a bout of rising concern. It appears that one major air disaster negates a year's worth of statistics supporting the industry's position that air travel is as safe as it ever was. Earlier in the decade, public opinion had a very different character. A 1984 Gallup survey for the *Wall Street Journal* showed a majority then expressing more confidence in airline safety and efficiency. The 1984 poll also seems to reflect consumer response to the early effects of airline deregulation, which created a competitive situation resulting in lower fares and more flights and flight times.

Loss of confidence over the past decade is seen even among those who fly fairly often. The more frequent flyers, however, are significantly more likely than other passengers (85% versus 73%) to say that air travel is basically safe, despite the well-publicized accidents of recent years.

SEPTEMBER 4
JOB SATISFACTION

Interviewing Date: 7/18–21/89
Survey #GO 89136

Asked of those who are employed: Which of the following best describes the place where you work?

Office	32%
Factory or manufacturing facility	15

Store, restaurant, or other retail outlet.......13
Construction site or other outside
    work site....................................11
School...8
Hospital, clinic, or medical facility...........7
Somewhere else..............................14

Also asked of those who are employed:

Are you an employee of a private company or business; an employee of the federal, state, or local government; or are you self-employed in your own business or professional practice?

Employee of private company
    or business...............................62%
Employee of government....................23
Self-employed...............................14
No response...................................1

Are you regularly scheduled to work only weekdays during daytime hours, or are you regularly scheduled for some evening or weekend work?

Weekdays, daytime hours....................62%
Some evenings or weekends.................24
No set schedule.............................14

In a typical week, about how many hours do you work?

Under 20 hours..............................4%
20–29 hours.................................6
30–34 hours.................................5
35–44 hours................................46
45–59 hours................................26
60 hours or more...........................13

How much do you travel in your job?

A lot......................................19%
Some.......................................15
Only a little..............................31
Not at all.................................35
No response..................................*

*Less than 1%

In general, how much time outside of work do you spend thinking about work?

A lot......................................29%
Some.......................................30
Only a little..............................29
None at all................................12
No opinion...................................*

*Less than 1%

How much of your social life is spent with people whom you've come to know through your work?

A lot......................................16%
Some.......................................34
Hardly any.................................39
None at all................................11
No opinion...................................*

*Less than 1%

Usually, is your work physically tiring?

Yes..45%
No...55

Here are two different ways of looking at your job. Some people get a sense of identity from their job. For other people, their job is just what they do for a living. Which of these best describes the way you usually feel about your job?

Sense of identity..........................57%
Just a living..............................40
No opinion...................................3

Overall, how satisfied are you with your job? Are you completely satisfied, mostly satisfied, mostly dissatisfied, or completely dissatisfied?

Completely satisfied.......................28%
Mostly satisfied...........................61
Mostly dissatisfied.........................8
Completely dissatisfied.....................3
No opinion...................................*

By Age

18–29 Years

Completely satisfied.......................23%
Mostly satisfied...........................66

Mostly dissatisfied 9
Completely dissatisfied.......................... 2
No opinion... *

30–49 Years

Completely satisfied 24%
Mostly satisfied..................................63
Mostly dissatisfied 9
Completely dissatisfied.......................... 4
No opinion... *

50 Years and Over

Completely satisfied 43%
Mostly satisfied..................................48
Mostly dissatisfied 7
Completely dissatisfied.......................... 1
No opinion... 1

*Less than 1%

For each job characteristic listed below, please tell me how satisfied you are with your current job in this regard:

Close to home?

Completely satisfied 51%
Mostly satisfied..................................36
Mostly dissatisfied 9
Completely dissatisfied.......................... 3
No opinion... 1

Contact with people?

Completely satisfied 50%
Mostly satisfied..................................45
Mostly dissatisfied 4
Completely dissatisfied.......................... 1
No opinion... *

*Less than 1%

Opportunity to use initiative?

Completely satisfied 49%
Mostly satisfied..................................39
Mostly dissatisfied 8
Completely dissatisfied.......................... 3
No opinion... 1

Flexible hours?

Completely satisfied 46%
Mostly satisfied..................................40
Mostly dissatisfied 10
Completely dissatisfied.......................... 3
No opinion... 1

Job security?

Completely satisfied 45%
Mostly satisfied..................................42
Mostly dissatisfied 8
Completely dissatisfied.......................... 3
No opinion... 2

Work important to society?

Completely satisfied 41%
Mostly satisfied..................................49
Mostly dissatisfied 6
Completely dissatisfied.......................... 2
No opinion... 2

Opportunity to learn new skills?

Completely satisfied 37%
Mostly satisfied..................................45
Mostly dissatisfied 12
Completely dissatisfied.......................... 4
No opinion... 2

Insurance, benefits?

Completely satisfied 32%
Mostly satisfied..................................39
Mostly dissatisfied 14
Completely dissatisfied.......................... 9
No opinion... 6

Opportunity for promotion?

Completely satisfied 29%
Mostly satisfied..................................38
Mostly dissatisfied 19
Completely dissatisfied.......................... 6
No opinion... 8

Pressure?

Completely satisfied 24%
Mostly satisfied..................................52
Mostly dissatisfied 17
Completely dissatisfied.......................... 6
No opinion... 1

Salary?

Completely satisfied 16%
Mostly satisfied...................................56
Mostly dissatisfied 19
Completely dissatisfied......................... 8
No opinion... 1

The following questions were asked of workers who are not self-employed.

How satisfied are you with the company or organization for which you work:

Job overall?

Completely satisfied 28%
Mostly satisfied...................................61
Mostly dissatisfied 8
Completely dissatisfied......................... 3
No opinion... *

*Less than 1%

Kind of work?

Completely satisfied 41%
Mostly satisfied...................................52
Mostly dissatisfied 6
Completely dissatisfied......................... 1
No opinion... *

*Less than 1%

Company?

Completely satisfied 30%
Mostly satisfied...................................54
Mostly dissatisfied 11
Completely dissatisfied......................... 4
No opinion... 1

How satisfied are you with your boss or immediate supervisor?

Completely satisfied 40%
Mostly satisfied...................................45
Mostly dissatisfied 9
Completely dissatisfied......................... 4
No opinion... 2

Note: Gallup recently polled employed adults to find out what they do for a living, how satisfied they are with their jobs, and other aspects of their occupations. The survey portrays a diverse workplace in which there is no such thing as a typical worker.

The vast majority (89%) are satisfied with their jobs to some degree. However, only a distinct minority say that they are completely satisfied (28%). Most workers are not very critical of their jobs overall, but significant percentages express dissatisfaction with the amount of pressure faced on the job (23%), the amount of money earned (27%), opportunities for promotion (25%), and health insurance and other benefits (23%). Interestingly, people give their boss better evaluations than they give their company or organization.

The survey shows that satisfaction is strongly related to whether or not the job helps define who the worker is as a person. As many as 40% look at their jobs as just a way to make a living, while 57% find that they get a sense of personal identity. In addition to being happier workers, those whose identity is tied to their jobs have a greater personal commitment to their work.

Moreover, the survey finds that there is no common work experience. The most typical setting is the office, but only 32% work in one. Factories and manufacturing facilities, once the dominant sector in American industry, now employ only 15% of the work force. The growth in the service sector is in evidence since one in every four workers is employed in stores and restaurants (13%), schools (8%), or hospitals (7%). One in ten (11%) works outdoors.

While the majority of Americans works for a private company (62%), one out of four workers (23%) is employed in a government job, and 14% are self-employed. And, although most (62%) work a regular weekday schedule, significant numbers (38%) are regularly scheduled to work evenings and/or weekends or report that they have no set schedule. Again reflecting the diversity of work in America, 45% say that their jobs are physically tiring, while the remaining 55% are not tired after a day's work.

Members of the postwar generations who have entered the labor force since the 1960s are significantly less satisfied with their jobs than older Americans. Whereas only one in four (24%) workers between the ages of 18 and 49 is completely satisfied, the rate of comparable satisfaction among older workers is nearly double, 43%. This lower level of job satisfaction among younger workers also may reflect the heightened competition for jobs found by members of the baby boom. These workers now are bumping into each other, competing for jobs and promotions just as they once overflowed school classrooms in the 1950s and 1960s.

SEPTEMBER 13
PRESIDENT BUSH/DRUG PROBLEM

Interviewing Date: 9/7–10/89 (U.S. only)
Survey #GO 89138

Do you approve or disapprove of the way George Bush is handling his job as president?

Approve...70%
Disapprove...17
No opinion..13

By Sex
Male

Approve...73%
Disapprove...15
No opinion..12

Female

Approve...67%
Disapprove...18
No opinion..15

By Ethnic Background
White

Approve...72%
Disapprove...16
No opinion..12

Nonwhite

Approve...54%
Disapprove...25
No opinion..21

By Education
College Graduate

Approve...74%
Disapprove...18
No opinion.. 8

College Incomplete

Approve...73%
Disapprove...18
No opinion.. 9

High-School Graduate

Approve...72%
Disapprove...15
No opinion..13

Less Than High-School Graduate

Approve...56%
Disapprove...19
No opinion..25

By Region
East

Approve...65%
Disapprove...22
No opinion..13

Midwest

Approve...74%
Disapprove...15
No opinion..11

South

Approve...71%
Disapprove...14
No opinion..15

West

Approve...69%
Disapprove...18
No opinion..13

By Age
18–29 Years

Approve...71%
Disapprove...16
No opinion..13

30–49 Years

Approve...72%
Disapprove...16
No opinion..12

50 Years and Over

Approve...67%
Disapprove...19
No opinion..14

By Income

$50,000 and Over

Approve..82%
Disapprove..11
No opinion..7

$30,000–$49,999

Approve..73%
Disapprove..20
No opinion..7

$20,000–$29,999

Approve..66%
Disapprove..16
No opinion..18

Under $20,000

Approve..64%
Disapprove..21
No opinion..15

By Politics

Republicans

Approve..85%
Disapprove..7
No opinion..8

Democrats

Approve..59%
Disapprove..27
No opinion..14

Independents

Approve..65%
Disapprove..17
No opinion..18

Selected National Trend

	Approve	Dis-approve	No opinion
1989			
August	69%	19%	12%
July	66	19	15
June	70	14	16
May	56	22	22
April	58	16	26
March	56	16	28
February	63	13	24
January	51	6	43

Presidential Performance Ratings
(In September of Inaugural Year)

		Approve	Dis-approve	No opinion
Reagan	1981	60%	29%	11%
Carter	1977	66	16	18
Nixon	1969	60	24	16
Johnson*	1965	88	4	8
Kennedy	1961	76	12	12
Eisenhower	1953	75	14	11
Truman*	1949	51	31	18

*Figures for Lyndon Johnson (August 1965) and Harry Truman (September 1949), both vice presidents who took office after the death of an incumbent president, indicate approval roughly seven months after each was elected to office in his own right. Since Gerald Ford was not elected, no figures are shown for him.

Do you approve or disapprove of the job President Bush is doing in dealing with the drug problem?

Approve..72%
Disapprove..18
No opinion..10

By Sex

Male

Approve..75%
Disapprove..17
No opinion..8

Female

Approve..70%
Disapprove..18
No opinion..12

By Ethnic Background

White

Approve..73%
Disapprove..17
No opinion..10

Nonwhite

Approve..64%
Disapprove..25
No opinion..1

By Education

College Graduate

Approve..69%
Disapprove.....................................23
No opinion...................................... 8

College Incomplete

Approve..70%
Disapprove.....................................23
No opinion...................................... 7

High-School Graduate

Approve..75%
Disapprove.....................................13
No opinion.....................................12

Less Than High-School Graduate

Approve..72%
Disapprove.....................................17
No opinion.....................................11

By Region

East

Approve..67%
Disapprove.....................................21
No opinion.....................................12

Midwest

Approve..75%
Disapprove.....................................13
No opinion.....................................12

South

Approve..78%
Disapprove.....................................14
No opinion...................................... 8

West

Approve..67%
Disapprove.....................................25
No opinion...................................... 8

By Age

18–29 Years

Approve..70%
Disapprove.....................................19
No opinion.....................................11

30–49 Years

Approve..74%
Disapprove.....................................18
No opinion...................................... 8

50 Years and Over

Approve..73%
Disapprove.....................................17
No opinion.....................................10

By Income

$50,000 and Over

Approve..68%
Disapprove.....................................22
No opinion.....................................10

$30,000–$49,999

Approve..78%
Disapprove.....................................22
No opinion.....................................10

$20,000–$29,999

Approve..72%
Disapprove.....................................19
No opinion...................................... 9

Under $20,000

Approve..76%
Disapprove.....................................17
No opinion...................................... 7

By Politics

Republicans

Approve..85%
Disapprove...................................... 9
No opinion...................................... 6

Democrats

Approve..65
Disapprove.....................................27
No opinion...................................... 8

Independents

Approve.. 6
Disapprove...................................... 1
No opinion...................................... 1

Did you happen to watch President Bush's speech on Tuesday evening [September 5] dealing with a plan to combat drugs, or did things come up that prevented you from watching? Did you see all of the speech, most of the speech, or just part of it?

Yes, watched 39%
    All of the speech.........................14
    Most of the speech 10
    Part of it 14
    Don't know...............................1
No, did not watch it.............................61

Asked of those who heard the president's speech: Do you think President Bush's plan, in the long run, will significantly reduce drug use, or not?

Will reduce drug use.............................49%
Will not reduce drug use.........................42
No opinion.......................................9

Also asked of those who heard the president's speech: Is it your impression that President Bush's plan calls for spending too much money to combat drug use, too little money, or the right amount of money?

Too much 15%
Too little...42
Right amount 34
No opinion..9

Would you, yourself, be willing to pay higher federal income taxes to help combat drug use?

Yes...62%
No..35
No opinion...3

Do you think the Colombian government is making a strong enough effort to reduce drug trafficking in that country?

Yes...31%
No..56
No opinion...13

The following questions were asked in both the United States and Colombia. (The Colombia poll was based on telephone interviews, made on September 6–10, 1989, with a representative sample residing in Bogotá and Medellín.)

I would like you to consider some concerns that people may have. For each one please tell me how concerned you are, if at all, that it will happen—very concerned, somewhat concerned, not too concerned, or not at all concerned:

Having family members develop an alcohol problem?

	United States	Colombia
Very concerned	49%	90%
Somewhat concerned	16	4
Not too concerned	15	4
Not at all concerned	20	1
No opinion	*	1

*Less than 1%

Having family members involved with drugs?

	United States	Colombia
Very concerned	60%	97%
Somewhat concerned	10	1
Not too concerned	12	1
Not at all concerned	18	1
No opinion	*	*

*Less than 1%

Becoming a victim of a crime as a consequence of the drug problem in this country?

	United States	Colombia
Very concerned	59%	95%
Somewhat concerned	20	1
Not too concerned	12	2
Not at all concerned	8	1
No opinion	1	1

Also asked in the United States and Colombia:

Do you think the U.S. government is doing all it can to help Colombia combat the major drug dealers?

	United States	Colombia
Yes	46%	39%
No	44	52
No opinion	10	9

Do you think the Colombian government is doing all it can to combat the major drug dealers?

	United States	Colombia
Yes	28%	58%
No	59	34
No opinion	13	8

Do you think the United States is putting too much, too little, or the right amount of pressure on Colombia to deal with this problem?

	United States	Colombia
Too much	6%	59%
Too little	47	12
Right amount	36	23
No opinion	11	6

Would you favor or oppose each of the following:

U.S. troops helping to fight or arrest drug traffickers in Colombia?

	United States	Colombia
Favor	46%	31%
Oppose	50	64
No opinion	4	5

U.S. military advisers assisting Colombian forces in fighting and arresting drug traffickers?

	United States	Colombia
Favor	69%	57%
Oppose	27	38
No opinion	4	5

The United States giving money to the Colombian government to help fight or arrest drug traffickers?

	United States	Colombia
Favor	53%	61%
Oppose	43	34
No opinion	4	5

The United States providing military equipment and supplies to help fight or arrest drug traffickers?

	United States	Colombia
Favor	70%	63%
Oppose	26	30
No opinion	4	7

Do you feel that the Colombian government will be able to significantly reduce the flow of drugs out of the country?

	United States	Colombia
Yes	44%	54%
No	47	39
No opinion	9	7

In your opinion, what's the more effective way to combat the drug problem—by reducing demand for drugs in the United States, or by reducing the supply of drugs coming out of Colombia?

	United States	Colombia
Reducing demand in the United States	48%	57%
Reducing supply coming out of Colombia	44	31
No opinion	8	12

Some of the Colombian drug dealers have asked the Colombian government not to prosecute them for past drug dealing in exchange for promising to stop dealing drugs. Do you think the Colombian government should or should not agree to do this?

	United States	Colombia
Should	23%	41%
Should not	70	51
No opinion	7	8

The following questions were asked in Colombia:

Do you think the U.S. government is making a strong enough effort to reduce drug use in that country?

	Colombia
Yes	33%
No	59
No opinion	8

Do you think the seriousness of the drug problem in the United States is being exaggerated?

	Colombia
Yes	45%
No	49
No opinion	6

What do you think is the most important problem facing this country today?*

	Colombia
Narcotics traffic/narcotics war	58%
Lack of safety	26
Terrorism	20
Unemployment	17
Guerrillas	15
Poverty/hunger	12
High cost of living	11
Corruption	4
Paramilitary groups	2
Other	5
No opinion	1

*Multiple responses were given.

Do you think the Colombian government should now request that U.S. troops be sent to help combat drug traffickers?

	Colombia
Yes	19%
No	77
No opinion	4

In the long run, do you think the crackdown on drug dealers is in the best interest of Colombia, or not?

	Colombia
Yes	45%
No	46
No opinion	9

If the drug dealing in Colombia is significantly reduced, what effect would it have on the economy in Colombia overall? Would it improve it, worsen it, or not have much of an effect?

	Colombia
Improve it	38%
Worsen it	34
Not have much effect	21
No opinion	7

Do you think the power of the major drug dealers in Colombia is being exaggerated?

	Colombia
Yes	41%
No	51
No opinion	8

Do you approve or disapprove of the way Virgilio Barco Vargas is handling his job as president?

	Colombia
Approve	45%
Disapprove	43
No opinion	12

Do you approve or disapprove of the job President Barco is doing in dealing with the drug problem?

	Colombia
Approve	60%
Disapprove	30
No opinion	10

Note: A new Gallup Poll in the United States and Colombia finds the people of both countries divided over the war now being waged against the Colombian drug cartels. While feeling personally threatened by the violence associated with the drug trade, many Colombians question whether their government's recent crackdown on the cocaine dealers will benefit the country in the long run.

Most Colombians see the demand for illegal drugs in the United States as the major source of the problem and are resentful of American pressure on their government to cut the supply. A majority would not welcome U.S. troops to help fight the drug war at this time. Most Colombians, however, would like Washington to provide assistance, including military advisers, to help their own government's efforts.

Among Americans, there is no consensus that going after the drug suppliers is the best way to attack the problem. Fewer than one half (44%) believe that reducing the flow of drugs coming into the country from abroad will be more effective than working to reduce demand here at home, and the public is divided about using U.S. forces in Colombia. Moreover, Americans are as skeptical about Colombia's ability to cut the supply of drugs as they are about the chances that President George Bush's new antidrug program will make much of a dent in the demand.

The survey provides ample evidence that Colombians feel personally threatened in the face of the violence that has erupted in their country in recent weeks. They cite lack of safety and terrorism second only to drug trafficking as their country's most important problem. Moreover, nearly all Colombians interviewed (95%), compared with six in ten Americans (59%), say that they are very concerned about becoming victims of drug-related crime.

The Colombians find much to criticize about the U.S. role in the drug wars now being fought in their country. Six in ten (59%) say that Washington is putting too much pressure on Bogotá to deal with the problem. By a margin of 57% to 31%, Colombians see reducing demand in the United States rather than cutting the flow of drugs from Colombia as the more effective way to fight the drug trafficking. Many Colombians (45%) even suggest that the seriousness of the drug problem in the United States is being exaggerated.

Washington is seen by Colombians as falling short on providing Bogotá with enough assistance in combating drugs—39% think that the United States has done all it can to help, while 52% disagree. These figures are reversed concerning Colombia's efforts, with 58% saying that the government is doing all it can to combat the major drug dealers.

In general, the people of Colombia seem to welcome all types of U.S. military assistance short of combat troops. Sixty-three percent want military equipment and supplies, 61% want money for the Colombian government's war on traffickers, and 57% want military advisers to assist Colombian troops in the

fight. Two thirds (64%), however, reject the idea of U.S. troops being dispatched to Colombia, while an even larger majority (77%) say that they oppose their government formally requesting such help from the United States at this time.

Americans, in turn, also are wary of the Colombians. A majority (56%) does not believe that Bogotá is doing all it can to cut the flow of drugs into the United States. A plurality (47%) thinks that Washington has not put enough pressure on the Colombian government to deal with the problem. Americans are more likely to favor sending troops than are Colombians to say that their government should solicit such help. The U.S. public is less likely than the Colombian public, however, to favor sending financial aid, probably reflecting a lack of trust in the Bogotá government's officials. Send weapons and advisers, but not cash, the Americans seem to be saying.

The Colombians are more likely than Americans to be optimistic that their own government will make major progress in cutting the supply of illegal drugs entering the United States. Fifty-four percent of Colombians, compared with 44% of Americans, believe that this effort will succeed. For the most part, Colombians say that their country's economy will not suffer adversely if drug activity is reduced significantly.

A large majority of Americans (70%) and a smaller majority (57%) of residents of Bogotá think that the Colombian government should not agree to give drug traffickers immunity from prosecution in return for their promise to stop all future drug dealing. However, a majority (55%) of the residents of Medellín, a city long reputed to be a center for the cocaine trade and more recently a combat zone because of the crackdown, generally says that the government should agree to the drug dealers' request.

Colombian President Virgilio Barco Vargas faces a more critical public than does Bush in rallying support for his policies to fight drugs. Barco receives positive marks for his handling of the drug problem from a majority (60%) of the Colombians interviewed, but his overall approval ratings are mixed, with 45% approving and 43% disapproving. Moreover, a substantial proportion (46%) believes that Barco's all-out war on the major drug dealers will not prove to be in the country's best interests. By contrast, 72% of Americans approve, while 18% disapprove, of President Bush's handling of the drug problem.

In his eighth month in office, Bush is more popular than his recent predecessors in the White House at similar points in their terms. His approval rating (70%) outdistances Ronald Reagan's (60%) and Richard Nixon's (60%) and is slightly higher than Jimmy Carter's (66%). It falls short, however, of Lyndon Johnson's (88%), John Kennedy's (76%), and Dwight Eisenhower's (75%).

SEPTEMBER 20
TELEVISION EVANGELISTS
AND MINISTERS

Interviewing Date: 9/7–10/89
Survey #GO 89138

I am going to read you some pairs of opposite phrases that have been used to describe television evangelists and ministers. From each pair of opposites, would you select the term you feel best describes television evangelists or ministers, in general:

Caring?

Care about people................................33%
Don't care about people.........................62
No opinion...5

By Sex
Male

Care about people................................32%
Don't care about people.........................62
No opinion...6

Female

Care about people................................34%
Don't care about people.........................61
No opinion...5

By Ethnic Background
White

Care about people................................33%
Don't care about people.........................62
No opinion...5

Nonwhite

Care about people................................37%
Don't care about people.........................56
No opinion...7

By Education
College Graduate

Care about people................................29%
Don't care about people.........................66
No opinion...5

College Incomplete

Care about people................................33%
Don't care about people.........................63
No opinion...4

High-School Graduate

Care about people................................35%
Don't care about people.........................60
No opinion...5

Less Than High-School Graduate

Care about people................................36%
Don't care about people.........................58
No opinion...6

By Region
East

Care about people................................29%
Don't care about people.........................66
No opinion...5

Midwest

Care about people................................34%
Don't care about people.........................60
No opinion...6

South

Care about people................................39%
Don't care about people.........................56
No opinion...5

West

Care about people................................30%
Don't care about people.........................65
No opinion...5

By Age

18-29 Years

Care about people...............................35%
Don't care about people.........................61
No opinion...4

30-49 Years

Care about people...............................35%
Don't care about people.........................60
No opinion...5

50 Years and Over

Care about people...............................31%
Don't care about people.........................62
No opinion...7

By Religion

Protestants

Care about people...............................40%
Don't care about people.........................55
No opinion...5

Catholics

Care about people...............................21%
Don't care about people.........................75
No opinion...4

Born-again Christians Only

Care about people...............................47%
Don't care about people.........................47
No opinion...6

Church Members Only

Care about people...............................37%
Don't care about people.........................58
No opinion...5

Those Who Say Religion Is Very Important in Their Life

Care about people...............................40%
Don't care about people.........................53
No opinion...7

Those Who Say Religion Is Fairly Important in Their Life

Care about people...............................27%
Don't care about people.........................70
No opinion...3

Those Who Say Religion Is Not Very Important in Their Life

Care about people...............................18%
Don't care about people.........................77
No opinion...5

Selected National Trend

	Care	Don't care	No opinion
1987	48%	38%	14%
1980	59	21	20

Sincerity?

Sincere 26%
Insincere..67
No opinion...7

By Sex

Male

Sincere 26%
Insincere..67
No opinion...7

Female

Sincere 25%
Insincere..68
No opinion...7

By Ethnic Background

White

Sincere 24%
Insincere..69
No opinion...7

Nonwhite

Sincere 34%
Insincere..59
No opinion...7

By Education

College Graduate

Sincere 20%
Insincere..74
No opinion...6

College Incomplete

Sincere 27%
Insincere..69
No opinion...4

High-School Graduate

Sincere 28%
Insincere..66
No opinion... 6

Less Than High-School Graduate

Sincere 26%
Insincere..62
No opinion..12

By Region

East

Sincere 19%
Insincere..74
No opinion... 7

Midwest

Sincere 30%
Insincere..63
No opinion... 7

South

Sincere 28%
Insincere..65
No opinion... 7

West

Sincere 25%
Insincere..69
No opinion... 6

By Age

18–29 Years

Sincere 27%
Insincere..70
No opinion..3

30–49 Years

Sincere 26%
Insincere..70
No opinion... 4

50 Years and Over

Sincere 25%
Insincere..62
No opinion..13

By Religion

Protestants

Sincere 30%
Insincere..62
No opinion... 8

Catholics

Sincere 17%
Insincere..80
No opinion...3

Born-again Christians Only

Sincere 42%
Insincere..50
No opinion... 8

Church Members Only

Sincere 30%
Insincere..63
No opinion... 7

Those Who Say Religion Is Very Important in Their Life

Sincere 32%
Insincere..59
No opinion... 9

Those Who Say Religion Is Fairly Important in Their Life

Sincere 19%
Insincere..77
No opinion... 4

Those Who Say Religion Is Not Very Important in Their Life

Sincere 12%
Insincere..82
No opinion... 6

Selected National Trend

	Sincere	In-sincere	No opinion
1987	34%	51%	15%
1980	56	25	19

Honesty?

Honest...23%
Dishonest..70
No opinion... 7

By Sex

Male

Honest...22%
Dishonest...70
No opinion.. 8

Female

Honest...23%
Dishonest...71
No opinion.. 6

By Ethnic Background

White

Honest...22%
Dishonest...72
No opinion.. 6

Nonwhite

Honest...27%
Dishonest...62
No opinion..11

By Education

College Graduate

Honest...18%
Dishonest...75
No opinion.. 7

College Incomplete

Honest...21%
Dishonest...75
No opinion.. 4

High-School Graduate

Honest...24%
Dishonest...71
No opinion.. 5

Less Than High-School Graduate

Honest...28%
Dishonest...60
No opinion..12

By Region

East

Honest...17%
Dishonest...78
No opinion.. 5

Midwest

Honest...27%
Dishonest...67
No opinion.. 6

South

Honest...23%
Dishonest...67
No opinion..10

West

Honest...23%
Dishonest...70
No opinion.. 7

By Age

18–29 Years

Honest...19%
Dishonest...77
No opinion.. 4

30–49 Years

Honest...23%
Dishonest...73
No opinion.. 4

50 Years and Over

Honest...24%
Dishonest...63
No opinion..13

By Religion

Protestants

Honest...28%
Dishonest...64
No opinion.. 8

Catholics

Honest...13%
Dishonest...82
No opinion.. 5

Born-again Christians Only

Honest..37%
Dishonest..54
No opinion.. 9

Church Members Only

Honest..29%
Dishonest..62
No opinion.. 9

Those Who Say Religion Is Very Important in Their Life

Honest..29%
Dishonest..61
No opinion..10

Those Who Say Religion Is Fairly Important in Their Life

Honest..14%
Dishonest..82
No opinion.. 4

Those Who Say Religion Is Not Very Important in Their Life

Honest..13%
Dishonest..84
No opinion.. 3

Selected National Trend

	Honest	Dis- honest	No opinion
1987	34%	53%	13%
1980	53	26	21

Relationship with God?

Have a special relationship....................23%
Do not have a special relationship...........67
No opinion.......................................10

By Sex

Male

Have a special relationship....................19%
Do not have a special relationship...........71
No opinion.......................................10

Female

Have a special relationship....................26%
Do not have a special relationship...........64
No opinion.......................................10

By Ethnic Background

White

Have a special relationship....................21%
Do not have a special relationship...........69
No opinion.......................................10

Nonwhite

Have a special relationship....................33%
Do not have a special relationship...........55
No opinion.......................................12

By Education

College Graduate

Have a special relationship....................15%
Do not have a special relationship...........78
No opinion....................................... 7

College Incomplete

Have a special relationship....................18%
Do not have a special relationship...........73
No opinion....................................... 9

High-School Graduate

Have a special relationship....................24%
Do not have a special relationship...........66
No opinion....................................... 9

Less Than High-School Graduate

Have a special relationship....................34%
Do not have a special relationship...........48
No opinion.......................................18

By Region

East

Have a special relationship....................18%
Do not have a special relationship...........74
No opinion....................................... 8

Midwest

Have a special relationship....................25%
Do not have a special relationship...........66
No opinion....................................... 9

South

Have a special relationship....................29%
Do not have a special relationship...........57
No opinion.......................................14

West

Have a special relationship....................16%
Do not have a special relationship..........75
No opinion.. 9

By Age
18–29 Years

Have a special relationship....................23%
Do not have a special relationship..........72
No opinion.. 5

30–49 Years

Have a special relationship....................23%
Do not have a special relationship..........69
No opinion.. 8

50 Years and Over

Have a special relationship....................23%
Do not have a special relationship..........61
No opinion..16

By Religion
Protestants

Have a special relationship....................29%
Do not have a special relationship..........59
No opinion..12

Catholics

Have a special relationship....................13%
Do not have a special relationship..........80
No opinion.. 7

Born-again Christians Only

Have a special relationship....................41%
Do not have a special relationship..........45
No opinion..14

Church Members Only

Have a special relationship....................27%
Do not have a special relationship..........61
No opinion..12

Those Who Say Religion Is Very Important in Their Life

Have a special relationship....................32%
Do not have a special relationship..........55
No opinion..13

Those Who Say Religion Is Fairly Important in Their Life

Have a special relationship....................14%
Do not have a special relationship..........80
No opinion.. 6

Those Who Say Religion Is Not Very Important in Their Life

Have a special relationship....................5%
Do not have a special relationship..........91
No opinion.. 4

Selected National Trend

	Special relation- ship	No special relation- ship	No opinion
1987	30%	56%	14%
1980	47	33	20

Trustworthiness?

Trustworthy with money.......................16%
Not trustworthy with money..................79
No opinion.. 5

By Sex
Male

Trustworthy with money.......................16%
Not trustworthy with money..................78
No opinion.. 6

Female

Trustworthy with money.......................16%
Not trustworthy with money..................79
No opinion.. 5

By Ethnic Background
White

Trustworthy with money.......................15%
Not trustworthy with money..................80
No opinion.. 5

Nonwhite

Trustworthy with money.......................19%
Not trustworthy with money..................73
No opinion.. 8

By Education

College Graduate

Trustworthy with money........................10%
Not trustworthy with money..................86
No opinion...4

College Incomplete

Trustworthy with money........................14%
Not trustworthy with money..................82
No opinion...4

High-School Graduate

Trustworthy with money........................18%
Not trustworthy with money..................77
No opinion...5

Less Than High-School Graduate

Trustworthy with money........................21%
Not trustworthy with money..................69
No opinion...10

By Region

East

Trustworthy with money........................12%
Not trustworthy with money..................83
No opinion...5

Midwest

Trustworthy with money........................18%
Not trustworthy with money..................77
No opinion...5

South

Trustworthy with money........................17%
Not trustworthy with money..................77
No opinion...6

West

Trustworthy with money........................17%
Not trustworthy with money..................79
No opinion...4

By Age

18–29 Years

Trustworthy with money........................13%
Not trustworthy with money..................85
No opinion...2

30–49 Years

Trustworthy with money........................15%
Not trustworthy with money..................81
No opinion...4

50 Years and Over

Trustworthy with money........................18%
Not trustworthy with money..................72
No opinion...10

By Religion

Protestants

Trustworthy with money........................22%
Not trustworthy with money..................73
No opinion...5

Catholics

Trustworthy with money........................7%
Not trustworthy with money..................90
No opinion...3

Born-again Christians Only

Trustworthy with money........................30%
Not trustworthy with money..................64
No opinion...6

Church Members Only

Trustworthy with money........................18%
Not trustworthy with money..................76
No opinion...6

Those Who Say Religion Is Very Important in Their Life

Trustworthy with money........................22%
Not trustworthy with money..................71
No opinion...7

Those Who Say Religion Is Fairly Important in Their Life

Trustworthy with money........................9%
Not trustworthy with money..................87
No opinion...4

Those Who Say Religion Is Not Very Important in Their Life

Trustworthy with money........................4%
Not trustworthy with money..................93
No opinion...3

Selected National Trend

	Trust-worthy	Not trust-worthy	No opinion
1987	23%	63%	14%
1980	41	36	23

Do you ever watch religious programs on television? In the past seven days, have you watched any religious programs on television?

Watch religious programs	49%
Within past seven days	21
Not in past seven days	28
Do not watch religious programs	51

Selected National Trend

	Within past seven days	Not in past seven days	Do not watch
1987	25%	24%	51%
1983	18	24	58

By any chance, have you contributed money to any television evangelists in the last twelve months?

	1989	1987
Yes	5%	4%
No	95	96

I am going to read you a list of institutions in American society. Would you please tell me how much confidence you, yourself, have in each one—a great deal, quite a lot, some, or very little:

	Great deal or quite a lot
The military	63%
Church or organized religion	52
U.S. Supreme Court	46
Public schools	43
Banks	42
Congress	32

Selected National Trend

	1986	1985	1981
The military	63%	61%	50%
Church or organized religion	57	66	64
U.S. Supreme Court	53	56	46
Public schools	49	48	42
Banks	49	51	46
Congress	41	39	29

Would you describe yourself as a "born-again," or evangelical, Christian?

Yes	34%
No	62

Do you happen to be a member of a church or synagogue?

	1989	1987
Yes	67%	69%
No	33	31

Did you happen to attend a church or synagogue in the last seven days, or not?

	1989	1987
Yes	42%	40%
No	58	60

How important would you say religion is in your own life?

	1989	1987
Very important	57%	53%
Fairly important	29	31
Not very important	13	15
No opinion	1	1

Note: As Jim Bakker's trial on charges of conspiracy and fraud unfolds, a new Gallup Poll finds that public opinion of television evangelists in general is at an all-time low. Several years of headlines on the sexual and financial scandals involving some leading evangelical preachers such as Bakker and Jimmy Swaggart have taken their toll.

In 1980, when Gallup first started gauging the public's image of television evangelists, most Americans held positive views of the characteristics of television ministers as a group. However, a 1987 poll taken one month after Bakker's resignation as head of the PTL ministry found sharp decreases in the numbers of adults describing television evangelists as caring, honest, sincere, trustworthy, and involved in a special relationship with God. The latest poll now finds that opinion of electronic preachers has continued to drop precipitously since Bakker's resignation. The declines registered between 1987 and 1989 are almost as sharp as those measured between 1980 and 1987.

Respondents' leading complaint against television evangelists continues to be that they are not trustworthy with money. Nearly eight in ten (79%) say that these preachers cannot be trusted with their supporters' donations. In 1980, before the financial scandals and opulent life-styles of certain popular televangelists were revealed, less than one half as many (36%) was distrustful of these evangelists' handling of funds. However, by 1987 a majority of the public (63%) already was expressing the view that television ministers could not be trusted with money.

The growing cynicism in attitudes toward television ministers is equally apparent in ratings about their spiritual and personal characteristics. Large majorities now describe them as dishonest (70%), insincere (67%), lacking a special relationship with God (67%), and uncaring (62%). In 1980 the public was more likely to rate these ministers positively rather than negatively on all of these characteristics, with majorities describing televangelists as caring (59%), sincere (56%), and honest (53%). Almost one half in 1980 (47%) thought that these preachers had a special relationship with God.

The television evangelists' sharpest critics are under 50 years of age, college graduates, middle- or upper-income adults, residents of the East, and whites. Self-described "born again," or evangelical, Christians and those who watch religious television on a weekly basis are the strongest supporters of television preachers, although even among these groups it is rare to find a majority describing televangelists in a positive way on any of the five characteristics about which Gallup inquired.

Despite the public's negative view, the electronic churches continue to reach a large audience, although the size of that audience shows signs of erosion. One half of all adults (49%) report that they have watched religious programming on television at least once, and one in five (21%) is considered a weekly viewer, having watched religious television in the past seven days.

After a period of growth between 1983 and 1987, the number of respondents who have ever tuned in to religious television has stayed at the same level during the past two years. However, the percentage of adults who watched religious programming in the past week declined four percentage points, from 25% to 21%, since 1987.

One in twenty adults (5%), representing roughly 8.5 million Americans, has contributed money to at least one television evangelist in the past year. This is statistically unchanged from the percentage reporting donations in 1987 (4%). Those most likely to be contributors are often those with the least discretionary income—older people, blacks, and those who do not have a high-school diploma.

The sharp decline in the public's view of television evangelists since 1987 is not reflected in lower evaluations of organized religion as a whole, nor in any change in the role that religion plays in adults' lives. One half of Americans (52%) say that they have a great deal or quite a lot of confidence in the church or organized religion. This public confidence suffered an earlier setback between 1985 and 1986 when, for the first time in Gallup's measurements, the church did not emerge as the institution receiving the highest level of confidence from among a list of various institutions that Gallup asked people to rate. In 1985 more than six in ten (66%) Americans said that they had a great deal or quite a lot of confidence in the church, with the figure falling to 57% by the following year.

Religion is at least as important to adults now as it was in 1987, with a majority (57%) currently saying that religion is very important in their own lives. In 1987, 53% gave this answer. Church membership and attendance remain at essentially the same levels that Gallup has observed for two decades, with two in three (67%) Americans belonging to a church or synagogue and 42% attending services within the past week.

SEPTEMBER 26
ALCOHOLIC BEVERAGES

Interviewing Date: 9/12–15/89
Survey #GO 89138-2

Do you have occasion to use alcoholic beverages such as liquor, wine, or beer, or are you a total abstainer?

		Those who drink
National		56%

Selected National Trend

		Those who drink
1988		63%
1987		65
1984		64
1981		70
1978		71
1976		71
1966		65
1958		55
1947		63
1939		58

Asked of those who drink (56% of the sample): When did you last take a drink of any kind of alcoholic beverage?

	1989	1988	1987
Within last 24 hours	32%	39%	38%
2–7 days ago	35	25	29
Over 7 days ago	32	34	32
Not sure	1	2	1

Also asked of those who drink: Approximately how many drinks of any alcoholic beverage did you drink in the past seven days?

	1989	1988	1987
None	33%	32%	29%
1–7 drinks	47	49	50
8–19 drinks	13	10	11
20 or more	5	6	6
Not sure	2	3	4

Also asked of those who drink: Do you sometimes drink more than you think you should?

	1989	1987	1985	1978
Yes	35%	29%	32%	23%
No	65	71	68	77

Also asked of those who drink: Do you plan to cut down or quit drinking within the next year?

	1989	1987	1984
Yes, to cut down	18%	12%	14%
Yes, to quit	7	3	2
Neither	74	82	83
No opinion	1	3	1

Asked of the entire sample: Has drinking ever been a cause of trouble in your family?

		Yes
National		19%

Selected National Trend

		Yes
1987		24%
1985		21
1984		17
1981		22
1978		22
1976		17
1974		12
1966		12
1950		14

Note: In the past year, the incidence of drinking alcoholic beverages has fallen precipitously and the level of concern about drinking has sharply increased. A new Gallup Poll finds that 56% of Americans drink alcoholic beverages, down from 63% last year. The current level of consumption is a statistical tie with the lowest level, recorded in 1958 (55%). When this question was first asked by Gallup in 1939—five years after Prohibition was repealed—58% said that they drank alcohol. The highest incidence was recorded in 1976 and 1978, when 71% of the population drank liquor, beer, or wine.

The Gallup Poll also reveals a decline in the frequency of drinking since last year. Fewer drinkers in the current survey report that they have had a drink within the last twenty-four hours, compared to those in the 1988 survey (32% versus 39%). Most of those who drink alcohol today do so moderately. Almost one half of those interviewed (47%) said that within the past week they had between one and seven drinks, while one third (33%) reported that they had not imbibed any alcohol at all. Moderate drinking, it is currently argued, may have some beneficial health effects.

The decline in consumption among Americans may be a result of many factors, such as increased awareness of alcohol-related health problems, stiffer drunk-driving penalties, and alarm about drug abuse in the

United States. In addition, one in five (19%) reports that alcohol has been a source of trouble in the family. This heightened awareness and proximity to the detrimental effects of alcohol have caused many Americans to quit drinking entirely, or at least to cut down. More than four in ten (44%) today say that they do not drink alcohol at all. And one quarter of those who currently drink say that they plan to cut down (18%) or quit (7%) within the next year, almost double the 1987 finding in which 15% said that they planned to cut back or quit.

The heightened awareness of the potential problems associated with alcohol use also is evident in the fact that more drinkers say that they are concerned about how much they consume. One third (35%) of those who drink are concerned that they sometimes drink too much. In 1987, only 29% of drinkers had this concern.

OCTOBER 2
AMERICA'S LARGE CITIES

Interviewing Date: 8/15–18/89
Survey #GO 89137-2

If you could live anywhere in the United States that you wanted to, would you prefer a city, suburban area, small town, or farm?

City..19%
Suburban area 24
Small town 34
Farm 22
No opinion.................................. 1

*Now, thinking about large cities— including both those you have visited and those you have never visited—in your opinion, which is the best large city in America? Which is the second best?**

New York 16%
San Francisco...............................14
Los Angeles.................................11
Seattle...................................... 9
San Diego................................... 9
Denver...................................... 8
Boston 8

Dallas...................................... 7
Chicago..................................... 7
Atlanta 6
Washington, DC 6

*In your opinion, which is the worst large city in America? Which is the second worst?**

New York 40%
Los Angeles.................................20
Chicago.....................................19
Detroit.....................................15
Miami 10
Washington, DC 9
San Francisco............................... 6
Philadelphia................................ 5
Cleveland................................... 4
Houston..................................... 3
Pittsburgh 3

*In your opinion, which large city has the fewest social problems, such as crime, drugs, and poverty? Which has the second fewest social problems?**

Seattle.....................................10%
Denver...................................... 7
Salt Lake City.............................. 6
Minneapolis 6
Phoenix..................................... 5
San Diego................................... 4
Dallas...................................... 4
Cincinnati.................................. 3
Boston 3
Indianapolis................................ 3
St. Louis 3

*In your opinion, which large city in America has the friendliest people? Which large city is second?**

Atlanta 12%
Dallas...................................... 8
Los Angeles................................. 6
New Orleans................................. 6
Seattle..................................... 6
Denver...................................... 6
San Francisco............................... 6
Chicago..................................... 5
San Diego................................... 5
Houston..................................... 5
New York 5

In your opinion, which large city in America has the best arts, entertainment, and nightlife? Which has the second best?*

New York	54%
Los Angeles	21
San Francisco	14
Chicago	11
Washington, DC	7
New Orleans	6
Atlanta	4
Boston	4
Philadelphia	4
Miami	4

In your opinion, which large city in America has the best food? Which large city is second?*

New York	29%
San Francisco	20
New Orleans	18
Chicago	9
Los Angeles	9
Boston	7
Dallas	5
Atlanta	4
Miami	4
Washington, DC	4

In your opinion, which large city in America is the most attractive? Which is the second most attractive?*

San Francisco	21%
New York	12
Los Angeles	10
Seattle	10
Washington, DC	10
San Diego	8
Denver	8
Honolulu	7
Boston	7
Atlanta	6
Miami	5
Dallas	5
Chicago	5

*First and second choices are combined.

Note: America's big-city lights are shining more brightly than they did in the 1970s. Urban areas once again are experiencing greater population growth than rural areas, and a recently completed special Gallup Poll finds that city life has regained some popularity over the past decade, especially among young people.

The survey probed public images of the country's largest cities and found that the biggest of our big cities, New York, wins top honors as both America's best and worst. However, for friendliness, attractiveness, and fewest social problems, southern and western cities draw the highest ratings.

Among the poll's key findings are the following:

• Nearly one in five (19%) Americans considers city life to be the ideal today, compared with a low of 13% in a 1972 Gallup Poll. However, a majority continues to prefer living in either suburbs (24%), small towns (34%), or on farms (22%).

• While New York gets the most votes as both the best and worst city in America, its traditional second-city rival, Chicago, only manages ninth place as best city but ties for second as worst. Among the best, New York (16%) is followed by the West Coast cities of San Francisco (14%) and Los Angeles (11%). Despite being one of the three best nationwide, Los Angeles receives relatively low ratings from people who have visited many times. Moreover, smaller cities such as Seattle, San Francisco, and Boston are more popular than New York when the evaluations are based on Americans who have spent a lot of time in each place.

• In keeping with the image of southern hospitality, people across the country believe that southern cities are among the friendliest. Atlanta (12%) is most frequently chosen, followed by Dallas (8%), Los Angeles, New Orleans, Seattle, Denver, and San Francisco (all 6%).

• New York is widely seen as the cultural capital. The Big Apple is named by 54% as the leader in arts, entertainment, and nightlife. Los Angeles is a distant second, at 21%. San Francisco (14%) and Chicago (11%) are the only other two in this category mentioned by at least one in ten.

• New York (29%) also draws the most mentions as the city with the best food, but this is not nearly as much of a runaway as the cultural contest. San Francisco (20%) and New Orleans (18%) are close seconds after New York.

• San Francisco is most often thought of as the most attractive city (21%). New York (12%) comes in second, followed by Los Angeles (10%), Seattle (10%), and Washington, DC (10%).

• Western cities head the list of those believed to have the fewest social problems, such as crime, drugs, and poverty. Seattle (10%) is chosen most frequently, followed by Denver (7%), Salt Lake City (6%), Minneapolis (6%), and Phoenix (5%).

Opinions of which cities are best vary considerably according to where people live; they naturally tend to give more credit to cities in their own regions. Overall, however, New York, San Francisco, and Los Angeles draw the best ratings from respondents in all parts of the country, while cities in the Midwest earn relatively fewer positive mentions nationwide. These cities include Detroit, Cleveland, Milwaukee, and Cincinnati.

OCTOBER 11
TAXES

Interviewing Date: 10/5–8/89
Survey #GO 89139

Which of the following worries you most about the future:

	October	February*
Increase in taxes	50%	42%
Increase in prices	16	24
You or your spouse may lose your job	15	14
Increase in interest rates	11	11
None	6	5
No opinion	2	4

*This survey was conducted for *Times Mirror* by the Gallup Organization.

Do you think the Bush administration will or will not be able to avoid raising taxes?

	October	January*
Will	18%	29%
Will not	71	64
No opinion	11	7

Do you approve or disapprove of raising income taxes as a way of reducing the federal budget deficit?

Approve	25%
Disapprove	69
No opinion	6

If you had a say in making up the federal budget this year, should spending be increased, decreased, or kept the same for the following programs:

To improve public education?

Increased	76%
Decreased	3
Kept the same	19
No opinion	2

To combat the drug problem?

Increased	75%
Decreased	7
Kept the same	16
No opinion	2

To help the homeless?

Increased	71%
Decreased	6
Kept the same	20
No opinion	3

Health care?

Increased	67%
Decreased	5
Kept the same	24
No opinion	4

To reduce air pollution?

Increased	59%
Decreased	9
Kept the same	30
No opinion	2

Research on AIDS?

Increased	59%
Decreased	9
Kept the same	29
No opinion	3

Job training and placement?

Increased...56%
Decreased 9
Kept the same....................................33
No opinion..2

To assist low-income families?

Increased...56%
Decreased 10
Kept the same....................................31
No opinion..3

Aid to farmers?

Increased...48%
Decreased 16
Kept the same....................................32
No opinion..4

Health insurance?

Increased...48%
Decreased 12
Kept the same....................................34
No opinion..6

Financial aid for college students?

Increased...44%
Decreased 15
Kept the same....................................39
No opinion..2

To provide child-care services?

Increased...41%
Decreased 13
Kept the same....................................42
No opinion..4

To assist first-time home buyers?

Increased...37%
Decreased 16
Kept the same....................................42
No opinion..5

Space exploration?

Increased...21%
Decreased 38
Kept the same....................................39
No opinion..2

Defense spending?

Increased...14%
Decreased 42
Kept the same....................................41
No opinion..3

As you may know, there has been discussion in Congress to lower the capital gains tax, which applies to income from the sale of stocks, bonds, and real estate. Do you approve or disapprove of lowering the capital gains tax?

Approve...46%
Disapprove...36
No opinion..18

By Income
$50,000 and Over

Approve...62%
Disapprove...31
No opinion..7

$30,000–$49,999

Approve...46%
Disapprove...37
No opinion..17

$20,000–$29,999

Approve...50%
Disapprove...34
No opinion..16

Under $20,000

Approve...37%
Disapprove...41
No opinion..22

Note: In an era when deficits have placed sharp limits on federal spending, most Americans say that they would pay higher taxes if necessary to tackle the social problems of the late 1980s, but they continue to balk at paying higher taxes as a means to reduce the deficit. Although substantial pluralities favor government spending increases for a wide range of programs, the public is only willing to take money out of its own pocket for a handful of problems. Most notably, reducing air pollution does not engender majority support as a cause worthy of personal financial sacrifice, even though most Americans say that the government should spend more on the problem.

Since the beginning of the year, the perception that a tax increase is inevitable has become more widespread. Currently, 71% of adults believe that the Bush administration will not be able to avoid raising taxes; 64% thought that way in January, when George Bush first took office. In relation to other personal economic worries—higher prices, joblessness, rising interest rates—the fear that taxes will go up is even more dominating a concern now than it was then.

While previous Gallup surveys have found expectations for a tax increase tied to a belief that taxes will have to be raised to cut the deficit, the public is solidly opposed to a hike in personal income taxes to reduce the deficit (69%). Even among groups most willing to support increased income taxes to bring the deficit down—men and college graduates—no more than 32% and 35%, respectively, give their approval to this proposal.

The overwhelming thumbs-down on new taxes as a way to cut the deficit, however, does not mean that people find any increase in taxes unacceptable. While the public lost its appetite for increased defense spending in the early part of the decade, it continues to favor increasing the spending level for a wide array of domestic concerns. When asked about current spending levels for fifteen specific purposes, a majority of the public favors more spending for eight of them: improving public education (76%); combating the drug problem (75%); programs to help the homeless (71%); long-term health care, including coverage of nursing home costs (67%); reducing air pollution (59%); research on AIDS (59%); job training and placement (56%); and programs to assist low-income families (56%).

As evident as the public's desire to spend more money on these government programs is its lack of willingness to cut spending on any specific budget item. Even in the cases of defense spending and space exploration, which rate as Americans' lowest priorities for new spending, most people think that we should at least maintain current spending levels.

In a poll completed after the House of Representatives voted to reduce the capital gains tax rate through 1991, but prior to Senate action on the proposal, a plurality of the public (46%) approves of lowering the capital gains tax. Slightly more than one third (36%) disapproves of cutting the tax, while a sizable proportion (18%) has no opinion on this issue.

The vote in the House is regarded as a major victory for President Bush and the GOP. In voting solidly in favor of lowering the capital gains tax (only one House Republican voted against the proposal), GOP legislators were reflecting the views of the party's rank-and-file. Republicans in the poll favor cutting the tax by a 2-to-1 margin (56% to 28%), while the Democratic faithful, by contrast, are nearly evenly divided on this issue.

Respondents with a household income of $50,000 or more, who can be expected to benefit disproportionately from such a tax cut, are most in favor of reducing the capital gains tax (62% approve, 31% disapprove). Those with a household income below $20,000 are least supportive of the change (37% approve, 41% disapprove).

OCTOBER 18
ABORTION—A TEN-YEAR COMPARISON

Interviewing Date: 10/5–8/89
Survey #89139

The Supreme Court's 1973 Roe v. Wade decision established a woman's constitutional right to an abortion, at least in the first three months of pregnancy. Would you like to see the Supreme Court completely overturn its Roe v. Wade decision, or not?

Yes...33%
No..61
No opinion...6

Compared to how you feel on other public issues, are your feelings about abortion:

| | Those who favor overturn of Roe v. Wade | | Those who oppose overturn of Roe v. Wade | |
	1989	1979	1989	1979
Extremely strong	41%	36%	17%	7%
Very strong	33	34	26	18

Fairly			
strong	20	24	41	45
Not strong			
at all	6	6	16	30

How important is a candidate's position on abortion when you decide how to vote in an election for governor or the state legislature?

	Those who favor overturn of Roe v. Wade		Those who oppose overturn of Roe v. Wade	
	1989	1979*	1989	1979*
Most				
important	27%	12%	8%	1%
Very				
important	38	44	26	17
Somewhat				
important	24	20	38	32
Not too				
important	11	24	28	50

*In 1979 the question referred to an election for Congress.

Note: Americans who believe that a woman has a right to an abortion have dramatically stepped up their activism on the issue during the past ten years, according to a new Gallup Poll. While a much higher percentage of those opposed to abortion engages in activism today than those holding the so-called prochoice position—a difference that has been observed since the Supreme Court's 1973 ruling in *Roe v. Wade*—prochoice advocates in 1989 are much more likely to take tangible steps as a result of their beliefs than they were in 1979. Today, equal numbers of people on both sides of the issue are writing letters and donating money in support of their position.

Almost one in ten (8%) of prochoice supporters says that a candidate's position on this issue is one of the most important considerations when deciding how to vote, whereas in 1979 only a tiny fraction (1%) of prochoice supporters were willing to say that they would translate their opinions into votes. Among right-to-life advocates, 27% report today that a candidate's stance is one of the most important considerations, compared to 12% in 1979.

About four in ten (43%) of those who support a woman's right to abortion say that

their feelings are extremely or very strong, up from one quarter (25%) who thought this way one decade ago. Commitment to this issue is even stronger among those holding the right-to-life position, with 74% feeling extremely or very strong today, compared to 70% in 1979.

The population as a whole favors the prochoice position. A clear majority (61%) of Americans does not want the Supreme Court to overturn its *Roe v. Wade* decision, while one third (33%) is in favor of a reversal. A 1979 survey conducted by researchers at the University of Michigan's Survey Research Center found a similar proportion of pro- and antiabortion sentiment in the general population, as is revealed in the current Gallup Poll.

However, the 1979 study also found that people opposed to abortion had much more strongly held opinions about the issue than those who favored abortion. And, due to the greater intensity of opinion on the antiabortion side, opponents of abortion ten years ago were much more likely than supporters to write letters to public officials, contribute money to organizations, and say that they would make voting decisions on the basis of a candidate's position on abortion.

The current Gallup Poll finds right-to-life forces still more activist than prochoice forces, but the balance is shifting. Perhaps fueled by concern over this summer's Supreme Court ruling in the Webster case that invited states to pass legislation restricting abortion, the new survey shows substantial increases in the overall number of abortion rights supporters who feel strongly about the issue and who are taking a politically active role.

Despite the increase in political involvement among abortion rights supporters, the right-to-life side continues to have more intense feelings on this issue and exert a disproportionately large and vocal opposition. Today, four in ten (41%) opponents of abortion say that their feelings about abortion are extremely strong, while less than one half as many abortion rights supporters (17%) report that their feelings are equally strong. Opponents of abortion are more than three times as likely as supporters to say that this issue is one of their most important considerations when deciding how to vote (27% versus 8%).

OCTOBER 19
CALIFORNIA EARTHQUAKE

Interviewing Date: 10/18/89
Special Survey

The following questions were asked in Alameda, Contra Costa, Marin, San Francisco, San Mateo, and Santa Clara counties:

Where were you when the earthquake hit?

At home	48%
At work	22
At school	2
Outside	10
In a car	7
In a bus/BART/other public transportation	1
Other	10

How frightened were you during the earthquake?

Very frightened	37%
Somewhat frightened	29
Not too frightened	18
Not at all frightened	15
No opinion	1

Were you, or was anyone in your household, injured in any way?

Yes	2%
No	98

Were any other family members injured in any way?

Yes	1%
No	99

Did the earthquake cause any damage to your home or personal property?

Yes	41%
No	59

Asked of those who suffered damage to home or property: Can you give me a rough estimate of the cost of the damage?

Less than $500	48%
$500–$999	26
$1,000–$4,999	12
$5,000–$9,999	1
$10,000 or over	*
No opinion	13

*Less than 1%

Do you feel that the Bay Area was prepared for dealing with an earthquake of this severity, or not?

Yes	62%
No	29
No opinion	9

Do you feel that you, yourself, were prepared for dealing with an earthquake of this severity, or not?

Yes	49%
No	47
No opinion	4

How would you rate the job the police in the Bay Area did in responding to the earthquake emergency?

Excellent	60%
Good	24
Only fair	4
Poor	1

How would you rate the job the other emergency services did in responding to the earthquake situation?

Excellent	62%
Good	25
Only fair	4
Poor	1
No opinion	8

How would you rate the job your neighbors did in responding to the earthquake emergency?

Excellent	41%
Good	29
Only fair	7
Poor	2
No opinion	21

Did you, yourself, do anything to help deal with the earthquake emergency?

Yes...33
No..65
Not sure 2

Some people have been predicting that the Bay Area would have a major earthquake. Do you think that Tuesday's [October 17] earthquake was the major one that was predicted, or do you think that the major earthquake is still to come?

Tuesday's was the major quake..................22%
Major quake is still to come....................58
There will not be a major
    quake (volunteered)...........................1
No opinion..19

Have you started to think about moving to a different place as a result of the earthquake?

Yes..7%
No...92
No opinion...1

Note: San Francisco Bay Area residents are a hardy breed. Despite the fact that many sustained property damage in the October 17 earthquake, most were frightened, and most think a bigger quake is yet to come, few are considering a move away from the area. These are the first reactions recorded in a special Gallup Poll conducted by telephone on October 18 in six of the California counties affected by the earthquake, after most restrictions on incoming telephone calls were lifted for the area. (Gallup interviewers could not reach those who suffered the most severe damage and personal injury, and interviews were not conducted in either San Benito or Santa Cruz counties.)

About one half (48%) of the adults contacted was at home when the earthquake hit at 5:04 p.m. One quarter (24%) of them was still at work or at school. Eighteen percent were outdoors or in transit, including a survey respondent who was on the San Francisco-Oakland Bay Bridge when a section of it collapsed. The remaining 10% were in a variety of other places.

Only 37% felt very frightened as the earthquake was happening, with 29% somewhat frightened, 18% not too frightened, and 15% not frightened at all.

Even though the hardest-hit areas were excluded from the survey, property damage was widespread, with 41% reporting damage to their homes or personal property. Almost two thirds (65%) of the Santa Clara County residents interviewed reported property damage. Most of this damage was minor, with 48% of those reporting damage estimating repairs at less than $500.

Six in ten (62%) Bay Area residents think that the community as a whole generally was prepared to deal with an earthquake as severe as that of October 17, while about one half (49%) think that they personally were prepared. Police and other emergency service workers draw overwhelmingly positive ratings for their responsiveness to the disaster. Sixty percent of respondents think that the police reaction was excellent, with an additional 24% rating the police responsiveness as good. Only 5% think that the police were only fair or poor. Equally high ratings are given to other emergency service workers, with six in ten (62%) residents evaluating the response as excellent, one quarter (25%) as good, and only 5% giving a lower rating.

Bay Area residents also think almost as highly of their neighbors. Forty-one percent say that their neighbors did an excellent job in responding to the disaster, and 29% think that their neighbors did a good job. Nine percent give lower ratings. Bay Area residents themselves (33%) pitched in to help deal with the emergency. Some people reported visits to reassure their elderly neighbors or placed calls to the relatives of neighbors who were without telephone service. Others helped out by such activities as donating blood and distributing generators to people without electricity.

A majority of residents believes that the earthquake was not the major one that experts have predicted would hit the area sooner or later. Almost six in ten (58%) think that the major earthquake is still to come, while 22% hope that Tuesday's quake was the big one. Despite widespread expectation that an even more severe earthquake will hit the Bay Area in the future, almost everyone plans to stay put. Perhaps reflecting their confidence in official preparedness and in the competence of emergency service workers, nine in ten (92%) residents say that they are not thinking about moving to another location. Only 7% have started to think about relocation.

HOMOSEXUALITY

Interviewing Date: 10/12–15/89
Survey #GO 89139-2

Do you think homosexual relations between consenting adults should or should not be legal?

Should...47%
Should not.......................................36
No opinion......................................17

By Sex

Male

Should...49%
Should not.......................................38
No opinion......................................13

Female

Should...45%
Should not.......................................34
No opinion......................................21

By Ethnic Background

White

Should...48%
Should not.......................................36
No opinion......................................16

Nonwhite

Should...45%
Should not.......................................36
No opinion......................................19

By Education

College Graduate

Should...61%
Should not.......................................28
No opinion......................................11

College Incomplete

Should...55%
Should not.......................................32
No opinion......................................13

High-School Graduate

Should...42%
Should not.......................................39
No opinion......................................19

Less Than High-School Graduate

Should...32%
Should not.......................................45
No opinion......................................23

By Region

East

Should...55%
Should not.......................................27
No opinion......................................18

Midwest

Should...41%
Should not.......................................40
No opinion......................................19

South

Should...40%
Should not.......................................44
No opinion......................................16

West

Should...56%
Should not.......................................30
No opinion......................................14

By Age

18–29 Years

Should...61%
Should not.......................................31
No opinion..8

30–49 Years

Should...53%
Should not.......................................33
No opinion......................................14

50 Years and Over

Should...32%
Should not.......................................43
No opinion......................................25

By Income

$50,000 and Over

Should..62%
Should not...27
No opinion...11

$30,000-$49,999

Should..48%
Should not...38
No opinion...14

$20,000-$29,999

Should..52%
Should not...35
No opinion...13

Under $20,000

Should..41%
Should not...41
No opinion...18

By Religion

Protestants

Should..42%
Should not...42
No opinion...16

Catholics

Should..54%
Should not...28
No opinion...18

Selected National Trend

	Should	Should not	No opinion
1987	33%	55%	12%
1986	33	54	13
1985	44	47	9
1982	45	39	16
1977	43	43	14

As you know, there has been considerable discussion in the news lately regarding the rights of homosexual men and women. In general, do you think homosexuals should or should not have equal rights in terms of job opportunities?

Should..71%
Should not...18
No opinion...11

Selected National Trend

	Should	Should not	No opinion
1982	59%	28%	13%
1977	56	33	11

Now, I'd like to ask you about the hiring of homosexuals in specific occupations. Do you think homosexuals should or should not be hired for each of the following occupations:

Salespersons?

Should..79%
Should not...13
No opinion... 8

Selected National Trend

	Those responding "should"
1987	72%
1985	71
1982	70
1977	68

The armed forces?

Should..60%
Should not...21
No opinion...11

Selected National Trend

	Those responding "should"
1987	55%
1985	55
1982	52
1977	51

Doctors?

Should..56%
Should not...32
No opinion...12

	Those responding "should"
1987	49%
1985	52
1982	50
1977	44

The clergy?

Should	44%
Should not	43
No opinion	13

	Those responding "should"
1987	42%
1985	41
1982	38
1977	36

Elementary-school teachers?

Should	42%
Should not	48
No opinion	10

	Those responding "should"
1987	33%
1985	36
1982	32
1977	27

High-school teachers?

Should	47%
Should not	43
No opinion	10

Is homosexuality something a person is born with, or is homosexuality due to other factors such as upbringing or environment?

Born with	19%
Other factors	48
Both (volunteered)	12
Neither (volunteered)	2
No opinion	19

	Born with	Other factors	Both, neither	No opinion
1982	17%	52%	15%	16%
1977	12	56	17	15

Do you think that, given the choice, most homosexuals would rather be homosexual, or that most would rather not be homosexual?

Would rather be	38%
Would rather not be	31
No opinion	31

Note: As the backlash toward homosexuals that grew out of the AIDS epidemic subsides, support for the civil rights of gays has increased dramatically compared to a few years ago. Previous Gallup Polls conducted in the mid-1980s showed an increasing intolerance of homosexuality at a time when fear of contracting AIDS was at its highest point among the general public, but a new survey shows that the trend is reversing.

The poll finds that almost one half (47%) of all adults thinks that homosexual relations between consenting adults should be legal, up from only one third (33%) who thought that way in 1987. Seven in ten (71%) now say that homosexuals should have equal job opportunities, compared to only six in ten (59%) who favored equal opportunity for gays in 1982.

Today, just over one third (36%) believes that homosexual relations should not be legal, whereas more than one half opposed legalization in 1987 (55%). Attitudes about legalization of homosexual relations are now where they were in 1982, before awareness of AIDS became so widespread.

The belief that homosexuals should not be discriminated against in employment is increasing. More Americans now say that homosexuals should be hired for a variety of occupations, thus reflecting a gradual increase in tolerance over the period since 1977 when Gallup first started to measure these attitudes.

However, respondents still make important distinctions in terms of those jobs considered appropriate. A large majority (79%) thinks that homosexuals should be hired as salespersons, and most also would have homosexuals as members of the armed forces (60%) and the medical profession (56%). The public is split on whether homosexuals should be employed as clergy (44% versus 43%), elementary-school teachers (42% versus 48%), and high-school teachers (47% versus 43%).

Americans tend to see homosexuality as a product of a person's environment or upbringing. About one half (48%) sees upbringing as the main cause, and an additional 12% also think that upbringing is a contributing factor. Only one in five (19%) thinks that a person is born with the tendency. These beliefs are essentially unchanged from those expressed in a 1982 Gallup Poll.

The public is divided, however, in its view about whether homosexuals prefer their own sexual orientation. About four in ten (38%) think that, given the choice, most homosexuals would rather remain gay, but 31% think that most homosexuals would opt for a heterosexual orientation if they could choose. These views represent a shift in opinion since 1982, when the public was equally likely to think that homosexuals would opt for a gay orientation (33%) as to think that they would choose heterosexuality (37%).

OCTOBER 27
NORTH ATLANTIC TREATY
ORGANIZATION (NATO)

Interviewing Date: 7/18–21/89 (U.S. only)
Survey #GO 89136-2

Asked in twelve of the sixteen NATO member countries: The relations between Russia and the West have been changing over the last few years. Both Russia and NATO have taken away and destroyed several types of nuclear weapons. Do you think the NATO alliance should be maintained, or is the alliance not necessary anymore?*

	Should be maintained	Not necessary	No opinion
Netherlands	81%	15%	4%
Canada	78	8	14
United States	75	10	15
Great Britain	71	15	14
Belgium	69	13	18
Luxembourg	69	10	21
West Germany	63	13	24

Italy	58	18	24
Turkey	50	14	36
Denmark	43	13	44
Spain	30	34	36
Portugal	26	9	65

*Four NATO member countries—France, Greece, Norway, and Iceland—were not surveyed.

Asked in eleven of the sixteen NATO member countries: Today, it is often claimed that Europe has enjoyed over forty years of peace against a Russian threat because the North Atlantic Treaty Organization (NATO) was founded forty years ago. Do you think this view is right or wrong?*

	Right	Probably right	Wrong	No opinion
Canada	26%	44%	11%	19%
Great Britain	27	41	15	17
West Germany	29	38	11	22
Netherlands	34	30	30	6
Luxembourg	20	44	12	24
Italy	31	29	18	22
Turkey	24	28	10	38
Belgium	14	37	16	33
Denmark	20	22	13	45
Spain	17	15	30	38
Portugal	8	20	5	67

*Five NATO member countries—United States, France, Greece, Norway, and Iceland—were not surveyed.

Asked in twelve of the sixteen NATO member countries: It has been proposed that as long as Russia has nuclear weapons that can reach targets in Western Europe, NATO should keep a number of similar weapons in Western Europe. Do you agree with that?*

	Agree	Disagree	No opinion
Netherlands	66%	29%	5%
United States	63	26	11
Canada	62	21	17
Great Britain	60	22	18
Belgium	59	20	21
Luxembourg	51	22	27

West Germany 46	22	32
Turkey.................42	18	40
Italy....................38	32	30
Denmark 27	24	49
Spain 22	40	38
Portugal..............21	11	68

*Four NATO countries—France, Greece, Norway, and Finland—were not surveyed.

Note: The relaxation of tensions between the West and the Soviet Union during the Gorbachev era has yet to push Western public opinion toward the view that NATO has outlived its usefulness. A 1989 Gallup International survey taken this summer in twelve of the sixteen NATO member countries, conducted forty years after the founding of the North Atlantic alliance, finds high levels of support throughout North America and Western Europe for maintaining NATO. Only in Spain, the newest member of the alliance, is there significant sentiment for doing away with NATO.

Three quarters (75%) of Americans favor the continuation of NATO, while 10% say that the alliance is no longer necessary. Only the Canadians (78%) and the Dutch (81%) rank higher. Following the United States in overall support for preserving NATO are Great Britain (71%), Belgium (69%), Luxembourg (69%), West Germany (63%), and Italy (58%).

While less than a majority in Turkey (50%), Denmark (43%), and Portugal (26%) say that the alliance should be maintained, relatively few in these countries take the contrary view. Instead, high proportions are uncertain or do not know enough about the situation to voice an opinion. Only in Spain do as many people think that NATO is unnecessary (34%) as believe it should be maintained (30%).

The survey also finds that respondents generally believe that the alliance has been instrumental in forestalling armed conflict in Europe over the last forty years. Only the Spaniards—the group least supportive of NATO—have a tendency to disagree (30%) that it has played an important role in keeping the peace.

The question of whether NATO should modernize its short-range nuclear weapons to counter similar Soviet missiles capable of reaching targets in Western Europe is more controversial than the question of whether NATO should continue to exist. Only in the United States (63%) and four other countries—the Netherlands (66%), Canada (62%), Great Britain (60%), and Belgium (59%)—does a clear majority think that NATO should maintain its short-range nuclear weapons in Western Europe. In Italy and Denmark, public opinion divides nearly evenly on the issue.

NOVEMBER 6
DIET AND NUTRITION

Interviewing Date: 9/12–15/89
Survey #GO 89138-2

How much do you worry about the quality and healthfulness of your diet?

A great deal...32%
A fair amount..................................31
Some...15
Not too much....................................10
Not at all...12

How much attention do you pay to the food warnings and nutritional recommendations you hear or read about?

A great deal.......................................26%
A fair amount..................................36
Some...16
Not too much....................................13
Not at all... 9

When you learn about food warnings or nutritional recommendations, how often do you try to follow the advice and make changes in your diet?

All of the time 9%
Most of the time................................38
Some of the time 34
Hardly ever 13
Never 6

Would you say that you personally are making a strong effort, some effort, or no effort at all to:

	Strong, some effort	No effort	No opinion
Eat fresh fruits, vegetables........	93%	7%	*
Eat green vegetables........	87	13	*

Avoid foods high in fat	87	13	*
Avoid foods high in cholesterol	81	18	1
Avoid a lot of salt	78	21	1
Avoid foods high in sugar	80	20	*
Eat foods high in fiber	82	17	1
Avoid fried foods	77	23	*
Eat foods high in calcium	73	25	2
Avoid beverages with caffeine	59	41	*
Avoid foods with additives	70	29	1
Avoid red meat	65	35	*

*Less than 1%

Now, I'd like to ask you some questions about the foods you eat. First, thinking back over the past two or three years, would you say your eating habits have changed a lot, changed a little, or have not changed?

Changed a lot.....................................34%
Changed a little................................31
Have not changed 35

Did you eat breakfast this morning?

Yes...68%
No..32

Did you eat lunch today?

Yes...82%
No..18

Did you eat dinner last night?

Yes...93%
No.. 7

The following questions were asked of those who ate dinner on the previous weekday night:

Where did you eat dinner last night?

At home...86%
At restaurant..................................... 9
Other... 5

While you were eating dinner last night, were you doing anything else such as working, studying, watching television, or reading?

Yes...45%
No..55

Did you eat dinner alone last night, or did you eat with other people?

Alone..22%
With others......................................78

Asked of those who are living with other people: In a typical week, how many nights do the members of your household eat dinner together?

Seven..37%
Six to four 34
Three to one.....................................22
None... 6
No opinion....................................... 1

In a typical week, how many of your dinner meals are homemade and eaten at home? By homemade, I mean dinners that are mostly made from scratch with fresh ingredients.

Seven..25%
Six to four 48
Three to one.....................................21
None... 5
No opinion....................................... 1

How would you describe your own personal weight situation?

Overweight.......................................33%
About right.......................................61
Underweight..................................... 6

How much do you enjoy cooking?

A great deal......................................32%
A fair amount....................................27
Some...16
Not too much....................................13
Not at all..12

How much do you enjoy eating?

A great deal......................................48%
A fair amount....................................36
Some...10

Not too much.......................................5
Not at all..1

Overall, how healthy would you say your diet is?

Very healthy 44%
Somewhat healthy 48
Not too healthy...................................6
Not at all healthy................................2

Note: The family dinner is undergoing a fundamental change in America. Mom is now less likely to do the cooking, the apple pie may have come from a freezer or take-out restaurant, and there is a good chance that conversation at the table will be tuned out by distractions. Changing sex roles, a devotion to convenience foods, mounting concern about diet, and busy life-styles are making a profound impact on the way Americans dine, according to the latest Gallup Mirror of America Poll.

Gallup recently surveyed American adults to find out their dining habits, how concerned they are with nutrition, and what, if anything, they are doing to improve their diets. Among the key findings:

• Of the 86% who dine at home on week nights, just over one half prepares a meal from scratch. The others dine on frozen or prepackaged food or else eat meals from take-out restaurants.

• Among those who dine at home in the company of others, nearly four in ten (45%) watch television, study, work, or read while eating.

The survey finds a majority of adults worried about the quality of their diets and attentive to food warnings and nutritional advice. More than six in ten (63%) say that they worry a great deal or a fair amount about the quality and healthfulness of the foods they eat. Despite this evidence showing some progress toward a more healthful diet, Americans are still eating large amounts of foods they have been advised by experts to avoid or cut back on.

The poll also shows that many people skip meals. Despite the theory that breakfast is the most important meal of the day, it is the one most frequently missed. One in three adults (32%) skips breakfast on a typical weekday morning, and nearly one in five (18%) skips lunch. Many fewer miss dinner (7%). This tendency to skip meals may be related to busy life-styles or to a desire to lose weight. One

third (33%) of all Americans say that they are overweight.

When Americans gather for a family dinner on weeknights these days, the odds are fairly high that they will be distracted by television, work, or study. Relaxation and conversation with dinner—the nurturing elements of home life—are enjoyed by only one in three adults. On a typical weeknight, about two in ten adults (22%) eat dinner alone. Of those dining with other members of their household, only 36% enjoy the meal without the distraction of watching television, working, or reading. Moreover, adults typically eat a homemade dinner (made mostly from scratch with fresh ingredients) even less often than they eat together as a family. Less than one half (48%) usually eats homemade meals as often as four to six nights per week.

Americans have clearly gotten the message that they should eat more fresh fruits and vegetables and avoid foods high in fat or cholesterol, despite the recent debate over whether a low-cholesterol diet can actually reduce the risk of heart disease for everyone. Today, more than one half of all adults say that they are making a strong or some effort to eat fresh fruits and vegetables (93%), eat green vegetables in the cabbage family (87%), or avoid foods with a lot of fat (87%).

Nearly one half is making either a strong or some effort to avoid foods high in cholesterol (81%) or foods containing a lot of salt (78%). At least four in ten say that they are making the effort to avoid foods with a lot of sugar (80%), eat foods high in fiber (82%), or avoid fried foods (77%). One in three (73%) is trying to eat foods high in calcium.

The dietary changes that people are least likely to attempt are avoiding old favorites such as coffee and beef. Four in ten (41%) adults are making no effort to reduce their caffeine consumption, 35% are not trying to avoid red meat, and 29% are not trying to avoid foods containing additives such as preservatives, colorings, and artificial flavorings.

The public's efforts at dietary change have been more successful in some areas than in others. The latest data on per-capita food consumption reveals that Americans are eating record amounts of fresh fruits and vegetables and have increased their consumption over the past twenty years of low-fat milk products, poultry, fish, seafood, pasta, cereals, and other grain products. People are eating fewer eggs and less whole milk than ever before.

However, the discrepancies between how Americans say they are trying to improve their diet and what they actually eat point out how difficult it is for people to make changes in something as basic as the foods they consume. Although large numbers of people are aware of the food warnings and nutritional recommendations that are so abundant today, only one in ten (9%) adults say that they follow the advice that they hear all of the time. Four in ten (38%) follow the advice and warnings most of the time, while 34% adhere to new recommendations some of the time and 19% hardly ever or never follow the advice.

NOVEMBER 15
PRESIDENT BUSH

Interviewing Date: 11/9–12/89
Survey #GO 89140

Do you approve or disapprove of the way George Bush is handling his job as president?

Approve...70%
Disapprove...17
No opinion...13

By Politics

Republicans

Approve...87%
Disapprove... 7
No opinion... 6

Democrats

Approve...55%
Disapprove...29
No opinion...16

Independents

Approve...69%
Disapprove...14
No opinion...17

Presidential Performance Ratings
(In November of Inaugural Year)

		Approve	Dis-approve	No opinion
Reagan	1981	49%	40%	11%
Carter	1977	56	30	14
Nixon	1969	67	19	14
Johnson	1965	62	22	16
Kennedy	1961	79	9	12
Eisenhower	1953	61	26	13
Truman	1949*	51	31	18

*September

How strongly would you say you approve or disapprove? Would you say very strongly, or not so strongly?

	Bush November 1989	Reagan November 1981
Approve	70%	49%
Very strongly	32	25
Not so strongly	38	24
Disapprove	17	40
Very strongly	8	24
Not so strongly	9	16
No opinion	13	11

At this point, would you say that George Bush is doing a better job as president than you expected, or not as good a job as you expected?

Better than expected.............................44%
Not as good as expected.........................21
About as well as expected (volunteered).....28
No opinion... 7

By Politics

Republicans

Better than expected.............................45%
Not as good as expected.........................18
About as well as expected (volunteered).....33
No opinion... 4

Democrats

Better than expected.............................42%
Not as good as expected.........................26

About as well as expected (volunteered) 25
No opinion...7

Independents

Better than expected............................45%
Not as good as expected........................20
About as well as expected (volunteered) 27
No opinion..8

Apart from whether you approve or disapprove of the way Bush is handling his job as president, what do you think of Bush as a person? Would you say you approve or disapprove of him?

	Bush November 1989	Reagan November 1981
Approve	84%	73%
Disapprove	7	17
No opinion	9	10

Do you approve or disapprove of the way Dan Quayle is handling his job as vice president?

Approve..43%
Disapprove...29
No opinion...28

By Politics

Republicans

Approve..57%
Disapprove...18
No opinion...25

Democrats

Approve..33%
Disapprove...38
No opinion...29

Independents

Approve..41%
Disapprove...29
No opinion...30

Now let me ask you about some specific problems facing this country. As I read off each one, would you tell me whether you approve or disapprove of the way President Bush is handling that problem:

Environmental issues?

Approve..46%
Disapprove...40
No opinion...14

Education policy?

Approve..53%
Disapprove...35
No opinion...12

Situation in Eastern Europe?

Approve..63%
Disapprove...16
No opinion...21

Economic conditions in this country?

	November	March
Approve	40%	52%
Disapprove	51	27
No opinion	9	21

Federal budget deficit?

	November	March
Approve	32%	40%
Disapprove	53	36
No opinion	15	24

The abortion issue?

	November	July
Approve	38%	43%
Disapprove	45	35
No opinion	17	22

The drug problem?

	November	Sept.
Approve	53%	72%
Disapprove	41	18
No opinion	6	10

Poverty and homelessness?

	November	August
Approve	30%	33%
Disapprove	59	53
No opinion	11	14

Foreign policy?

	November	March
Approve	65%	62%
Disapprove	21	15
No opinion	14	23

Relations with the Soviet Union?

	November	March
Approve	81%	70%
Disapprove	11	10
No opinion	8	20

Situation in Central America?

	November	March
Approve	40%	37%
Disapprove	39	33
No opinion	21	30

Do you approve or disapprove of the job President Bush has done so far in explaining his policies and plans for the future to the American people?

Approve	61%
Disapprove	33
No opinion	6

Selected National Trend

	Approve	Dis-approve	No opinion
May	52%	37%	11%
March	65	28	7

Do you think President Bush is doing enough to help the Soviet Union deal with the political and social changes taking place there, or should he do more?

Doing enough	61%
Should do more	24
Doing too much (volunteered)	5
No opinion	10

Do you think President Bush is doing enough to further reduce the military tensions between the United States and the Soviet Union, or should he do more?

Doing enough	61%
Should do more	24
Doing too much (volunteered)	5
No opinion	10

Do you think President Bush is doing enough to help Eastern European countries such as Poland, East Germany, and Hungary deal with the political and social changes taking place there, or should he do more?

Doing enough	59%
Should do more	27
Doing too much (volunteered)	5
No opinion	9

How much progress, if any, do you think the Bush administration has made in combating drugs?

A lot	7%
Some	48
Not too much	30
None at all	12
No opinion	3

Note: One year after he won the presidency in a sometimes bitter and divisive campaign, George Bush receives broad-based public approval for his performance in office. In the latest Gallup Poll, 70% of Americans approve of the way he is handling his job, while fewer than one in five disapproves (17%). To find a president with a higher rating at this point in his first term, one must go back to John F. Kennedy, who earned 79% approval in a November 1961 Gallup Poll.

The new survey, conducted as the opening of the Berlin Wall takes most of the world by surprise, identifies the reduction of East-West tensions as one of the keys to Bush's high approval rating. When asked to evaluate the president's handling of specific policy areas, the public gives Bush his best marks for U.S.-Soviet relations (81% approve) and foreign policy in general (65%). Central America remains one area of foreign policy that is not a clear positive for Bush. The public divides about evenly (40% approve, 39% disapprove).

By a margin of 63% to 16%, Americans also approve of the president's handling of the situation in Eastern Europe. Similarly, by 59% to 27%, respondents say that Bush is doing enough to help the Eastern bloc countries deal with political and social change. His conciliatory style is another key factor behind his high approval ratings. Unlike Ronald Reagan, whose strongly conservative views on many issues tended to alienate certain segments of the public, Bush attracts little strong opposition. Americans today are only one third as likely to strongly disapprove of Bush's job performance (8%) as they were to think that way about Reagan eight years ago (24%). While those who approve of Bush generally express moderate (38%) rather than strong approval (32%), the president still receives more strong approval ratings than did Reagan in his first term (25%).

Bush's personal popularity—that is, opinions of him as a person rather than of his job performance—compares favorably with that of his predecessor. Currently, 84% of the public say that they approve of Bush as a person, while only 7% disapprove. The figures for Reagan at a comparable point in his presidency were significantly less positive, 73% to 17%. In fact, Bush's personal popularity is now as high as Reagan's was at any time during his eight years in office.

Bush's job performance on specific issues outside the area of foreign policy and East-West relations, however, fail to match his overall approval rating. Although he has pledged to be the "education president," his ratings on education—53% approve, 35% disapprove—do not come close to the overall approval figure.

Perhaps most worrisome for Bush are his ratings on economic issues. Opinion now runs against him—51% disapprove, 40% approve—for his general handling of economic conditions, and respondents are twice as likely to disapprove of the president's handling of the economy now as they were in March. Similarly, Bush draws lower ratings for his efforts to deal with the deficit; more than one half (53%) now disapproves, while only one third (32%) approves.

In addition to the economy, Bush seems vulnerable on the abortion issue and on the problems of poverty and homelessness. On these growing concerns, a plurality expresses disapproval of the way he has handled the situation (45% and 59%, respectively).

Bush gets better marks on the environment than did Reagan, but even so a large proportion (40%) expresses disapproval of his handling of environmental issues. Ratings of his performance in combating the drug problem now are more closely divided—53% versus 41%—after being overwhelmingly positive (72%) shortly after Bush's televised speech of September 5 on the issue.

NOVEMBER 16
SOVIET-MADE PRODUCTS

Interviewing Date: April–May 1989 (USSR only)
Special Survey*

The following questions were asked in three cities of the Soviet Union—Moscow, Kursk, and Kiev.

Over the next five years do you expect the quality of Soviet-made products such as farm products, grocery items, or manufactured goods such as clothing, furniture, or electrical appliances to improve a great deal, improve somewhat, stay the same, get somewhat worse, or get much worse?

Improve a great deal 8%
Improve somewhat 34
Stay the same 28
Get somewhat worse 7
Get much worse 5
No opinion 18

*This survey was conducted jointly by the Gallup Poll and the Institute of Sociology of the Soviet Academy of Sciences. Results cannot be projected to the entire Soviet Union because only three locations are covered in this survey. The three cities selected for this survey were chosen to provide a composite sample that would be typical of the Russian Republic and the Ukraine.

Which, if any, of the types of products listed on this card do you (or some other member of your family living with you) have at the present time? Which, if any, of these products do you think you (or some other member of your family living with you) will purchase in the next two years?

	Have at present time	Will purchase in next two years
Refrigerator	97%	16%
Television	97	10
Wristwatch	96	16
Furniture	92	43
Radio	82	7
Washing machine	78	22
Cassette tape recorder	68	15
Record player	60	6
Still camera	57	6
Bicycle	43	12
Cooking stove	35	4

Automobile	23	16
Motorcycle/moped	10	3
Movie camera	8	3
Video tape player	4	10
Video camera	2	3
None; no opinion	1	24

Note: Soviet consumers do not expect a dramatic change in the quality of goods available in their markets. Only 8% of the consumers surveyed think that product quality will improve a great deal over the next five years. Indeed, most believe that quality will improve only somewhat (34%) or that it will stay about the same (28%).

Soviet respondents are more likely to own and purchase household rather than personal items. Asked which products they expect to buy within the next two years, furniture is mentioned most often (43%). One in five (22%) plans to buy a washing machine. Sixteen percent intend to purchase a refrigerator within the next twenty-four months, and the same percentage intends to buy an automobile. Wristwatches (16%), cassette tape recorders (15%), bicycles (12%), televisions (10%), and video tape players (10%) are the only other items named by at least 10% of those surveyed of products that they plan to buy.

Individual ownership of cooking stoves and automobiles is relatively low in the Soviet Union. Only one third (35%) indicates having a stove. (Among apartment dwellers, stoves are often part of communal property and are shared by a number of families.) Merely 23% say that they own a car.

Virtually all of the Soviet households interviewed report having a television (97%) and refrigerator (97%). At least four in five have a radio (82%) or washing machine (78%), while over two thirds (68%) say that they have a cassette tape recorder. Smaller proportions own record players (60%), cameras (57%), or bicycles (43%). While only 4% of respondents report that they currently own a video tape player, 10% indicate that they would be interested in buying one. Intent, not surprisingly, is higher among young people and those with higher incomes.

NOVEMBER 22
VOLUNTARISM

Interviewing Date: 11/9–12/89
Survey #GO 89140

Do you, yourself, happen to be involved in any charity or social service activities, such as helping the poor, the sick, or the elderly?

	Yes
National	41%

By Sex

Male	36%
Female	46

Selected National Trend

	Yes
1987	39%
1986	36
1984	31
1982	29
1977	27

Asked of those who responded in the affirmative: In the past thirty days, roughly how many hours, if any, did you spend on volunteer activities? Just your best estimate:

None	29%
Less than 6 hours	20
6–14 hours	24
15 or more hours	23
Don't know	4

Also asked of those who replied in the affirmative: How much do you enjoy the volunteer work you do? Would you say you enjoy it:

A great deal	70%
Somewhat	17
A fair amount	12
Not too much; not at all; no opinion	1

Now I'd like to focus on the past twelve months and talk about all the ways in which people can help others through charitable organizations and other groups which help people—for example, health organizations, social welfare groups, local community groups, youth organizations, educational groups, and religious charities.

Have you done any unpaid volunteer work for any of these types of organizations within the past twelve months?

	Yes
National	42%

During the past twelve months have you contributed money to any charitable organization or other group, not including your church, that used your donation to help other people?

	Yes
National	70%

Have you made any contributions to your church during the past twelve months that were used specifically for the church's charitable activities?

	Yes
National	60%

During the past twelve months have you contributed any food, clothing, or other property to a charitable organization or other group that helps people?

	Yes
National	74%

People help other people in ways besides giving money, time, or other things to organized groups. Sometimes people help the needy directly. During the past twelve months did you give money, food, or clothing to any of the following types of people:

	Yes
The homeless or street people	36%
A needy neighbor	50
A needy relative	54
A needy friend	53
Another needy person	38

Now think about the next two weeks. Do you plan to donate any money or food to a charitable group during the next two weeks?

	Yes
National	63%

Compared to two years ago, do you think the number of people in your community who volunteer their time to help other people has increased, decreased, or stayed the same?

Increased	40%
Decreased	9
Stayed the same	41
No opinion	10

Asked of those who have done volunteer work or who have made donations within the past twelve months: Which of the following types of people have been helped by either your volunteer work or your donations of money or property in the past twelve months?

	Have been helped
The handicapped	51%
Sick people	54
Children	61
Teenagers, young adults	49
The elderly	62
Poor, homeless people	63
Victims of crime, abuse, or disaster	40

Also asked of those who have done volunteer work or who have made donations within the past twelve months: Thinking again about the types of people who have been helped by either your volunteer work or donations of money or property during the past twelve months, were they mostly:

People in your local community	58%
People in your area of the country	15
People across the country	11
People all over the world	12
No opinion	4

Note: The vast majority of Americans report taking steps in their personal lives to help the nation's less fortunate by donating money, belongings, or time to charitable organizations, according to a new Gallup Poll. The survey shows that voluntarism has been increasing gradually throughout the decade, and the level is about the same now as it was before President George Bush took office.

The latest Gallup Poll finds that in the last twelve months:

• Seven in ten people (70%) contributed money to a charitable organization, and six in ten (60%) gave money to their church that was earmarked for charitable activities. Altogether,

85% of Americans gave money to an organized charity.

• Three quarters (74%) of the public donated food, clothing, or other property to an organization that helps needy people.

• Four in ten (42%) did unpaid volunteer work for a charitable organization. The average volunteer worker contributed six hours of time on unpaid work in the past month. A large majority of unpaid volunteers (70%) enjoy their work a great deal.

Many adults contributed either their time, money, or property directly to a person in need in the past year, without using a charitable organization as an intermediary. About one half helped a needy relative, friend, or neighbor directly. Over one third (36%) helped a homeless person, street person, or another needy individual directly.

Most giving today is focused in local communities. Six in ten contributors (58%) report that most of the people who benefited from their generosity were part of the local community. Fifteen percent directed most of their charitable activity to people in their area of the country. Eleven percent helped those all across the country, while 12% focused their contributions on people living in other nations around the world.

Young children (61%), the elderly (62%), and the poor and homeless (63%) are the recipients of most charitable activity in the United States. Six in ten contributors benefit these groups of needy people, while about one half helps sick people (54%), the handicapped (51%), and teenagers or young adults (49%). Another 40% make donations to victims of crime, abuse, or disaster.

Gallup has tracked Americans' involvement in social service for more than ten years and finds that this activity has been rising gradually throughout the decade. In 1977 only 27% of Americans reported some charitable or social work. Now, 41% are involved. However, the current levels of voluntarism are essentially unchanged from two years ago, when 39% reported social service.

Nonetheless, many Americans believe that the spirit of voluntarism is on the rise in their communities. Four in ten (40%) think that the number of people in their community who volunteer time to help others has increased in the past two years. Only 9% think that volunteer activity has decreased, while 41% perceive no change.

NOVEMBER 29
AIDS

Interviewing Date: 11/16–19/89
Survey #GO 89140-2

How concerned are you that you, yourself, will get AIDS—very concerned, a little concerned, not very concerned, or not at all concerned?

Very...15%
A little..21
Not very..21
Not at all...42
No opinion...1

Selected National Trend

	Very, a little	Not very, not at all	No opinion
October 1988	38%	62%	*
October 1987	42	58	*

*Less than 1%

How concerned are you that a member of your family will get AIDS—very concerned, a little concerned, not very concerned, or not at all concerned?

Very...27%
A little..30
Not very..19
Not at all...22
No opinion...2

Do you think it is likely or not likely that AIDS will eventually become an epidemic for the population at large?

Likely 68%
Not likely...26
No opinion...6

	Likely	Not likely	No opinion
October 1988	69%	23%	8%
October 1987	51	42	7

As I read off each item, one at a time, would you tell me whether you think each of the following is or is not a way for people to catch AIDS from someone who has it:

Sharing hypodermic needles?

Is	98%
Is not	1
Don't know	1

	Is	Is not	Don't know
October 1988	96%	2%	2%
October 1987	97	1	2

Intimate sexual contact with a person of the same sex?

Is	96%
Is not	2
Don't know	2

	Is	Is not	Don't know
October 1988	95%	2%	3%
October 1987	95	2	3

Intimate sexual contact with a person of the opposite sex?

Is	95%
Is not	3
Don't know	2

	Is	Is not	Don't know
October 1988	92%	5%	3%
October 1987	88	10	2

Receiving blood transfusions?

Is	90%
Is not	9
Don't know	1

	Is	Is not	Don't know
October 1988	91%	7%	2%
October 1987	86	11	3

Donating blood?

Is	44%
Is not	54
Don't know	2

	Is	Is not	Don't know
October 1988	29%	65%	6%
October 1987	29	66	5

From a drinking glass?

Is	16%
Is not	78
Don't know	6

	Is	Is not	Don't know
October 1988	18%	72%	10%
October 1987	26	66	8

Being coughed or sneezed upon?

Is	14%
Is not	79
Don't know	7

	Is	Is not	Don't know
October 1988	13%	72%	15%
October 1987	25	65	10

From toilet seats?

Is	11%
Is not	84
Don't know	5

	Is	Is not	Don't know
October 1988	15%	73%	12%
October 1987	18	72	10

Working alongside or in close proximity to someone with AIDS?

Is 7%
Is not 89
Don't know 4

Selected National Trend

	Is	Is not	Don't know
October 1988	5%	89%	6%
October 1987	11	84	5

Do you personally know anyone who has contracted AIDS?

	Yes
National	13%

Selected National Trend

	Yes
November 1986	6%
August 1985	4

Do you think it is likely that scientists will develop a vaccine for AIDS in the next five years, in the next ten years, later, or never?

Next five years 33%
Next ten years 39
Later 15
Never 6
No opinion 7

Note: A large and growing segment of the public mistakenly believes that AIDS can be transmitted through blood donations. This misperception has increased dramatically over the past year, even as the public has rejected other inaccurate beliefs about how the virus is transmitted.

The latest Gallup Poll shows that respondents have been attentive to the specific warnings of health officials about behaviors that increase the risk of getting AIDS. There is widespread awareness that the virus can be transmitted by sharing hypodermic needles (98%), by intimate sexual contact with a person of the same (96%) or the opposite (95%) sex, and by receiving a blood transfusion (90%).

However, many Americans hold notions about AIDS that have been discredited by health officials. More than four in ten (44%) believe that donating blood can lead to infection, while one in seven thinks AIDS can be caught from a drinking glass (16%) or from being coughed or sneezed upon by a victim (14%). Eleven percent see a risk of catching it from toilet seats, and 7% think that AIDS can be contracted by working in close proximity to a victim.

For the most part, the public has become better informed during the past year. A comparison of current knowledge with that recorded in an October 1988 Gallup survey shows growing public sophistication. Significantly more people now are aware of the risks of sharing needles and of having intimate sexual contact, while significantly fewer now believe that AIDS can be transmitted by toilet seats, drinking glasses, or coughs and sneezes.

A notable exception to this increasing awareness is belief about the risk of blood donations. Misinformation about the transmission of AIDS in this way is up sharply over last year's survey. Americans now are closely divided between those who think that AIDS can be transmitted through blood donations (44%) and those who do not (54%). In 1988 people who correctly perceived that this poses no threat outnumbered those holding the incorrect view by more than two to one (65% to 29%).

Personal concern about contracting AIDS has been fairly stable over this same period of time. One in seven adults (36%) is now very or a little concerned that he or she personally will get the disease, compared with 38% last year and 42% in 1987. Now 63% say that they are not very or not at all concerned, statistically equal to 1988's 62% and 1987's 58%.

More Americans are worried about AIDS affecting a family member than about their own risk of contracting the disease. Almost three in ten (27%) adults say that they are very concerned that a family member will get AIDS, 30% are a little concerned, 19% are not very concerned, and only 22% are not at all concerned. Nonwhites in particular are worried about their family's vulnerability.

Indeed, two thirds of the public (68%) think that AIDS eventually will become an epidemic for the population at large. This view has not changed since last year, when 69% thought it was likely, but it differs sharply from the view in 1987 when 51% thought a widespread epidemic likely.

again would become a military threat to its neighbors. Indeed, as the future reunification of East and West Germany becomes a more realistic prospect each day, Americans say that such a major political change would be good (63%), not bad (21%), for the West.

One important reason why Americans are so hopeful about the future of political reform in the Communist world may be their high opinion of Soviet leader Mikhail Gorbachev. After his summit meeting at Malta with President George Bush, Gorbachev's favorability rating among the U.S. public in the Gallup Poll is even higher than it was one year ago, when he finished second only to Ronald Reagan in Gallup's annual list of America's ten most admired men. More than three fourths (77%) of Americans now say that they have a favorable opinion of Gorbachev, including 24% who describe their opinion as very favorable. Bush himself is finishing the year with a very respectable approval rating of 71%.

Americans see Gorbachev as a different kind of Soviet leader, and they are willing to give him the benefit of the doubt when it comes to issues such as human rights and Soviet involvement in regional conflicts. By a 2-to-1 margin (66% to 27%) the public rejects the view of some of Bush's conservative critics that the president should take advantage of the turmoil in Eastern Europe by pressuring Gorbachev on such issues. There is a consensus in favor of giving him more time to achieve the reforms that he has championed in the USSR.

With a new kind of leader in Moscow, the change in Eastern Europe is thought to represent a permanent rather than a short-lived phenomenon. Only one in five Americans (21%) expects that the movement toward more political and economic freedom will be cut short by a hard-line crackdown. Indeed, 68% expect the reform process to continue. Whether or not events in Eastern Europe indicate the beginning of the end of communism, however, is another matter. As many Americans are likely to disagree (47%) as agree (46%) with this contention.

Almost all Americans (88%) say that the next few years will be characterized by increasing political freedom for the citizens of Eastern Europe and 71% believe that economic well-being in the region will improve over the same period. Moreover, the church, which has

vied for power with the state throughout the history of countries such as Poland, is expected to be a beneficiary of the reform movement. Three quarters (74%) say that religion will come to play a more important role in the lives of the people of Eastern Europe over the next few years.

While hard-line communism will not be missed, many Americans do foresee one area of difficulty associated with economic change in Eastern Europe. A plurality of 46% believes that social problems such as poverty, hunger, and alcoholism will worsen over the next few years, while 35% foresee improvement in this area.

DECEMBER 20
CIVIL RIGHTS

Interviewing Date: 12/7–10/89
Survey #GO 89141

Now I'd like to ask some questions about civil rights in this country. First, do you approve of the job President Bush is doing to protect the civil rights of individuals?

Approve..62%
Disapprove...23
No opinion...15

Over the past year or so, how much progress do you think has been made in the area of civil rights in this country—a lot of progress, some progress, not very much progress, or no progress at all?

A lot of progress..................................11%
Some progress....................................44
Not very much progress........................30
No progress at all...............................12
No opinion...3

For each of the following groups I read, please tell me whether you think there has been too much attention or not enough attention to the civil rights of this group:

Blacks?

Too much 39%
Not enough...40
Right amount (volunteered)....................17
No opinion.. 4

Asian-Americans?

Too much 25%
Not enough...45
Right amount (volunteered)....................17
No opinion...13

Women?

Too much 29%
Not enough...49
Right amount (volunteered)....................18
No opinion.. 4

The elderly?

Too much 4%
Not enough...84
Right amount (volunteered)....................10
No opinion.. 2

The disabled and handicapped?

Too much 6%
Not enough...81
Right amount (volunteered)....................11
No opinion.. 2

Hispanics?

Too much 28%
Not enough...46
Right amount (volunteered)....................15
No opinion...11

People who have AIDS?

Too much 31%
Not enough...51
Right amount (volunteered)....................13
No opinion.. 5

Jews?

Too much 20%
Not enough...43
Right amount (volunteered)....................22
No opinion...15

Some people say that to make up for past discrimination, women and members of minority groups should be given preferential treatment in getting jobs and places in colleges. Others say that their ability, as determined in test scores, should be the main consideration. Which point of view comes closer to how you feel on the subject?

Give preferential treatment....................10%
Determine by test scores........................84
No opinion.. 6

Selected National Trend

	Preferential treatment	Test scores	No opinion
January 1984	10%	84%	6%
December 1980	10	83	7
October 1977	11	81	8

On the whole, do you think most white people want to see blacks get a better break, or do they want to keep blacks down, or don't you think they care either way?

See blacks get better break....................39%
Keep blacks down....................................20
Don't care..34
No opinion.. 7

By Ethnic Background
White

See blacks get better break....................40%
Keep blacks down....................................19
Don't care..34
No opinion.. 7

Black

See blacks get better break....................34%
Keep blacks down....................................24
Don't care..36
No opinion.. 6

Selected National Trend

	See blacks get better break	Keep blacks down	Don't care	No opinion
Whites only				
February 1988	52%	6%	31%	11%
August 1984	44	17	30	9

Blacks only

February 1988	34%	24%	36%	6%
August 1984	22	41	30	7

Who do you think is more to blame for the present conditions in which blacks find themselves—white people or blacks themselves?

White people...18%
Blacks themselves................................55
Neither (volunteered)...........................4
Both (volunteered)...............................18
No opinion...5

Do you think further improvements in the standard of living of blacks in general will reduce the standard of living of whites, or do you think that the situation of blacks can improve without hurting the situation of whites?

Improvements in black standard of living
    will hurt whites...............................12%
Black standard of living can improve
    without hurting whites......................82
No opinion...6

For the next few questions I'd like you to think about your own community. In general, do you think blacks have as good a chance as white people in your community to get any kind of job for which they are qualified, or don't you think they have as good a chance?

	December 1989	July 1978	March 1963
Blacks have as good a chance as whites	65%	67%	43%
Blacks do not have as good a chance as whites	28	24	48
No blacks/whites in this community (volunteered)	5	–	–
No opinion	2	9	9

Do you think blacks have as good a chance as white people in your community to get any kind of housing they can afford, or don't you think they have as good a chance?

Blacks have as good a chance
    as whites.......................................68%
Blacks do not have as good a chance
    as whites.......................................27
No blacks/whites in this
    community (volunteered)....................3
No opinion...2

Do you think black children have as good a chance as white children in your community to get a good education, or don't you think they have as good a chance?

Black children have as good a chance
    as white children.............................80%
Black children do not have as good a
    chance as white children....................15
No blacks/whites in
    this community (volunteered)..............4
No opinion...1

Note: By an overwhelming margin the public wants to see the civil rights of the elderly and disabled receive more attention, yet Americans are much less supportive of increased efforts on behalf of groups that have been the traditional focus of civil rights programs and legislation. Large majorities think that blacks now have the same opportunities as whites in their communities in terms of obtaining jobs, housing, and education, although sharp racial differences in this perception continue to exist.

The public is divided over how much progress in civil rights has been made by the Bush administration. Only 11% think that there has been a lot over the past year or so, comparable to the 12% who see no progress at all. More than four in ten (44%) think that some progress has been made, while 30% believe that there has not been very much progress.

The current poll also finds that 62% approve of the job that President George Bush is doing to protect the civil rights of individuals. Only 23% disapprove and 15% offer no opinion. This level of support for Bush is close to his current overall job-performance rating of 71% approval and much higher than any of the performance ratings that he received last month on a wide range of domestic issues.

One reason that the public may approve of the president's performance on civil rights is that his administration has been working to broaden the concept so that it encompasses issues related to the disabled, the elderly, and people who have been diagnosed as having AIDS. While this approach has been controversial among some civil rights leaders who see it as an orientation away from enforcement of laws against racial discrimination, the public overwhelmingly supports a change in emphasis.

More than eight in ten Americans think that there has been insufficient attention paid to the civil rights of the elderly (84%) and of disabled and handicapped people (81%). This support cuts across party lines, with Republicans, Democrats, and independents sharing a belief in the need for intensified action for the elderly and the disabled. Only about one in twenty thinks that there has been too much attention already paid to these groups.

For a variety of other groups that have suffered the effects of disadvantage, discrimination, or prejudice, the public tends to favor more rather than less emphasis on their civil rights, although not nearly to the extent recorded for those of the elderly and disabled. One half (51%) believes that there should be more attention focused on people who have AIDS, although 31% think that AIDS patients have received too much attention.

Moreover, just under one half thinks that there has been insufficient attention given to the civil rights of women (49%), Hispanics (46%), and Asian-Americans (45%). Just over one quarter thinks that each of these three groups has received too much. About four in ten (43%) think that the civil rights of Jewish people have not received enough attention, while only 20% say that Jews have been the focus of too much.

In contrast, the public is evenly split between those who think that the civil rights of blacks have received too much (39%) and not enough (40%) consideration. However, most Americans think that blacks have the same opportunities as whites in their communities for jobs, housing, and education. About two thirds think that blacks have as good a chance as whites to obtain any kind of job for which they are qualified (65%) and to find any kind of housing that they can afford (68%). Eight in ten (80%) think that black children have as good a chance as white children to get a good education in their community. The public's views on job opportunities are unchanged from those expressed in a 1978 Gallup survey.

Not surprisingly, blacks themselves have distinctly different perceptions of their opportunities in these three areas. About one half think that their job (54%) and housing opportunities (45%) are not as good as those afforded whites in their communities. And one third (33%) thinks that educational opportunities for black children are not as good.

The public overwhelmingly rejects (84%) the notion that some groups should receive preferential treatment in employment and higher education in order to make up for past discrimination, while only 10% support this view. Blacks take the opposite side, although their opinions are mixed. Over one half (56%) of blacks endorses preferential treatment, while one third (32%) rejects it.

Similar to the opinion registered by Gallup more than twenty years ago, 55% of the public think that black people are more to blame for the present conditions in which they find themselves, while 18% blame whites. Another 18% say that whites and blacks share equally in the blame for blacks' current situation.

The public is divided over the continuing role of whites in blacks' pursuit of a higher standard of living in America. Four in ten (39%) think that most white people want to see blacks get a better break, but 34% think that most white people do not care one way or the other. A significant minority of the public (20%) thinks that most whites want to keep blacks down. Whites now are more critical of their own feelings toward blacks than they were just two years ago. In a survey conducted by Gallup in February 1988 for *Newsweek*, 52% of whites thought that most whites wanted to see blacks get a better break, while only 6% thought that most whites wanted to keep blacks down. The opinions of blacks have not changed since last year.

On a related issue, 82% of respondents think that further improvements in the standard of living of blacks will not reduce that of whites, while only 12% disagree and think that whites' standard of living will be hurt by further black progress.

DECEMBER 27
MOST ADMIRED MAN

Interviewing Date: 12/7–10/89
Survey #GO 89141

What man whom you have heard or read about, living today in any part of the world, do you admire the most? And who is your second choice?

The following are listed in order of frequency of mention, with first and second choices combined:

George Bush
Mikhail Gorbachev
Ronald Reagan
Pope John Paul II
Billy Graham
Lech Walesa
Donald Trump
Lee Iacocca
Jesse Jackson
Jimmy Carter } tied
Bill Cosby

By way of comparison, the following are the results of the 1988 survey:*

Ronald Reagan
Mikhail Gorbachev
George Bush
Pope John Paul II
Jesse Jackson
Billy Graham
Lee Iacocca
Edward Kennedy
Bill Cosby
Donald Trump

*Published in this volume on January 5, 1989

Note: Among Americans, Soviet leader Mikhail Gorbachev once again places second on the list of the ten most admired men in the world, while the ranking of former President Ronald Reagan and President George Bush are reversed from those reported in 1988. Gorbachev's popularity in this country has increased dramatically since his first appearance on the list when, just two years ago, he finished eighth. As the pace of change within the Soviet Union and Eastern European nations has accelerated, his popularity in the United States has continued to rise. A recent Gallup Poll shows 77% of Americans expressing a favorable opinion of him, thus putting him on a par with Bush.

Pope John Paul II and the Reverend Billy Graham complete the ranks of the top five most admired men. The pope has finished in the top ten consistently since his first appearance in 1977, often placing first or second on the list. Since 1955, Graham has failed to appear on the list only once, in 1962. Indeed, Graham has been found on the list thirty-two times since this question was first asked in 1946—more often than any other person.

In a year that has seen upheaval in Poland, Lech Walesa—leader of that country's Solidarity movement—has returned to the list for the first time since 1983. Walesa places sixth, followed by businessman Donald Trump, Chrysler Chairman Lee Iacocca, and the Reverend Jesse Jackson. Former President Jimmy Carter and entertainer Bill Cosby tie for tenth place.

DECEMBER 27
MOST ADMIRED WOMAN

Interviewing Date: 12/7–10/89
Survey #GO 89141

What woman whom you have heard or read about, living today in any part of the world, do you admire the most? And who is your second choice?

The following are listed in order of frequency of mention, with first and second choices combined.

Margaret Thatcher
Mother Teresa of Calcutta
Barbara Bush
Nancy Reagan
Corazon Aquino
Oprah Winfrey
Betty Ford
Princess Diana
Sandra Day O'Connor
Jacqueline Kennedy Onassis

By way of comparison, the following are the results of the 1988 audit:*

Margaret Thatcher
Mother Teresa of Calcutta
Nancy Reagan
Oprah Winfrey
Betty Ford
Barbara Walters
Corazon Aquino
Jacqueline Kennedy Onassis
Elizabeth Taylor
Barbara Bush

*Published in this volume on January 8, 1989

Note: For the second straight year British Prime Minister Margaret Thatcher is the woman most admired by Americans. Thatcher has stayed among the top ten for eleven consecutive years. Mother Teresa of Calcutta, who first appeared on the list in 1979, is the second most admired woman. First Lady Barbara Bush, moving up from her tenth-place finish last year, now is third.

Former First Lady Nancy Reagan is fourth, her lowest ranking since she first appeared in 1980 in eighth place. Philippine President Corazon Aquino and television talk-show hostess Oprah Winfrey are in fifth and sixth place, respectively. Former First Lady Betty Ford, who has appeared in the top ten consistently since 1974, ranks seventh. Princess Diana of Great Britain and Supreme Court Justice Sandra Day O'Connor, both missing from the top ten since 1985, hold the eighth and ninth positions. Although not named every year, Jacqueline Kennedy Onassis's position as the tenth most admired woman this time marks her twenty-fifth appearance on the list since her first mention in 1960.

Frequently mentioned this year, but not among the top ten, are Queen Elizabeth II of Great Britain, former UN Ambassador Jeane Kirkpatrick, and Secretary of Labor Elizabeth Dole. Absent from this year's top ten after having made the 1988 list are actress Elizabeth Taylor and television personality Barbara Walters.

DECEMBER 28
NEW YEAR'S EVE

Interviewing Date: 10/12–15/89
Survey #GO 88156-2

Do you usually do something special to celebrate the new year on New Year's Eve?

	Yes
National	44%

By Age

18–29 years	69%
30–49 years	42
50 years and over	30

Where did you spend New Year's Eve last year?

Spent quiet evening at home	55%
Went out to a party	17
Had party at home	5
Went out to restaurant or nightclub	8
Went somewhere else	14
Can't recall	1

Last year, did you spend New Year's Eve with family members, with friends, with both, or were you alone?

Family only	44%
Friends only	21
Both friends and family	21
Alone	12
Other	1
Can't recall	1

Note: After the excitement of Christmas, many Americans choose to avoid yet another celebration on New Year's Eve and opt for a quiet evening at home with the family. A recent Gallup Poll on holiday celebrations finds 56% saying that they usually do not do anything special to celebrate New Year's Eve, while 44% make it a special night.

If this New Year's Eve is anything like last year's, only a minority of adults will attend parties (22%) or ring in the new year at a restaurant or nightclub (8%). More than one half (55%) spent a quiet evening at home last year, and 65% were with members of their family. Roughly four in ten (42%) adults spent last New Year's Eve with friends, while only 12% were alone.

The new year is greeted most enthusiastically by adults under the age of 30. The large majority (69%) of 18 to 29-year-olds usually does something special on New Year's Eve, compared to less than one half (42%) of all 30 to 49-year-olds and only 30% of older adults.

DECEMBER 31
WAR AND PEACE

Interviewing Date: 12/7–10/89
Survey #GO 89141

Asked in thirty-five countries plus Hong Kong: Do you think that 1990 will be a peaceful year more or less free of international disputes, a troubled year with much international discord, or remain the same?

	Peaceful	Troubled	Remain the same	No opinion
Soviet Union (Moscow)	64%	11%	16%	9%
Iceland	48	6	39	6
Chile	46	26	22	6
Argentina	43	23	23	11
United States	37	26	32	5
Uruguay	36	30	22	12
Israel	36	23	20	21
Italy**	36	20	36	8
Brazil	35	37	18	9
Sweden	35	16	41	8
South Korea	34	28	18	21
Turkey	33	23	14	30
Denmark**	31	31	29	10
Ireland**	31	18	40	11
West Germany**	30	25	32	1
New Zealand	30	22	45	3
Switzerland	29	27	34	10
Great Britain**	29	26	38	7
Mexico	28	42	31	4
Luxembourg**	28	37	32	4
Hong Kong	28	34	31	7
Spain**	26	28	27	19
Netherlands**	25	30	41	3
South Africa†	25	28	36	11
Finland	25	20	50	5
Costa Rica	24	35	26	15
Philippines	24	29	45	2
Canada	24	27	46	4
Portugal**	24	17	30	30
Austria	23	31	37	9
Hungary	22	31	29	17
Australia	20	28	44	7
Greece**	19	20	33	28
Belgium**	16	33	48	3
Japan	12	22	36	30
France**	10	39	42	9

*Some totals do not add to 100% due to rounding.
**Member of the European Economic Community
†National data for blacks and whites. In contrast to previous years, separate breakdowns are not available.

Note: At the end of a year that has seen revolution in Eastern Europe, Soviet citizens generally look forward to 1990 as a period of international peace. A new Gallup international survey taken in thirty-five countries around the globe finds close to two thirds (64%) of Moscow residents predicting peace in the new year. For the third straight year, Muscovites rate as the most optimistic in this regard.

Relative to their predictions of one year ago, Americans also are more likely to see the chances of war diminishing. Among a nationally representative sample of U.S. adults, those who see the prospects for peace as improving (37%) are more numerous that those who predict that 1990 will be characterized by greater conflict between nations (26%).

In Europe, where considerations of German reunification may be causing concern in neighboring countries, the public's outlook for peace in the new year is more mixed. The West Germans themselves and the British divide fairly evenly in their predictions: about three in ten (30% in West Germany, 29% in Great Britain) see the prospects for peace improving, while slightly fewer believe that problems will worsen (25% in West Germany, 26% in Great Britain).

In four nations on the continent that belong to the European Economic Community (EEC)—Belgium, France, Luxembourg, and the Netherlands—there now is more pessimism about the future in the poll's findings than was evident one year ago. In France and in Luxembourg, nearly four in ten (39% and 37%, respectively) see more troubled times ahead, while the percentages decrease somewhat in Belgium (33%) and the Netherlands (30%).

Among the citizens of the other EEC countries the Italians, the Irish, and the Danes are most optimistic in their forecasts. Close to one third of the Italians (36%) and the Irish and Danes (each 31%) count on world peace in the new year. Outside the EEC, in Europe the citizens of Iceland (48%) are the most positive, while those of Hungary (22%) and Austria (23%) are the least.

In Latin America, Chile (46%) and Argentina (43%) are most optimistic about world peace, while Mexico (42%) leads in expectations for international discord. In other parts of the world the outlook for peace is mixed. It is worth noting, however, that one country that has seen its share of conflict during the postwar era—Israel—shows an above average level of optimism. Over one third (36%) of Israelis see a more peaceful world in 1990, while 23% take the opposite view. And in another nation known for its own ongoing problems—South Africa—the reverse is true. There, only 25% expect world peace in 1990, while 36% would not be surprised by international discord.

Among the Asian nations surveyed, only the South Koreans lean toward an optimistic appraisal (34%) of the prospects for peace. And after an attempted coup in the Philippines, it is not surprising that the Filipino people are a great deal less optimistic about peace in the new year than they were one year ago. In their predictions for 1990, 29% see the chances for peace worsening, while 24% see a reduction in tensions. Last year, in their predictions for 1989, 41% expected a more peaceful year, but 25% saw trouble ahead.

INDEX

A

Abortion

  approval rating of Supreme Court's decision
    allowing states to restrict, 160–62

  as result of Court's ruling, call elected official to
    register your opinion on, 167

  as result of Court's ruling, contribute to
    organization supporting your position on,
    167

  as result of Court's ruling, take part in
    demonstration in support of your position
    on, 167–68

  as result of Court's ruling, take political
    candidate's position on more into account,
    166

  importance of candidate's position on, in
    election for governor or state legislature,
    212

  likely that state law will be passed to make it
    difficult for a woman to get, 165

  more medical knowledge on first stages of life
    and your opinion on, 24–27

  overturn 1973 Supreme Court ruling (*Roe v.
    Wade*) on, 20–22, 162–64, 211

    national trend, 164

  restriction on, of not allowing abortions unless
    required to save woman's life, 164

  restriction on, of passing laws to make it difficult
    for clinics performing abortions to continue,
    165

  restriction on, of requiring test to see if five-
    month fetus might survive outside womb,
    164–65

  restriction on, of requiring that women under 18
    get parental consent, 165

  strength of your feelings about, 211–12

  which political party better reflects your views
    on, 165

  your own position is right on, 22–24

Abortion issue

  handled by Bush, 166, 223

Accomplishment

  importance of having sense of, 57

    national trend, 58

Adult relationships

  marry/get romantically involved with same
    person again, 31–33

  quality of communication between you and your
    partner, 29–31

  satisfied with sexual relationship with your
    partner, 37–40

  you can trust your partner, 35–37

  your partner fulfills your emotional needs, 33–35

Aerobics and dancercize

  your participation in, 28

    by women, 28

AIDS

  attention paid to civil rights of people who have,
    234

  catch by donating blood, 229

    national trend, 229

  catch by intimate contact with person of
    opposite sex, 229

    national trend, 229

  catch by intimate contact with person of same
    sex, 229

    national trend, 229

  catch by receiving blood transfusions, 229

    national trend, 229

  catch by sharing hypodermic needles, 229

    national trend, 229

  catch by working alongside someone with, 230

    national trend, 230

  catch from being coughed or sneezed upon, 229

    national trend, 229

  catch from a drinking glass, 229

    national trend, 229

  catch from toilet seats, 229

    national trend, 229

  government spending for research on, 104, 209

  how concerned are you that a member of your
    family will get, 228

  how concerned are you that you will get, 228

    national trend, 228

  likely that scientists will develop vaccine for,
    230

  likely to become an epidemic, 228

    national trend, 229

  as most important problem, 120

  personally know anyone who has contracted,
    230

    national trend, 230

Airline safety

  air travel not very safe or basically safe compared
    with other means of transportation, 186

  flying on commercial airliners has become safer,
    53–54

  government doing all it can to make aviation
    safe, 54

  types of airplanes that you try to avoid, 186

  when you fly, how often are you frightened, 54–
    55, 185

    national trend, 55, 185–86

Airline safety (*continued*)
    your confidence in safety and efficiency,
        compared to few years ago, 185
        national trend, 185
Alcoholic beverages
    do you plan to cut down or quit drinking, 206
    drinking as cause of trouble in your family, 206
        national trend, 206
    how many did you drink in past seven days, 206
    increase taxes on, to reduce federal budget deficit,
        104
    sometimes drink more than you should, 206
    when did you last drink, 206
    your use of, 205–6
        national trend, 206
Alcoholism
    will increase in Eastern Europe, 232
Alcohol problem
    concern that family members will develop, 193
    as principal reason you got a divorce, 109
    See also Designated driver
American Cancer Society
    your overall opinion of, 102
American Civil Liberties Union (ACLU)
    your overall opinion of, 102
Aquino, Corazon
    as most admired woman, 4, 237, 238
Argentina, respondents in
    1990 as peaceful or troubled year, 239
Armstrong, Neil
    first person to walk on moon, 170
    spoke "That's one small step for a man . . . ," 170
Asian-Americans
    attention paid to civil rights of, 234
Atlanta
    as best large city, 207
    as city with best arts, entertainment, and
        nightlife, 208
    as city with best food, 208
    as city with friendliest people, 207
    as most attractive large city, 208
Australia, respondents in
    1990 as peaceful or troubled year, 239
Austria, respondents in
    1990 as peaceful or troubled year, 239
Automobile
    have or will purchase, in Soviet Union, 226

B

Baez, Joan
    fan of, at Woodstock, 176
The Band
    fan of, at Woodstock, 176
Banks
    your confidence in, 204
        national trend, 204
Barco Vargas, Virgilio
    approval rating of his dealing with drug problem,
        195

    approval rating as president of Colombia, 195
Baseball
    bet on professional sports event such as, in past
        twelve months, 132
        national trend, 133
    how many Major League games are fixed, 137
    how often have you bet on Major League, 136
    legalize betting on professional sports such as,
        130
    your participation in, 28
Basketball
    bet on college sports event such as, in past
        twelve months, 133
    bet on professional sports event such as, in past
        twelve months, 132
        national trend, 133
    how many college games are fixed, 137
    how many pro games are fixed, 137
    how often have you bet on college, 135
    how often have you bet on pro, 135
    legalize betting on professional sports such as,
        130
    your participation in, 28
        by men, 28
Belgium, respondents in
    Europe has enjoyed years of peace against
        Russian threat because NATO was founded,
        218
    NATO alliance should be maintained, 218
    NATO should keep nuclear weapons in Western
        Europe, 218
    1990 as peaceful or troubled year, 239
Bicycle
    have or will purchase, in Soviet Union, 225
Bicycle touring and racing
    your participation in, 28
Bicycling
    your participation in, 28
        by men and women, 28
        national trend, 28
Billiards
    your participation in, 28
        by men, 28
Blacks
    attention paid to civil rights of, 234
    black children have as good a chance as white
        children in your community to get a good
        education, 235
    further improvements in standard of living of
        blacks will reduce that of whites, 235
    have as good a chance as white people in your
        community to get housing, 235
    have as good a chance as white people in your
        community to get job, 235
    most white people want to see blacks get better
        break, 234
        national trend, 234–35
    not wanted as neighbors, 67–69
    satisfaction index of, 20
    who is to blame for the conditions in which
        blacks find themselves, 235

Bodybuilding
  your participation in, 28
Boston
  as best large city, 207
  as city with best arts, entertainment, and
    nightlife, 208
  as city with best food, 208
  as city with fewest social problems, 207
  as most attractive large city, 208
Bowling
  your participation in, 28
    by men and women, 28
    national trend, 28
Brazil, respondents in
  1990 as peaceful or troubled year, 239
Budget, federal
  proposed constitutional amendment requiring
    government to balance, 57
  See also Government spending
Budget deficit, federal
  Bush administration will reduce, 44–45
  handled by Bush, 82, 223
    compared to Reagan, 83
  reduce by increasing taxes on alcoholic
    beverages, 104
  reduce by limiting defense spending, 104
  reduce by lowering Medicare benefits, 104–5
  reduce by national lottery, 104
  reduce by national sales tax, 104
  reduce by raising income taxes, 209
  reduce by reducing Social Security COLAs, 104
  reduce by taxing Social Security benefits as
    ordinary income, 105
  as serious problem for country, 52
    national trend, 52
  use Social Security surplus to help reduce, 105
  See also Economic affairs
Bush, Barbara
  as most admired woman, 4, 237, 238
Bush, George
  and abortion issue, 166, 223
  approval of his cabinet appointments, 80
  approval of his explaining his policies and
    plans, 80, 224
    national trend, 224
  approval of his job to protect civil rights of
    individuals, 233
  approval rating, 41, 79–80, 103, 111, 139, 180,
    190–91, 222, 231
    compared to Reagan, 41–42, 83, 222
    national trend, 103, 111, 139, 180, 191,
    231
  approval rating compared to predecessors, 42,
    103, 191, 222
  approval rating as person, 223
  and budget deficit, 82, 223
    compared to Reagan, 83
  and Central America situation, 82, 224
  did you watch his speech dealing with plan to
    combat drugs, 193

doing better job as president than you expected,
  222–23
doing enough to help Eastern European countries
  deal with changes there, 224
doing enough to help Soviet Union deal with
  changes there, 224
doing enough to reduce military tensions between
  United States and Soviet Union, 224
and drug problem, 81–82, 191–92, 223
  compared to Reagan, 83
and economic conditions, 81, 223
  compared to Reagan, 83
and education policy, 223
and environmental issues, 223
and foreign policy, 81, 223
  compared to Reagan, 83
his plan to combat drug use calls for too much
  money, 193
his plan will significantly reduce drug use, 193
and hostage situation in Middle East, 181
  national trend, 181
and inflation, 82
and Middle East situation, 82
as most admired man, 3, 237
as outstanding president, 42
and poverty and homelessness, 183, 223
and recent events in China, 139
and relations with Soviet Union, 81, 224
  compared with Reagan, 83
and situation in Eastern Europe, 223
your opinion of, 112
  national trend, 112
Bush administration
  and disapproval of use of force against students in
    China, 139
  progress of, in combating drugs, 224
  should improve relations with Iran, 91–92
  will avoid raising taxes, 47
  will get drug crisis under control, 45
  will improve educational standards, 46
  will improve the lot of minorities and the poor,
    46–47
  will improve quality of the environment, 45
  will increase respect for United States abroad, 46
  will keep America prosperous, 45
  will keep nation out of war, 45–46
  will reduce crime rate, 46
  will reduce federal budget deficit, 44–45

C

Cabinet
  approval of Bush's appointments to, 80
  See also Tower, John
California earthquake
  Bay Area was prepared for dealing with, 213
  cause any damage to your home or personal
    property, 213

California earthquake (*continued*)
did you, yourself, help deal with, 213–14
estimate of cost of damage to your personal
property, 213
how frightened were you during, 213
rate the job of Bay Area police in responding to,
213
rate the job of other emergency services in
responding to, 213
rate the job of your neighbors in responding to,
213
think about moving to different place as result of,
214
Tuesday's [October 17] was the major quake, 214
were any other family members injured, 213
were you injured, 213
where were you when earthquake hit, 213
you, yourself, were prepared for dealing with, 213
Calisthenics
your participation in, 28
by women, 28
Camera
have or will purchase, in Soviet Union, 225
See also Movie camera; Video camera
Camping
your participation in, 28
by men and women, 28
Canada
fair trade policy with United States, 106
U.S. tariffs on goods from, 106
your overall opinion of, 98, 180
Canada, respondents in
Europe has enjoyed years of peace against
Russian threat because NATO was founded,
218
NATO alliance should be maintained, 218
NATO should keep nuclear weapons in Western
Europe, 218
1990 as peaceful or troubled year, 239
Carter, Jimmy
approval rating compared to Bush, 42, 103, 222
approval rating compared to Reagan, 7, 43, 191
as most admired man, 3, 237
as outstanding president, compared to Ford, 10
Cassette tape recorder
have or will purchase, in Soviet Union, 225
Catholics
not wanted as neighbors, 63–64
national trend, 64
Central America situation
handled by Bush, 82, 224
Chicago
as best large city, 207
as city with best arts, entertainment, and
nightlife, 208
as city with best food, 208
as city with friendliest people, 207
as most attractive large city, 208
as worst large city, 207

Child abuse
know any children whom you suspect have been
abused, 96
more prevalent today than in the past, 96–97
were you ever a victim of, 96
Child-care services
government spending to provide, 210
Children
helped by your volunteer work or donations, 227
Chile, respondents in
1990 as peaceful or troubled year, 239
China
Bush administration's disapproval of use of force
against students in, 139
Bush's dealing with recent events in, 139
current problems are typical or indicate weakness
of Communist system, 140
demonstrate disapproval of, by breaking off
diplomatic relations with, 140
demonstrate disapproval of, by permitting
Chinese students now in United States to
remain, 139
demonstrate disapproval of, by recalling U.S.
ambassador to, 140
demonstrate disapproval of, by restricting
American investments in, 140
demonstrate disapproval of, by suspending sale
of U.S. arms to, 139
multiparty system will emerge or leaders will
resist democratic reforms, 140
popular uprising likely to erupt, 140
send U.S. military aid if civil war were to break
out, 140
student uprising in, of importance to United
States, 139
will implement free-market reforms or revert to
closed economic system, 140
your overall opinion of, 98, 180
Cigarettes
rising prices of, 94, 95
Cigarette smoking
ever made serious effort to stop, 126
have you smoked in past week, 125
national trend, 125
how many do you smoke each day, 125–26
national trend, 126
would you like to give up, 126
national trend, 126
Cincinnati
as city with fewest social problems, 207
Cities
best large (list), in America, 207
most attractive (list), 208
prefer city, suburban area, small town, or farm,
207
with best arts, entertainment, and nightlife (list),
208
with best food (list), 208
with fewest social problems (list), 207

with friendliest people (list), 207
worst large (list), in America, 207
Civil rights
    approval of Bush's job to protect, 233
    attention paid to Asian-Americans, 234
    attention paid to blacks, 234
    attention paid to the disabled and handicapped, 234
    attention paid to the elderly, 234
    attention paid to Hispanics, 234
    attention paid to Jews, 234
    attention paid to people who have AIDS, 234
    attention paid to women, 234
    black children have as good a chance as white children in your community to get a good education, 235
    blacks have as good a chance as white people in your community to get housing, 235
    blacks have as good a chance as white people in your community to get job, 235
    further improvements in standard of living of blacks will reduce that of whites, 235
    most white people want to see blacks get better break, 234
        national trend, 234–35
    over the past year, how much progress has been made in, 233
    who is to blame for the conditions in which blacks find themselves, 235
    women and minority groups should be given preferential treatment, 234
        national trend, 234
Civil rights movement
    got involved in, in 1960s and 1970s, 177
Clergy
    homosexuals hired as, 217
    national trend, 217
Cleveland
    as worst city, 207
Clothing
    contributed food, clothing, or other property to charitable organization, 227
    given money, food, or clothing to the homeless or needy, 227
    not enough money to buy, 148, 149
        national trend, 148, 149
    rising prices of, 95
Cocker, Joe
    fan of, at Woodstock, 176
College students
    government spending for financial aid for, 210
Colombia
    its government making strong enough effort to reduce drug trafficking, 193
Colombia, respondents in
    approval rating of President Barco in dealing with drug problem, 195
    approval rating of Virgilio Barco Vargas as president, 195

Colombian government doing all it can to combat major drug dealers, 194
Colombian government should agree not to prosecute dealers in exchange for their promising to stop dealing drugs, 194
Colombian government should request that U.S. troops be sent to combat drug traffickers, 195
Colombian government will be able to significantly reduce flow of drugs out of the country, 194
concern that family members will become involved with drugs, 193
concern that family members will develop alcohol problem, 193
concern that you will become victim of crime as consequence of drug problem, 193
crackdown on drug dealers is in best interest of Colombia, 195
effect on economy in Colombia if drug dealing is reduced, 195
most important problem (list) facing country today, 195
power of major drug dealers in Colombia is being exaggerated, 195
reduce demand for drugs in United States or reduce supply coming out of Colombia, 194
seriousness of drug problem in United States is being exaggerated, 195
United States giving money to Colombian government to help fight drug traffickers, 194
United States providing military equipment [to Colombia] to help fight drug traffickers, 194
United States putting pressure on Colombia to deal with drug problem, 194
U.S. government doing all it can to help Colombia combat major drug dealers, 194
U.S. government making strong enough effort to reduce drug use, 195
U.S. military advisers assisting Colombian forces in fighting drug traffickers, 194
U.S. troops helping to fight drug traffickers in Colombia, 194
Common Market countries
    fair trade policy with United States, 106
    as leading economic power, 106
    U.S. tariffs on goods from, 106
Communication. *See* Adult relationships
Communism
    changes in Eastern Europe and Soviet Union reduce tensions between Communist and non-Communist countries, 232
    current problems in China are typical or indicate weakness of Communist system, 140
    current situation in Soviet Union and Eastern Europe means end of, 231
Congress
    charges are serious enough to justify Jim

more likely to keep United States out of war, 173
national trend, 173
your opinion of Democratic congressional
leaders, 114
Denmark, respondents in
Europe has enjoyed years of peace against
Russian threat because NATO was founded,
218
NATO alliance should be maintained, 218
NATO should keep nuclear weapons in Western
Europe, 219
1990 as peaceful or troubled year, 239
Denver
as best large city, 207
as city with fewest social problems, 207
as city with friendliest people, 207
as most attractive large city, 208
Designated driver
seen television commercials promoting, 1–2,
101
select a, at social occasions, 1, 100–101
Detroit
as worst large city, 207
Diana, Princess
as most admired woman, 237
Diet and nutrition
are you making effort to eat fresh fruits,
vegetables (fat, salt, others on list), 219–20
describe your own personal weight situation, 220
did you eat breakfast, 220
did you eat dinner, 220
did you eat dinner alone or with other people, 220
did you eat lunch, 220
do you enjoy cooking, 220
do you enjoy eating, 220–21
do you pay attention to food warnings and
nutritional recommendations, 219
do you worry about healthfulness of your diet,
219
how healthy is your diet, 221
how many nights do members of your household
eat dinner together, 220
how many of your dinner meals are homemade and
eaten at home, 220
when you learn about food warnings, do you
follow the advice, 219
where did you eat dinner, 220
while you were eating dinner, were you doing
anything else, 220
your eating habits have changed, over past two or
three years, 220
Divorce. See Marriage and divorce
Doctors
homosexuals hired as, 216
national trend, 217
Dole, Elizabeth
as most admired woman, 4
Drug abuse
as most important problem, 120

Drug problem
approval rating of President Barco in dealing
with, 195
approval rating of Virgilio Barco Vargas as
president of Colombia, 195
Bush administration will get drug crisis under
control, 45
Bush's plan to combat drug use calls for too much
money, 193
Bush's plan will significantly reduce drug use,
193
Colombian government doing all it can to
combat major dealers, 194
Colombian government making strong enough
effort to reduce trafficking, 193
Colombian government should agree not to
prosecute dealers in exchange for their
promising to stop dealing, 194
Colombian government should request that U.S.
troops be sent to help combat traffickers,
195
Colombian government will be able to
significantly reduce flow of drugs out of the
country, 194
concern that you will become victim of crime as
consequence of, 193
crackdown on dealers is in best interest of
Colombia, 195
cut drug supply, to help reduce crime, 142
did you watch Bush's speech dealing with, 193
effect on economy in Colombia if drug dealing is
reduced, 195
government spending for combating, 104, 209
handled by Bush, 81–82, 191–92, 223
compared to Reagan, 83
large cities (list) with fewest social problems,
such as, 207
narcotics traffic as most important problem
facing Colombia today, 195
power of major dealers in Colombia is being
exaggerated, 195
as principal reason you got a divorce, 109
progress of Bush administration in combating,
224
reduce demand for drugs in United States or reduce
supply coming out of Colombia, 194
seriousness of in United States is being
exaggerated, 195
United States giving money to Colombian
government to help fight traffickers, 194
United States providing military equipment [to
Colombia] to help fight traffickers, 194
United States putting pressure on Colombia to
deal with, 194
U.S. government doing all it can to help
Colombia combat major dealers, 194
U.S. government making strong enough effort to
reduce drug use, 195
U.S. military advisers assisting Colombian

Drug problem (*continued*)
    forces in fighting traffickers, 194
    U.S. troops helping to fight traffickers in
      Colombia, 194
    willing to pay higher income taxes to combat
      drug use, 193
Drugs
    change to more liberal attitudes toward, in 1960s,
      177
    concern that family members will become
      involved with, 193
    experimented with, in 1960s and 1970s, 177
    as factor most responsible for crime, 142
    prescription, rising prices of, 95

E

Earthquake, in California. *See* California earthquake
Eastern Europe
    Bush doing enough to help Eastern European
      countries deal with changes there, 224
    changes there will increase chances of world
      peace or of war, 232
    current situation in, means end of communism,
      231
    economic well-being of people will improve,
      232
    people will have more political freedom, 232
    political reforms will continue in, 231
    religion will play more important role in, 232
    social problems will increase in, 232
Eastern Europe situation
    handled by Bush, 223
East Germany
    Bush doing enough to help Eastern European
      countries deal with changes there, 224
    continue under Soviet Union or seek
      independence, 140
    if reunited with West Germany, it might become
      aggressor nation, 232
    reunification with West Germany good for United
      States and its allies, 231–32
Economic affairs
    Gallup analysis of Americans' knowledge of,
      107–8
Economic conditions
    handled by Bush, 81, 223
      compared to Reagan, 83
Economic problems
    lower crime rate by attacking, 145
    as most important problem, 120
Education
    amount now being spent to improve quality of
      public, 169
      national trend, 169
    black children have as good a chance as white
      children in your community to get a good,
      235
    Bush administration will improve standards, 46
    government spending to improve public, 209

investment in space is worthwhile or would be
    better spent on domestic programs such as,
    171–72
    lower crime rate through better, 145
    as most important problem, 120
    your confidence in public schools, 204
      national trend, 204
Education policy
    handled by Bush, 223
Eisenhower, Dwight
    approval rating compared to Bush, 42, 103, 222
    approval rating compared to Reagan, 7, 43, 191
Elderly people
    attention paid to civil rights of, 234
    government spending for programs for, 104
    helped by your volunteer work or donations, 227
    involved yourself in helping, 226
      national trend, 226
Electricity
    rising prices of, 95
Environment
    are you a strong environmentalist, 121–22
    Bush administration will improve quality of the,
      45
    consider boycott of Exxon's products, 123
    favor ban on chlorofluorocarbons, 124
    as most important problem, 120
    pollution as most important problem, 120
    which have you done (list) to improve the quality
      of the, 123
    worry about acid rain, 123
    worry about contamination by radioactivity from
      nuclear facilities, 123
    worry about contamination by toxic waste, 122–
      23
    worry about damage to earth's ozone layer, 123
    worry about "greenhouse effect," 123
    worry about loss of natural habitat for wildlife,
      123
    worry about loss of tropical rain forests, 123
    worry about ocean and beach pollution, 123
    worry about pollution of rivers, lakes, and
      reservoirs, 122
Environmental issues
    handled by Bush, 223
Environmental protection
    government spending for, 104

F

Family life
    breakdown of, as factor most responsible for
      crime, 142
    importance of having a good, 56
      national trend, 58
    your satisfaction with, 19
      by ethnic background, 20
Family ties
    during last year, have you been to ceremony for a
      relative, to family get-together, or given gift
      to a relative, 157

how often do you talk to your brother/sister on
the telephone, 154–55
how often do you talk to your grandparents on the
telephone, 157
how often do you talk to your parents on the
telephone, 151–52
how often do you usually see your brother/sister,
153–54
how often do you usually see your grandparents,
156–57
how often do you usually see your parents, 151
things (list) you have done for your parents
during past year, 152–53
things (list) your parents have done for you
during past year, 152
your knowledge of your family, 157–58
your relationship with your grandparents, 155–
56
your relationship with your parents/siblings as
close or distant, 155
your relationship with your parents/siblings as
fun or boring, 155
your relationship with your parents/siblings as
tense or easygoing, 155
your relationship with your parents/siblings as
warm or cold, 155

Farmers
government spending for aid to, 210
Ferraro, Geraldine
as most admired woman, 4
Finances, personal
better off next year than now, 49–50, 150
national trend, 50, 150
better off now than a year ago, 47–49, 149
national trend, 49, 50, 149
Finland, respondents in
1990 as peaceful or troubled year, 239
Firearms
deal with crime by enacting tougher gun control
laws, 144–45
have gun in house, 88
national trend, 89
laws covering sale of, 83–84
national trend, 85
legislation banning guns invisible to metal
detectors, 87–88
legislation banning "Saturday night specials,"
86–87
legislation banning semiautomatic assault guns,
85–86
number of guns kept in house, 89
your gun a pistol, shotgun, rifle, or assault gun,
89
national trend, 89
Fishing
your participation in, 28
by men and women, 28
national trend, 28
Food
contributed food, clothing, or other property to
charitable organization, 227

given money, food, or clothing to the homeless
or needy, 227
large cities (list) with best, 208
not enough money to buy, 147–48, 149
national trend, 147–48, 149
plan to donate any money or food to charitable
group during next two weeks, 227
rising prices of dairy products, 95
rising prices of fruits and vegetables, 95
rising prices of meats and poultry, 95
See also Diet and nutrition
Food programs
amount now being spent to provide, for low-
income families, 169–70
national trend, 170
Football
bet on college sports event such as, in past
twelve months, 133
bet on professional sports event such as, in past
twelve months, 132
national trend, 133
how many college games are fixed, 137
how many pro games are fixed, 137
how often have you bet on college, 136
how often have you bet on pro, 135
legalize betting on professional sports such as,
130
Ford, Betty
as most admired woman, 4, 237, 238
Ford, Gerald
approval rating compared to Bush, 42
approval rating compared to Reagan, 7, 43
as outstanding president, compared to Carter, 10
Foreign aid
as most important problem, 120
Foreign investment, in United States. See also
Economic affairs
Foreign policy
handled by Bush, 81, 223
compared to Reagan, 83
France, respondents in
1990 as peaceful or troubled year, 239
Furniture
have or will purchase, in Soviet Union, 225

G

Gambling
bet on a boxing match in past twelve months,
133
bet on college sports event in past twelve
months, 133
bet on a dog race in past twelve months, 134
bet on a horse race in past twelve months, 135
national trend, 135
bet on jai-alai in past twelve months, 134
bet on professional sports event in past twelve
months, 132
national trend, 133

NATO should keep nuclear
weapons in Western Europe, 218
1990 as peaceful or troubled year, 239
satisfaction index of, 20
Greece, respondents in
1990 as peaceful or troubled year, 239
Guthrie, Arlo
fan of, at Woodstock, 176

H

Handgun Control Inc.
your overall opinion of, 102
Handicapped people
attention paid to civil rights of disabled and, 234
helped by your volunteer work or donations, 227
Hart, Gary
as most admired man, 3
Havens, Richie
fan of, at Woodstock, 176
Health
importance of having good, 56
national trend, 58
your satisfaction with, 19
by ethnic background, 20
See also Diet and nutrition
Health care
amount now being spent to improve, 169
national trend, 169
government spending for, 209
investment in space is worthwhile or would be
better spent on domestic programs such as,
171–72
not enough money to pay for, 148, 149
national trend, 148, 149
Health insurance
government spending for, 210
Hendrix, Jimi
fan of, at Woodstock, 176
Hiking
your participation in, 28
by women, 28
Hispanics
attention paid to civil rights of, 234
not wanted as neighbors, 70–71
national trend, 72
Home buyers
government spending to assist first-time, 210
Homelessness
handled by Bush, 183, 223
Homeless people
given money, food, or clothing to, 227
government spending to help, 209
helped by your volunteer work or donations, 227
lack of effort or circumstances beyond his control
to blame if person is homeless, 184
Homosexuality
change to greater tolerance of, in 1960s, 178

relations between consenting adults should be
legal, 215–16
national trend, 216
something a person is born with, or due to other
factors, 217
national trend, 217
Homosexuals
equal rights in terms of job opportunities, 216
national trend, 216
given the choice, most would rather be
homosexual or not, 217
hired as clergy, 217
national trend, 217
hired as doctors, 216
national trend, 217
hired as elementary-school teachers, 217
national trend, 217
hired as high-school teachers, 217
hired as salespersons, 216
national trend, 216
serving in armed forces, 216
national trend, 216
Hong Kong, respondents in
1990 as peaceful or troubled year, 239
Honolulu
as most attractive city, 208
Hostage situation, in Middle East
Colonel Higgins was killed because Israelis
captured Sheik Obeid, 181
efforts now under way to free American hostages
in Lebanon will bring about release, 181
handled by Bush, 181
national trend, 181
if current U.S. efforts fail, United States should
take military action against hostage holders,
181
more chance that American hostages in Iran will
be released, now that Khomeini has died, 181
more important to free Americans or not
encourage future hostage taking, 181
which type of military action should United
States take, 182
your approval of Israelis' decision to abduct
Sheik Obeid, 181
Housing
blacks have as good a chance as white people in
your community to get any kind of, 235
your satisfaction with, 19
by ethnic background, 20
compared to Great Britain, 20
Houston
as city with friendliest people, 207
as worst city, 207
Hungary
Bush doing enough to help Eastern European
countries deal with changes there, 224
continue under Soviet Union or seek
independence, 140
Hungary, respondents in
1990 as peaceful or troubled year, 239

Hunger
    will increase in Eastern Europe, 232
Hunting
    your participation in, 28
        by men, 28

I

Iacocca, Lee
    as most admired man, 3, 237
Iceland, respondents in
    1990 as peaceful or troubled year, 239
Income, household
    your satisfaction with, 19
        by ethnic background, 20
        compared to Great Britain, 20
Independents
    affiliation with, 174
        national trend, 174
Indianapolis
    as city with fewest social problems, 207
Indians
    not wanted as neighbors, 72–73
Inflation
    handled by Bush, 82
Interest rates
    increase in, as worry in future, 94, 209
Iran
    Bush administration should improve relations
        with, 91–92
    more chance that American hostages will be
        released, now that Khomeini has died, 181
    United States retaliate against, by applying
        economic sanctions against, 91
    United States retaliate against, by assassinating
        Khomeini, 91
    United States retaliate against, by bombing oil
        fields, 91
    United States retaliate against, by breaking off
        diplomatic relations with, 91
    United States retaliate against, by encouraging
        coup to remove Khomeini, 91
    United States to retaliate against, if Rushdie were
        killed, 90–91
    your overall opinion of, 98, 180
        national trend, 180
    See also Satanic Verses
Iran-*contra* affair
    Oliver North's role in, 118–19
    Oliver North's sentence for his involvement in
        was fair or too harsh, 159
Ireland, respondents in
    1990 as peaceful or troubled year, 239
Israel
    your overall opinion of, 98, 180
        national trend, 180
    See also Hostage situation; Middle East situation
Israel, respondents in
    1990 as peaceful or troubled year, 239
Italy, respondents in

Europe has enjoyed years of peace against
    Russian threat because NATO was founded,
    218
NATO alliance should be maintained, 218
NATO should keep nuclear weapons in Western
    Europe, 219
1990 as peaceful or troubled year, 239

J

Jackson, Jesse
    as most admired man, 3, 237
Japan
    contributing enough to defense of Pacific region,
        106
    fair trade policy with United States, 106
    greater role in its own defense, 106
    as leading economic power, 105–6
    more responsibility for military defense, 106
    more responsibility for military defense, even if
        United States would no longer be dominant
        power, 106–7
    U.S. tariffs on goods from, 106
    your overall opinion of, 98, 180
Japan, respondents in
    1990 as peaceful or troubled year, 239
Jefferson Airplane
    fan of, at Woodstock, 176
Jews
    attention paid to civil rights of, 234
    not wanted as neighbors, 66–67
        national trend, 67
Job
    blacks have as good a chance as white people in
        your community to get any kind of, 235
    equal rights for homosexuals in terms of job
        opportunities, 216
        national trend, 216
    may lose your, as worry in future, 94, 209
    women and minority groups should be given
        preferential treatment, 234
        national trend, 234
Job satisfaction
    an employee of private company, of government,
        or self-employed, 187
    how many hours do you work, 187
    how much do you travel, 187
    how much of your social life is spent with people
        whom you know through your work, 187
    how much time outside of work do you spend
        thinking about work, 187
    is your work physically tiring, 187
    regularly scheduled to work weekends or for some
        evening or weekend work, 187
    sense of identity from your job or just a living,
        187
    which (list) describes the place where you work,
        186–87
    with being close to home, 188
    with the company, 189

Marriage and divorce (*continued*)
    whose idea was it to get divorced, 109
    you made the right decision by separating, 109
    you might have solved your problems, 109
Marriage and romance. *See* Adult relationships;
    Unmarried people
Medicare
    lower payments for, to reduce federal budget
        deficit, 104–5
Mexico
    your overall opinion of, 98
Mexico, respondents in
    1990 as peaceful or troubled year, 239
Miami
    as city with best arts, entertainment, and
        nightlife, 208
    as city with best food, 208
    as most attractive large city, 208
    as worst large city, 207
Middle East situation
    approval of U.S. talks with Palestine Liberation
        Organization, 15–17
    handled by Bush, 82
    have you followed, 13
    Israelis rely too much on force in dealing with
        Palestinian Arabs, 181
    U.S.-Palestine Liberation Organization talks
        improve chances for peace, 17–19
    your sympathies more with Israelis or Palestinian
        Arabs, 13–15, 180–81
        national trend, 181
    See also Hostage situation
Military
    homosexuals serving in armed forces, 216
        national trend, 216
    your confidence in, 204
        national trend, 204
Minneapolis
    as city with fewest social problems, 207
Minorities
    Bush administration will improve the lot of, 46–
        47
    should be given preferential treatment, 234
        national trend, 234
    See also by name of group
Morality
    importance of following strict moral code, 57
        national trend, 58
    moral decline, as most important problem, 120
Mother Teresa of Calcutta
    as most admired woman, 4, 237, 238
Motorboating
    your participation in, 28
        national trend, 28
Motorcycle/moped
    have or will purchase, in Soviet Union, 226
Movie camera
    have or will purchase, in Soviet Union, 226

N

National Organization for Women (NOW)
    your overall opinion of, 102
National Rifle Association (NRA)
    your overall opinion of, 102
National Right to Life Committee
    your overall opinion of, 102
Netherlands, respondents in
    Europe has enjoyed years of peace against
        Russian threat because NATO was founded,
        218
    NATO alliance should be maintained, 218
    NATO should keep nuclear weapons in Western
        Europe, 218
    1990 as peaceful or troubled year, 239
New Orleans
    as city with best arts, entertainment, and
        nightlife, 208
    as city with best food, 208
    as city with friendliest people, 207
New Year's Eve
    last year, did you spend with family members,
        with friends, or were you alone, 239
    usually do something special on, 238
    where did you spend (list), last year, 239
New York
    as best large city, 207
    as city with best arts, entertainment, and night
        life, 208
    as city with best food, 208
    as city with friendliest people, 207
    as most attractive large city, 208
    as worst large city, 207
New Zealand, respondents in
    1990 as peaceful or troubled year, 239
Nixon, Richard
    approval rating compared to Bush, 42, 103, 222
    approval rating compared to Reagan, 7, 43, 191
North, Oliver
    his role in Iran-*contra* affair, 118–19
    his sentence was fair or too harsh, 159
    his trial jury made the right decision about, 118
    as most admired man, 3
    should be punished or pardoned, 119
    your opinion of, 116–18
        national trend, 118
North Atlantic Treaty Organization (NATO)
    as long as Russia has nuclear weapons that can
        reach Western Europe, NATO should keep
        similar weapons in Western Europe, 218–19
    due to changing relations between Russia and the
        West, NATO alliance should be maintained,
        218
    Europe has enjoyed years of peace against
        Russian threat because NATO was founded,
        218

O

O'Connor, Sandra Day
  as most admired woman, 237
Onassis, Jacqueline Kennedy
  as most admired woman, 4, 237, 238

P

Pakistanis
  not wanted as neighbors, 72–73
Palestine Liberation Organization
  approval of U.S. talks with, 15–17
  talks of, with United States, improve chances for
    peace, 17–19
Palestinian Arabs. *See* Middle East situation
Peace
  changes in Eastern Europe and Soviet Union will
    increase chances of world, 232
  1990 as peaceful or troubled year, asked in thirty-
    five countries, 239
Peace (keeping out of war)
  did you side with those who supported or opposed
    the Vietnam War, 177
  got involved in antiwar movement in 1960s and
    1970s, 177
  Republican or Democratic party more likely to
    keep United States out of war, 173
    national trend, 173
Philadelphia
  as city with best arts, entertainment, and
    nightlife, 208
  as worst large city, 207
Philippines, respondents in
  1990 as peaceful or troubled year, 239
Phoenix
  as city with fewest social problems, 207
Pittsburgh
  as worst city, 207
Planned Parenthood Federation
  your overall opinion of, 102
Poland
  Bush doing enough to help Eastern European
    countries deal with changes there, 224
  continue under Soviet Union or seek
    independence, 140
  Solidarity's victory in, of importance to United
    States, 139
Pollution
  government spending to reduce air, 209
  as most important problem, 120
  See also Environment
Pool
  your participation in, 28
    by men, 28
Poor people
  are you now more or less sympathetic to
    problems of, than five years ago, 183

are your friends now more or less sympathetic to
  problems of, than five years ago, 183
Bush administration will improve the lot of, 46–
  47
government spending to assist low-income
  families, 169–70, 210
  national trend, 170
helped by your volunteer work or donations, 227
involved yourself in helping, 226
  national trend, 226
living conditions of, better or worse over last
  five years, 183
most prefer welfare or would rather earn own
  living, 184
welfare benefits give people a chance or make
  them dependent, 184
which group (list) has greatest responsibility for
  helping, 184
Portugal, respondents in
  Europe has enjoyed years of peace against
    Russian threat because NATO was founded,
    218
  NATO alliance should be maintained, 218
  NATO should keep nuclear weapons in Western
    Europe, 219
  1990 as peaceful or troubled year, 239
Poverty
  anyone in your family ever lived in, 183
  anyone in your own family now living in, 183
  does government know how to eliminate, 184
  ever be done away with in this country, 183
    national trend, 183
  handled by Bush, 183, 223
  lack of effort or circumstances beyond his control
    to blame if person is poor, 183
    national trend, 183
  large cities (list) with fewest social problems,
    such as, 207
  as most important problem, 120
  as most important problem facing Colombia
    today, 195
  percentage of Americans living below the
    poverty line, 183
  will increase in Eastern Europe, 232
  See also Poor people
Prices
  increases in, as worry in future, 94, 209
  See also Cost of living
Problems
  most important, 120
    asked in Colombia, 195
Prosperity
  Bush administration will keep America
    prosperous, 45
  Republican or Democratic party better at keeping
    country prosperous, 173–74
    national trend, 174
Protestants
  not wanted as neighbors, 64–66
    national trend, 66

Q

Quayle, Dan
 approval rating, 223

R

Radio
 have or will purchase, in Soviet Union, 225
Reagan, Nancy
 as most admired woman, 4, 237, 238
Reagan, Ronald
 approval rating, 4–5
  national trend, 6
 approval rating compared to Bush, 42, 103, 222
 approval rating compared to predecessors, 7, 43, 191
 approval rating as person, 10–12
  compared to Bush, 41–42, 83
  national trend, 12
 his handling of foreign and domestic problems (list), compared to Bush, 83
 as most admired man, 3, 237
 as outstanding president, 7–10
  national trend, 10
Record player
 have or will purchase, in Soviet Union, 225
Refrigerator
 have or will purchase, in Soviet Union, 225
Religion
 describe yourself as a "born-again," or evangelical, Christian, 204
 how important in your own life, 204
 member of church or synagogue, 204
 will play more important role in Eastern Europe, 232
 your attendance at church or synagogue in last seven days, 204
 your confidence in church or organized, 204
  national trend, 204
 See also Television evangelists and ministers
Religious fundamentalists
 not wanted as neighbors, 76–77
  national trend, 77
Religious sects or cults
 members of, not wanted as neighbors, 77–79
  national trend, 79
Republican party
 affiliation with, 174
  national trend, 174
 better for keeping country prosperous, 173–74
  national trend, 174
 better reflects your views on abortion, 165–66
 more likely to keep United States out of war, 173
  national trend, 173
 your opinion of Republican congressional leaders, 114
Rock music. See Woodstock
Roosevelt, Franklin
 approval rating compared to Reagan, 7

Running
 your participation in, 28
  by women, 28
Rushdie, Salman
 heard or read about Satanic Verses, 90
 United States to retaliate against Iran, if Rushdie were killed, 90–91

S

St. Louis
 as city with fewest social problems, 207
Salespersons
 homosexuals hired as, 216
  national trend, 216
Sales tax, national
 to reduce federal budget deficit, 104
Salt Lake City
 as city with fewest social problems, 207
San Diego
 as best large city, 207
 as city with fewest social problems, 207
 as city with friendliest people, 207
 as most attractive large city, 208
San Francisco
 as best large city, 207
 as city with best arts, entertainment, and nightlife, 208
 as city with best food, 208
 as city with friendliest people, 207
 as most attractive large city, 208
 as worst large city, 207
 See also California earthquake
Santana
 fan of, at Woodstock, 176
Satanic Verses (Rushdie)
 bookstores were right to remove, 90
 heard or read about, 90
Satisfaction
 with seven aspects of life, index of, 19–20
Savings and loan associations. See Economic affairs
Schroeder, Pat
 as most admired woman, 4
Scientific research
 government spending for, 104
Seattle
 as best large city, 207
 as city with fewest social problems, 207
 as city with friendliest people, 207
 as most attractive large city, 208
Sebastian, John
 fan of, at Woodstock, 176
Self-image
 importance of having good, 56
  national trend, 58
Sex
 change to more acceptance of premarital, in 1960s, 178
 change to more openness about, in 1960s, 178

in television programs, likely to make you feel uncomfortable, 99

Sexual relationships. *See* Adult relationships

Sick people
helped by your volunteer work or donations, 227
involved yourself in helping, 226
national trend, 226

Sly & the Family Stone
fan of, at Woodstock, 176

Social problems
lower crime rate by attacking, 145

Social Security
government spending for, 103, 104
reduce COLAs, to reduce federal budget deficit, 104
reserve surplus for future or use, to reduce federal budget deficit, 105
tax benefits as ordinary income, to reduce federal budget deficit, 105
See also Economic affairs

Social values
ranked by importance, 55–58
national trend, 58

Society, betterment of
importance of working for, 57
national trend, 58

Softball
your participation in, 28
by men, 28
national trend, 28

South Africa
your overall opinion of, 98

South Africa, respondents in
1990 as peaceful or troubled year, 239

South Korea
fair trade policy with United States, 106
U.S. tariffs on goods from, 106
your overall opinion of, 98

South Korea, respondents in
1990 as peaceful or troubled year, 239

Soviet Union
as long as Russia has nuclear weapons that can reach Western Europe, NATO should keep similar weapons in Western Europe, 218–19
Bush doing enough to help Soviet Union deal with changes there, 224
Bush doing enough to reduce military tensions between United States and, 224
changes there will increase chances of world peace or of war, 232
current problems are typical or indicate weakness of Communist system, 140
current situation in, means end of communism, 231
discontent in, will result in uprisings or change will come peacefully, 140
due to changing relations between Russia and the West, NATO alliance should be maintained, 218
Eastern Europe will continue under, or seek independence, 140

Europe has enjoyed years of peace against Russian threat because NATO was founded, 218
further ahead in space research, 170
national trend, 170
Gorbachev's attempts to restructure economy will succeed or fail, 140
if Gorbachev's policies fail, will his regime be replaced, 140
as leading economic power, 106
likely to be ally of United States by year 2000, 231
new openness will continue, or return to closed society in, 140
relations with, handled by Bush, 81, 224
compared with Reagan, 83
your overall opinion of, 98, 180

Soviet Union, respondents in
1990 as peaceful or troubled year, 239
over next five years, expect quality of Soviet-made products to improve, 225
which products (list) do you have at present, and which do you think you will purchase in next two years, 225–26

Space program
amount now being spent for, 169
national trend, 169
concentrate on unmanned missions like *Voyager 2*, or on maintaining manned program like space shuttle, 170–71
did you watch first manned moon landing, 170
government spending for space exploration, 210
important for United States to be first to land person on Mars, 170
investment in space research is worthwhile or would be better spent on domestic programs, 171–72
people like ourselves living on other planets, 170
top priority (list) for, 171
United States, Soviet Union, or a European country is further ahead in space research, 170
national trend, 170
who spoke "That's one small step for a man . . . ," 170
who was first person to walk on moon, 170

Spain, respondents in
Europe has enjoyed years of peace against Russian threat because NATO was founded, 218
NATO alliance should be maintained, 218
NATO should keep nuclear weapons in Western Europe, 219
1990 as peaceful or troubled year, 239

Sports
your participation in, 28–29
by men and women, 29
national trend, 29

Standard of living
further improvements in, of blacks will reduce

Standard of living (*continued*)
    that of whites, 235
    importance of having nice home, car, and other
      belongings, 58
    national trend, 58
    your satisfaction with, 19
      ethnic background, 20
      compared to Great Britain, 20
Stove
    have or will purchase, in Soviet Union, 225
Supreme Court
    as result of ruling, call elected official to register
      your opinion on abortion, 167
    as result of ruling, contribute to organization
      supporting your position on abortion, 167
    as result of ruling, take part in demonstration in
      support of your position on abortion, 167–
      68
    as result of ruling, take political candidate's
      position on abortion more into account, 166
    decision allowing states to pass laws that restrict
      abortion, 160–62
    overturn 1973 ruling (*Roe v. Wade*) on abortion,
      20–22, 162–64, 211
      national trend, 164
    your confidence in, 204
      national trend, 204
    your opinion of, 112–14
      national trend, 114
Sweden, respondents in
    1990 as peaceful or troubled year, 239
Swimming
    your participation in, 28
      by men and women, 28
      national trend, 28
Switzerland, respondents in
    1990 as peaceful or troubled year, 239

T

Tariff policy, U.S.
    on goods from Canada, 106
    on goods from Common Market countries, 106
    on goods from Japan, 106
    on goods from South Korea, 106
    See also Economic affairs
Taxes
    Bush administration will avoid raising, 46, 209
    discussion in Congress to lower capital gains
      tax, 210
    national sales, to reduce federal budget deficit,
      104
    willing to pay higher, to combat drug use, 193
    See also Budget deficit, federal; Economic affairs;
      Government spending
Tax reform
    increase in taxes as worry in future, 94, 209
    1986 bill a fairer distribution of tax load, 93
    taxes next year will increase, 93–94
Taylor, Elizabeth

    as most admired woman, 4, 238
Teachers
    homosexuals hired as elementary-school, 217
      national trend, 217
    homosexuals hired as high-school, 217
Television evangelists and ministers
    as caring, 197–98
      national trend, 198
    contributed money to, in last twelve months, 204
    ever watch religious programs on television, 204
      national trend, 204
    as having special relationship with God, 201–2
      national trend, 202
    as honest, 199–201
      national trend, 201
    as sincere, 198–99
      national trend, 199
    as trustworthy, 202–3
      national trend, 204
Television programs
    how frequently do you feel uncomfortable with,
      compared to one year ago, 99
    how many do you watch with your children per
      week, 98–99
    how often do you feel uncomfortable about, 99
    violence on, as factor most responsible for
      crime, 142
    what do you do (list), if you feel uncomfortable
      about, 99
    what is likely (list) to make you feel
      uncomfortable with, 99
Television set
    have or will purchase, in Soviet Union, 225
Tennis, your participation in
    national trend, 28
Thatcher, Margaret
    as most admired woman, 4, 237, 238
Tobacco Institute
    your overall opinion of, 102
Tower, John
    favor his confirmation as secretary of defense,
      60–61
    good for Senate to investigate personal lives of
      cabinet nominees, 62
    have heard or read about, 60
    his pledge not to drink was major reason to favor
      his confirmation, 61–62
    reasons listed for opposing his confirmation, 62
    Senate inquiry into his personal life has been
      fair, 62
Trade policy, U.S.
    with Canada, 106
    with Common Market countries, 106
    with Japan, 106
    with South Korea, 106
    See also Economic affairs
Truman, Harry
    approval rating compared to Bush, 42, 222
    approval rating compared to Reagan, 7, 43, 191
Trump, Donald
    as most admired man, 3, 237

West Germany, respondents in
    Europe has enjoyed years of peace against
        Russian threat because NATO was founded,
        218
    NATO alliance should be maintained, 218
    NATO should keep nuclear weapons in Western
        Europe, 219
    1990 as peaceful or troubled year, 239
The Who
    fan of, at Woodstock, 176
Winfrey, Oprah
    as most admired woman, 4, 237, 238
Woman, most admired
    choice for, 4, 237–38
Women
    attention paid to civil rights of, 234
    changes in the role of, in 1960s, 178
    participation in sports by, 28
    should be given preferential treatment, 234
        national trend, 234
Woodstock
    changes in the role of women, 178
    change to greater tolerance of homosexuality,
        178
    change to more acceptance of premarital sex, 178
    change to more liberal attitudes toward marijuana
        and other drugs, 177
    change to more openness about sex, 178
    change to more willingness to question authority
        of government, 178
    "conformist" applies more to young people of
        today than twenty years ago, 177
    consider myself a rock music fan, 175
    did you approve or disapprove of unmarried

        couples living together, 177
    did you have much in common with the young
        people who attended, 176
    did you side with those who favored or opposed
        legalized marijuana, 177
    did you side with those who supported or opposed
        the Vietnam War, 177
    "idealistic" applies more to young people of
        today than twenty years ago, 176
    fan of artists (list) who appeared at, 176
    how many people attended, 176
    know the state where Woodstock took place,
        175–76
    "materialistic" applies more to young people of
        today than twenty years ago, 176
    "patriotic" applies more to young people of
        today than twenty years ago, 177
    "reckless" applies more to young people of today
        than twenty years ago, 177
    rock musicians are more creative now than then,
        176
    "selfish" applies more to young people of today
        than twenty years ago, 176
    which alternative live-style (list) did you
        participate in, in 1960s and 1970s, 177
    which period of rock music do you enjoy most,
        175
Wright, Jim
    charges are serious enough to justify his being
        replaced, 115
    your opinion of, 115
Wristwatch
    have or will purchase, in Soviet Union, 225